THE NEW TESTAMENT
AN ORTHODOX PERSPECTIVE

The New Testament:
An Orthodox Perspective

Volume One
Scripture, Tradition, Hermeneutics

Theodore G. Stylianopoulos

Foreword by
Krister Stendahl

HOLY CROSS ORTHODOX PRESS
Brookline, Massachusetts 02146

Reprint 2002
© 1977 Holy Cross Orthodox Press
Published by Holy Cross Orthodox Press
50 Goddard Avenue
Brookline, Massachusetts 02146

On the cover: The Evangelist Matthew offering his Gospel to John Chrysostom. Codex 364. John Chrysostom, 45 Homilies on Matthew A.D. 1042-1050. From Weitzmann, Kurt and Galavaris, George, THE MONASTERY OF ST. CATHERINE AT MT. SINAI, THE ILLUMINATED GREEK MANUSCRIPTS @ 1990 by Princeton University Press. Reprinted with permission of Princeton University Press.

We are grateful to the following for permission to reprint passages from:
Fathers of the Church Volume 37, St. John of Damascus, trans. Frederic H. Chase, Jr. © 1958 by Catholic University of America Press.
Symeon the New Theologian: The Discourses, trans. C.J. deCatanzaro © 1980 by The Missionary Society of St. Paul the Apostle in the State of New York. Used by permission of Paulist Press.

Library of Congress Cataloging–in–Publication Data
Stylianopoulos, Theodore G.
The New Testament: an Orthodox Perspective / Theodore G. Stylianopoulos; foreword by Krister Stendahl.
p.   cm.
Includes bibliographical references and index.
Contents: v. 1. Scripture, tradition, hermeneutics.
ISBN 1-885652-13-5 (pbk.)
1. Bible. N.T. — Introductions. 2. Orthodox Eastern Church — Doctrines. 3. Bible. N.T. — Criticism, interpretation, etc.
I. Title.
BS2330.2.S78 1997
225.6 ' 1' 088219 — dc21   96-40125
                                                               CIP

In memory of
Bishop Gerasimos of Abydos
(1910–1995)
teacher, mentor, saint

Πολλῆς οὖν ἡμῖν χρεία τῆς νήψεως, πολλῆς τῆς σπουδῆς, πολλῆς τῆς τῶν θείων Γραφῶν ἐρεύνης.

There is then for us need of much sobriety, much diligence, much search of the divine Scriptures.

St. Symeon the New Theologian
Catechetical Discourse 3

Πᾶσα γὰρ σπουδὴ καὶ πᾶσα ἄσκησις μετὰ καμάτων πολλῶν ἡ μὴ καταντῶσα εἰς τὴν ἀγάπην ἐν τῷ συντετριμμένῳ τῷ πνεύματι, ματαία ἐστὶ καὶ εἰς οὐδὲν καταλήγουσα χρήσιμον.

For all diligence and all ascetic discipline with many labors, which does not attain to love in a contrite spirit, is in vain and yields nothing useful.

Catechetical Discourse 1

Contents

Abbreviations

ABD	Anchor Bible Dictionary
BTZ	Berliner Theologische Zeitschrift
CT	Christianity Today
CQR	Church Quarterly Review
CTR	Compass Theological Review
CC	Cross Currents
DeltBibMel	Deltion Biblikon Meleton
Dial	Dialogue
FT	First Things
GOTR	The Greek Orthodox Theological Review
IDB	Interpreter's Dictionary of Bible, G A. Buttrick (ed.)
Int	Interpretation
JTS	Journal of Theological Studies
LF	Lutheran Forum
NJBC	The New Jerome Biblical Commentary.
OC	One in Christ
Or	Origins
P.G.	J. P. Migne, Patrologia, series Graeca
Sob	Sobornost
SVTQ	St. Vladimir's Theological Quarterly
ThDNT	Theological Dictionary of the New Testament

Foreword

The reader may well ask why there should be this many pages, even a whole Volume One, before an Introduction to the New Testament arrives at, say, the Gospel of Matthew. My answer is simple. Professor Stylianopoulos is an honest man, well aware of the many ways in which the Bible has been read, and can be read, and will be read. He knows how naive – even dishonest – it is to say, "I read the text just as it stands."

In this volume on what the learned call hermeneutics–how to understand the texts–he describes the process by which he as an Orthodox Christian approaches the Scriptures. He discerns three steps or moves: the exegetical, the evaluative/interpretive, and the transformative.

In the ways he elaborates these moves or modes I see the impact of "the sociology of learning" on the American theological scene. For neither in Europe nor in other parts of the world are the scholars of the churches educated in faculties that are inter-denominational in composition and ethos to the extent that was already the case when Professor Stylianopoulos received his doctorate from Harvard Divinity School.

Thus his emphasis on how at the exegetical stage there is a common base in asking and answering the question of what a text meant to its author and/or to its originally intended readers, given the setting of time and place. This enterprise cannot be called Orthodox or Protestant or whatever. In this context, Professor Stylianopoulos refers to my article in IDB (see Chap. 7, note 6), and I agree with him that this search for "what was meant" should not foreclose the transcendent dimensions of Scripture's truth claims (Chap. 7, p. 193).

My intention both in stressing the various tenses of meaning – meant/came to mean/comes to mean – and in insisting that we ask, "meaning to whom?" was to show how necessary and valid the second, the interpretive, move is. And now I happily learn from him about a third, the transformative stage. It is here that I feel the most palpable impact of Professor Stylianopoulos' life as a biblical scholar nurtured by the traditions of Eastern Orthodoxy. Biblical hermeneutics is the art of lifting up into consciousness the processes that actually do take place in our reading and responding to the Scriptures. When Professor Stylianopoulos lifts up the transformative dimension, I recognize that serious Christians have always counted on something like that, but have not given it a distinct status in the scheme of hermeneutics.

Here I find a further link between Professor Stylianopoulos and scholars identified with the Evangelical end of the Protestant spectrum. There is of course what Professor Stylianopoulos calls an "enlightened conservatism" that brings them together. And there is the–to me one-sided–critique of the Enlightenment's subjectivism versus truth claims about "who God is." And there is Professor Stylianopoulos' positive reaction to some Evangelical scholars' newfound awareness of tradition as a corrective to manic biblicism. But on a deeper level there is also the convergence of the transformative move in Orthodoxy and the basic Evangelical insistence on the personal relation to Christ.

To be sure, the language by which Evangelicals and Orthodox speak of the transformation differs, and Professor Stylianopoulos speaks clearly about how he wants to bridge that classical divide between Eastern and Western theology and spirituality.

> Within their normative patterns of faith and practice all Christian traditions understandably exercise a kind of *sensus plenior* producing numerous interpretations and applica-

tions of biblical texts. The community of faith, whether in
Scripture or after Scripture, was always dependent more
on established communal norms of faith and practice than
on historical exactitude and precise exegesis. The burning
hermeneutical point is to submit the norms themselves to
critical evaluation in the light of total witness of Scripture.
The "justification theology" focusing on the issue of faith
and works is not less traditional simply because a Protestant declares it "biblical." Nor is the "theosis theology"
focusing on union with Christ in the Spirit unbiblical simply because an Orthodox declares it "traditional." An
exegetical approach may well find that both the "participatory" and "forensic" views of salvation are part of the
larger biblical witness, and that deeper appreciation of both
may be achieved precisely by seeing them in positive
comparative light. But the hermeneutical point is that,
functionally, whether by selection or omission, Scripture
and tradition play equally important roles in every faith
community. The difference is that, because of their
respective biases, Protestants tend to ignore the role of
tradition, whereas the Orthodox tend to boast about it
(Chap. 7, pp. 209-210).

When Professor Stylianopoulos' hermeneutical reflections
bring him close to the Evangelical segment of the scholarly community, it accounts for the relative absence of their counterparts
among Roman Catholic theologians. To be sure Raymond Brown
is mentioned as well as the recent Pontifical Biblical Commission's
document on "The Interpretation of the Bible in the Church"
[*Origins*, 23 (29, 1994), pp. 498-524]. But this should not be
misconstrued since the salient point in contemporary Roman
Catholic hermeneutics is the very one which in the ecumenical
world is associated with the name Professor Stylianopoulos. Let
me elaborate.

It was Professor Stylianopoulos who had been chosen to give
the keynote address at the opening of the Vancouver Assembly
for the World Council of Churches in 1983. The theme was

"Jesus Christ–The Light of the World." I found his address both impressive and helpful. I came away with a lasting insight – a gift from the Eastern Christendom – that the creeds of the church should be understood also as doxologies. I knew of course as a scholar that all the earliest credal elements in the New Testament are found in poetic form (think of Phil. 2), but it renewed my faith to think of my creeds as ways of praising the Triune God. Put in other terms, the question of genre is decisive for our understanding of Scripture and of theology. We must be on the right wavelength in order to be able to listen right. A story is not a hymn, and a commandment is not a statement. I now recall this sensitivity to genre from Professor Stylianopoulos' address in Vancouver in connection with recent insights in Roman Catholic hermeneutics. As Raymond Brown has pointed out (*The New Jerome Biblical Commentary*, 1990), this very recognition of literary form proved to be the key to the new scholarly creativity in Roman Catholic biblical studies: The encyclical *Divino Afflante Spiritu* (Pius XII, 1943) and Vatican II have made this approach imperative for all serious Catholic students of the Bible (*NJBC*, p. 1151, cf. 1170-71). It is good to know that Professor Stylianopoulos brings also such a perspective to the work now before him.

As Professor Stylianopoulos will lead us into the world of the New Testament having now, like Moses, stood at the Jordan, looking into the Promised Land, it will be exciting to go with him. This rich and honest first volume allows us to anticipate an introduction in which the three steps/moves/modes – the exegetical, the interpretive, the transformative – become not just stages one, two, three, but prove mutually stimulating in a dynamic interplay. I think, of course, on the analogy of the Holy Trinity as the Orthodox can think it, not as a hierarchical or psychological model, but as ultimate mutuality and interpenetration. And personally, I will especially watch out for the ways in which the transformative reality of the Scriptures will work itself out. For the Eastern understanding of the aim of the Divine exercise as *theosis*, of God becoming human that we be restored to the *imago dei*, certainly gives a focus that both intensifies the role of Christ and at the same time overcomes the almost heretical Christomonism of many Western and especially Protestant traditions. Imagine that we are about to receive an Orthodox introduction to the New Testament fully conversant with the "canons" of the contemporary Biblical Studies on these shores.

Krister Stendahl
Harvard Divinity School
Cambridge, Massachusetts

Preface

The present work is the first of two volumes planned as a comprehensive introduction to the New Testament in its historical and theological witness. This first volume deals with the fundamental issues, presuppositions, and contexts which largely determine how the Bible is read and interpreted. Although the main concern is the New Testament, the exposition necessarily engages the Old Testament as well, since apart from the Old the New cannot be fully understood. Thus the discussion centers around topics which pertain to Scripture as a whole — its nature and authority, its relationship to tradition, the patristic and modern approaches to Scripture, and the burning issue of interpretation. The second volume will concentrate on the individual books of the New Testament and include brief sections on the early Church and the broader background of Judaism and the Greco-Roman world.

The primary readers in view are theological students preparing for various pastoral ministries. Effective Christian ministry requires that such students be knowledgeable about the contemporary critical approaches to Scripture, but above all that they have a firm grasp of its theological and evangelical message. Students exposed to the formal study of Scripture for the first time are often confused by the diversity and radicalism of modern biblical criticism. They can hardly connect critical studies with the biblical narrative and its horizon of faith. They often struggle between simplistic pietism and debilitating doubt. Re-

Amen

sponsible teaching must provide a way for students to work out
a sound balance between faith and scholarship in order to avoid
the extremes of fideism and skepticism. A mature use of the
Bible presupposes that the historical complexities of the biblical
tradition not be ignored, not least because they carry significant
theological implications. At the same time, however, if priestly
and ministerial aspirants are to possess conviction and vigor in
their work, they need to acquire an informed and robust view of
the revealed character and canonical authority of the Scriptures.

The chief presupposition here is that the biblical writings indeed constitute Holy Scripture – a sacred record of God's self-
revelation received and transmitted by the Church of all ages –
to be read and used with discernment for the proclamation of
the gospel. The benefits of biblical criticism are affirmed and its
challenges examined. Nevertheless, the weight is placed on the
ultimate goal of biblical study: the explication of the theological
truths and spiritual witness of Scripture. In this sense the claim
"Orthodox perspective" in the title of this work contains an ecumenical appeal; it intends to express the ecclesial and theological interests not only of the Orthodox with a capital "O," but
also of all Christians who hold to the historic faith of the Church
and perceive themselves as orthodox with a small "o," though
not necessarily surrendering to pietistic or fundamentalist ways
of thinking. The exposition seeks to avoid scholarly jargon and
to explain technical terms for the benefit of all interested readers. The writer hopes, as well, that certain key positions advocated in this work, especially in the chapters dealing with
hermeneutics, that is, the art of interpretation, may be of interest to colleagues whose constructive criticism will be greatly appreciated.

Most of the persons to whom I owe expressions of gratitude
cannot be named here. A work such as this richly draws from
the thought of former professors at various schools, as well as
from the published works of numerous colleagues cited in the
notes. However, I wish to mention three persons who influenced me in particular ways: the late Bishop Gerasimos

Bishop Gerasimos
John Romanides

Papadopoulos of blessed memory by his spiritual witness; John Romanides by his theological insights, and Krister Stendahl by his descriptive exegetical methodology. I am also grateful to His Grace Bishop Methodios, former President of Hellenic College and Holy Cross Greek Orthodox School of Theology, for a sabbatical leave in 1995 during which most of this first volume was written. John Chryssavgis and Nicholas Constas, colleagues at Hellenic College and Holy Cross, read portions of the manuscript and offered valuable suggestions. My wife Fotini edited the first draft of several chapters. My assistant Anthony Belcher scrutinized the final draft, offering countless stylistic corrections and also preparing part of the bibliography. Anton Vrame contributed invaluable services in proof-reading the text and overseeing all technical aspects of publication. To all of these and others who helped in the publication of this work, I express my sincere thanks.

Finally, readers will take note that in the English transliteration of Greek names, I have preferred a rendering closer to the Greek rather than Latin forms, for example "Athanasios" instead of "Athanasius." The Latin forms now strike many authors and readers as patronizing. However, in cases where Greek names have been anglicized and have become standard, for example, "Gregory," I have naturally retained the English form rather than "Gregorios." Nevertheless, stylistic consistency in these matters is virtually impossible and I ask for the reader's indulgence.

Theodore G. Stylianopoulos
Holy Cross Greek Orthodox
School of Theology
Brookline, Massachusetts
April 4, 1996

Introduction

Why study the Bible? Most readers turn to the Scriptures because of religious and theological interest. They presuppose that the Bible is a sacred and authoritative book bearing testimony to the word of God. St. Paul refers to the Scriptures as "the oracles of God" (τὰ λόγια τοῦ Θεοῦ, Rom 3:2). He commends the Christians in Thessalonike for receiving the gospel, now recorded in the New Testament, "not as a human word but as what it really is, the word of God" (1 Thess 2:3). Throughout the ages, Christian believers, whether in public worship or in private reading, have looked to the Bible as a source of saving truth and spiritual guidance. They have perceived that the Scriptures, notwithstanding conflicts of interpretation and problems of misuse, offer an invitation to a life with God, a way of love and righteousness uniquely exemplified by the person and ministry of Jesus Christ.

The Bible is also read for literary enjoyment. The account of creation, the story of Israel, and the life of Christ have inspired countless men and women. The Psalms, Job, the Gospel of John, and Revelation all have exceptional literary merit. In modern times, the philological aspects of the Bible have been studied in formal and technical ways pertaining to its composition, narratives, poetry, and visions.[1] Moreover, it is well known that the

---

[1] L. Ryken and T. Longman, III, eds., *A Complete Literary Guide to the Bible* (Grand Rapids: Zondervan, 1993); L. Ryken, *The New Testament in Literary Criticism* (New York: Continuum, 1985); and J. B. Gabel, C. B. Wheeler, and A. D. York, *The Bible as Literature: An Introduction* (New York: Oxford University Press, 1996).

language and ideas of Scripture have influenced the literature of many peoples. In Western culture, for example, one can hardly appreciate Dante, Milton, or Tolstoy without knowledge of the imagery and teachings of the Bible. Literature has always grappled with the themes of good and evil, sacrifice and greed, hope and despair. The Scriptures have stirred the hearts and minds of many a poet and creative thinker pondering the meaning of life, freedom, justice, suffering, and death.

The Bible can be read because of historical interest, too. Most of the information about the origins and beliefs of Judaism and Christianity derive from the Scriptures. By reading the Bible, the careful reader can catch glimpses of the life and culture of other ancient peoples as well: the Egyptians, Assyrians, Babylonians, Persians, Greeks, and Romans. In modern times, the historical study of the Bible has reached systematic and professional standards.[2] It is commonplace to acknowledge that the Scriptures have emerged from particular cultural contexts and historical circumstances. In addition, there is greater awareness that the Bible has had an immense impact on the history of civilization by its influence not only on the social mores and legislation of laws, but also on cultural expressions in education, art, and music.[3] The imagination of some of the great explorers was inspired by a sense of biblical mission. Christopher Columbus, for example, wrote a brief work entitled *Book of Prophecies* in which he indicates that he was driven by the desire to spread

---

[2] A broad perspective can be gained from W. Keller, *Bible as History* (New York: Bantam, 1983); John Bright, *A History of Israel* (Philadelphia: Westminster, 1981); Martin Noth, *The Old Testament World*, trans. V. I. Gruhn (Philadelphia: Fortress, 1966); W. F. Albright, *From the Stone Age to Christianity* (New York: Doubleday, 1957); J. A. Thompson, *The Bible and Archaeology* (Grand Rapids: Eerdmans, 1982); and S. Freyne, *New Testament Message 2: The World of the New Testament* (Wilmington: Glazier, 1980).

[3] Pertaining to American culture, law, politics, and education, see N. O. Hatch and M. A. Noll, eds., *The Bible in America: Essays in Cultural History* (New York: Oxford University Press, 1982); J. T. Johnson, ed., *The Bible in American Law, Politics, and Political Rhetoric* (Alpharetta: Scholars Press, 1984); R. J. Neuhaus, *Bible, Politics, and Democracy* (Grand Rapids: Eerdmans, 1987); and D. Barr and N. Piediscalzi, *The Bible in American Education* (Alfaretta: Scholars Press, 1982).

the gospel throughout the world and prepare the way for the millennium prior to his discovery of America.[4] It may well be that, as some have claimed, the rise of modern science and technology, was in part motivated by the biblical idea of an orderly creation and God's directive to humanity to conquer the earth and have dominion over all things (Gen 1:28).[5]

These three aspects of biblical study, the theological, literary, and historical, are closely interconnected. They are related to the fundamental character of Scripture as a collection of historical documents recording the religious convictions and theological insights of Jews and Christians derived from what they understood to be profound encounters with God in the context of community. Although one aspect may be accented more than another for particular reasons, all three require due attention for a full understanding of the Scriptures. This holds especially true in modern times in which revolutionary advances in the hard and soft sciences have established a new and controversial sense of critical thinking based on the scientific experimental method. The proliferation of new knowledge about the world and humanity from science, history, and psychology, together with the philosophical presuppositions of the Enlightenment, has resulted in a general decline of confidence in the authority of the Bible as a source of truth.[6] The application of the scientific critical method in biblical study has led to radically different approaches to the Bible. Thus the question "why study the Bible?" is sharpened by many other questions. Who is studying the Bible?

---

[4] L. I. Sweet, "The Revelation of Saint John and History," *Christianity Today*, May 11, 1973, p. 10.

[5] *Science and the Theology of Creation* by the Bossey Seminar (Bossey: World Council of Churches, 1988), published in the *Church and Society Documents* No. 4, August 1988, and various articles in *Science and Religion*, ed. by Ian G. Barbour (New York: Harper & Row, 1968).

[6] See Alan Richardson, *The Bible in the Age of Science* (London: SCM Press, 1961); Van A. Harvey, *The Historian and the Believer* (New York: Macmillan, 1963); G. H. Reventlow, *The Authority of the Bible and the Rise of the Modern World*, trans. J. Bowden (Philadelphia: Fortress, 1985); and Brian J. Walsh and Richard J. Middleton, *Truth Is Stranger Than It Used to Be: Biblical Faith in a Postmodern Age* (Downers Grove: InterVarsity, 1995).

In what context is the Bible being read and studied? How is the Bible to be interpreted and applied? Does the Bible contain divine revelation or is it merely a cultural achievement of antiquity from which to draw expedient lessons for the advancement of praiseworthy causes? In what sense does the Bible constitute the sacred Scriptures of the Church and what are the implications of this fact?

Modern biblical studies have displayed tendencies toward disintegration. The theological and historical approaches to Scripture have drifted apart for over a century. The dominance of the historical-critical approach accommodating modernist assumptions has produced analytic results and revisionist theories to the degree that some have mused whether the wine of Scripture has been turned into the water of critical study. A few scholars themselves from within the guild have harshly critiqued historical-critical methodology as yielding a "mammoth misinterpretation" of the Bible and as being "bankrupt" because of its seeming uselessness for the life of the Church and society.[7] In reaction to the historical approach a growing number of biblical critics have attempted to open up fresh directions under the influence of the "new literary criticism" in order to extract relevant meaning from the Bible according to the sensibilities of modern readers.[8] However, these new approaches still appear to devalue the theological witness of the biblical writings by viewing them as ancient religious literature rather than as normative records of revelation. Along with the historical and literary approaches, and using their methodologies, other critics have exploited the Bible for ideological reasons in order to promote

---

[7] The former expression is by Roy A. Harrisville, "Introduction," in Peter Stuhlmacher, *Historical Criticism and Theological Interpretation of Scripture*, trans. Roy A. Harrisville, (Philadelphia: Fortress, 1977), p. 9. The latter is a term popularized by Walter Wink, *The Bible in Human Transformation* (Philadelphia: Fortress, 1973). Peter Stuhlmacher himself writes in the above book, p. 76, that biblical studies without theological interpretation is "a theological discipline which has abolished its relevance by its critical work."

[8] Edgar V. McKnight, *Post-Modern Use of the Bible* (Nashville: Abingdon, 1988). For further bibliography, see Chapter Five, note 7.

social and political causes such as liberationism and feminism.[9] Biblical studies show no trend toward coherence or consensus.

What can an Orthodox perspective on Scripture offer? Orthodox scholars, as discussed in various parts of the present volume,[10] have accepted the judicious application of the critical method because the spirit of Orthodoxy encourages discerning inquiry after truth and freedom of research. But wary of the prevalence of modernist assumptions in scholarship, Orthodox theologians have guarded against the radical inferences of historical criticism by leaning toward conservative positions and by being mindful of the dogmatic teaching of the Church. This fact holds true not only in the study of the Bible but also in the study of all the theological disciplines, including Church history, patristics, liturgics, canon law, and systematic theology. In the area of Scripture, formal academic studies have developed most notably in Greece where numerous scholars, affiliated with the Universities of Athens and Thessalonike, have published consistently and impressively since the mid-nineteenth century. Many of their contributions will be appropriately engaged in the present work, especially in the second volume which deals with the New Testament in greater detail.

Currently there are substantial introductions to the New Testament by three Greek biblical scholars: Savas Agouridis, John Karavidopoulos, and John Panagopoulos.[11] The first two, though deferential to traditional positions, follow a style and methodology familiar in international biblical scholarship. The third, by

[handwritten margin notes: Savas Agouridis / John Karavidopoulos / John Panagopoulos]

---

[9] For bibliography, see Chapter Five, notes 10 and 11.

[10] See especially Chapter Two, section three; Chapter Six, section four; and Chapter Seven, section four.

[11] All are in modern Greek. The introduction by S. Agouridis, Εἰσαγωγὴ εἰς τὴν Καινὴν Διαθήκην, was first published in 1971 and is now in its third edition (Ἀθῆναι: Ἐκδόσεις Γρηγόρη, 1991). The one by J. Karavidopoulos Εἰσαγωγὴ στὴν Καινὴ Διαθήκη, first appeared in 1983 and was reprinted several years ago (Ἀθῆναι: Ἐκδόσεις Π. Πουρναρᾶ, 1991). The most recent is by J. Panagopoulos Εἰσαγωγὴ στὴν Καινὴ Διαθήκη (Ἀθῆναι: Ἐκδόσεις Ἀκρίτας, 1995). Older New Testament introductions by Greek biblical scholars include those by Vasileios Ioannidis (1960), Vasileios Antoniadis (1937), and Nicholas Damalas (1876).

Panagopoulos, while utilizing international scholarship, adopts an explicit hermeneutical stance based on the Church fathers and produces a deliberately "Orthodox" introduction to the New Testament. Panagopoulos has also been composing a masterful, multi-volume work on the patristic exegetical tradition of which the first volume has been published.[12] Savas Agouridis in other contributions has written on the subject of hermeneutics as well. The hermeneutical positions of these scholars are discussed respectively in Chapters Six and Seven of the present volume.[13]

The hermeneutical position of the present work is a mediating one. While it takes very seriously the theological implications of the exegetical work of the Church fathers, it also equally insists on the descriptive critical study of the biblical documents on the grounds that nuanced historical study provides access to the original witness of the New Testament. The task of defining a distinctive "Orthodox approach" to Scripture, to which the present work seeks to make a contribution, still lies ahead. Whatever the definitive features of the Orthodox study of the Bible may be, they must include not only fidelity to the authority of Scripture and the Church fathers, but also honest grappling with all contemporary methodologies and sources of knowledge. The ideal which we must pursue, following the example of the Alexandrian, Antiochian, and Cappadocian fathers, is to achieve a harmonious synergy between true faith and sound reason. The intellectual achievement of the Church fathers, as well as the catholicity of the Christian faith, demand nothing less.

Therefore, the term "Orthodox" is neither a cultural nor denominational designation identifying Eastern Christianity as a merely historical phenomenon. It is a reference to the universal Christian tradition in the classic sense of what is true in all times and at all places. The goal is to define an ecumenical perspective oriented to a holding center, the Bible itself, yet one which embraces diversity in unity and unity in diversity in the

---

[12] This work is discussed in Chapter Four, under "The Patristic Exegetical Heritage."

[13] The position of Agouridis is presented in Chapter Six, section 3, and that of Panagopoulos in Chapter Seven, section four.

total Christian tradition. An Orthodox approach to the Bible
does not concern itself with this or that particular methodology
in biblical studies. Each methodology is to be valued on its own
merits. It would be in any case presumptuous to claim methodological contributions in a field where Orthodox scholars are
still learning from their Western colleagues. Rather, an Orthodox approach has to do with a comprehensive and balanced
appreciation of Holy Scripture in its own nature, authority, and
witness as the word of God, while at the same time being
committed to standards of critical study and freedom of research.
It may be proposed that such a perspective would include, among
others, three major features.

The first is holistic study itself, integrating literary, historical, and
theological aspects. Although the theological pertains to the essence
of the Bible as Holy Scripture, the historical and literary aspects are
to be properly valued as well because they are intrinsic to the biblical documents. And all aspects require critical study on the grounds
that inquiry after truth necessarily involves discerning insight and
critical judgment. A holistic approach to Scripture is theologically
anchored on the mystery of the incarnation of the Word (Λόγος)
and the universality of the gospel, requiring openness to all peoples,
all cultures, and all truth. It is an integrative perspective which takes
seriously, not only a theology of redemption, but also a theology of
creation. This is the vision of the great Church fathers from St.
Justin the Martyr to the Cappadocians who were all first-rank scholars of their age and shirked from engaging neither faith with reason,
nor gospel with the universal quest for truth.[14] Among Orthodox
theologians in the twentieth century it was, above all, the late Georges
Florovsky who invoked this patristic vision of reality and coined the
expression "neo-patristic synthesis" for the abiding task of theology
in every age.

[14] See Werner Jaeger, *Early Christianity and Greek Paideia* (Cambridge: Harvard
University Press, 1961); Henry Chadwick, *Early Christian Thought and the Classi-
cal Tradition* (New York: Oxford University Press, 1966); Frederick W. Norris,
*Faith Gives Fullness to Reasoning: The Five Theological Orations of Gregory of
Nazianzen* (Leiden: E. J. Brill, 1991); and Jaroslav Pelikan, *Christianity and Cul-
ture* (New Haven: Yale University Press, 1993).

N. T. Wright

Among Western theologians, a similar position is currently expounded in a far more detailed way by the British biblical scholar N. T. Wright in his work, *The New Testament and the People of God*.[15] In what he calls "critical realism," Wright develops a strong case for the integrated theological, historical, and literary study of Scripture on the premise that all three aspects of biblical study face the common question of knowledge and truth.[16] For him, the true function of critical thinking applied to Scripture is to recall Christianity to its historical roots. Theology cannot withdraw from contemporary intellectual discourse as if it could ignore the modernist challenge and be satisfied with the liturgical and devotional reading of the Bible. Scripture deserves to be studied critically in and of itself in order to draw from it the full overtones of its authentic witness.[17]

At the same time, Wright chides critical thinkers, who, as heirs of the Enlightenment, have often lapsed into shrill denunciations of traditional Christianity and have treated the religious and theological aspects of the Bible as peripheral. He also critiques the phenomenological approach of the new literary criticism which tends toward subjectivism. If the Bible's own normative theological claims are neglected, Wright asks, why should one read the Bible at all and not read, as of equal value, any other ancient or modern literature for relevant meaning?[18] The goal of Wright's own "relational epistemology," linking truth that is beyond sense-data to the knowing subject, is biblical theological truth concerning above all the question of God itself.[19] For example, Wright's comprehensive analysis of the "worldviews" of Judaism and Christianity finds that the triadic understanding of God is a genuine and distinct development of

---

[15] N. T. Wright, *The New Testament and the People of God* (Minneapolis: Fortress, 1992), especially pp. xiii-xvii, 1-144, and 467-476. This book is the first of several volumes planned by the author as an ambitious project of a comprehensive account of the origins of early Christianity.

[16] *Ibid.*, pp. 31-35.

[17] *Ibid.*, pp. 4, 10, and 12.

[18] *Ibid.*, pp. 9 and 24-25.

[19] *Ibid.*, pp. 35-46 and 467-476.

the biblical tradition, moving beyond the position of Judaism. According to Wright, the standard New Testament claim, which must be given full critical acknowledgment, is that "the god of Israel had now made himself known in and through, and even *as*, Jesus and the divine spirit."[20] Wright's perspective serves as an instructive example of the first feature of an Orthodox approach to biblical study in critical form.

2. A second major feature involves the communal or ecclesial dimension which is the object of theological reflection within the New Testament itself, notably the Letter to the Ephesians. Wright's proposal includes reference to the communal nature of all knowledge and the accompanying rejection of an alleged, purely objective history or detached critical study.[21] For Wright this applies not only to the contemporary reader's grid of hopes and assumptions rooted in community, but also to the whole range of religious experiences and theological convictions of the biblical authors themselves who are equally grounded in community. An Orthodox perspective welcomes this reference and would emphasize it even more strongly. The word of God is intimately linked with the receptive human subjects. Revelation never occurs in a vacuum. Scripture and tradition are part of the same dynamic and organic reality of God's dealing with people over the ages. From these considerations derives the emphasis of the present volume on the Bible as a book of the Church as well as a book of God.

In particular, the canonization of the Bible demonstrates the authoritative role of the Church and its living tradition in the discernment of theological truth, a role which is not only functional and receptive but also substantive and creative.

---

[20] *Ibid.*, p. 474. According to Wright, the Christian understanding of God is distinctive from the Jewish understanding and yet growing out of the latter in the matrix of the early Christian experience of Christ and the Spirit, so that it can neither be played off as secondary nor be castigated as an alleged pagan development. In fact, for Wright, the question of God constitutes the most important and most essential difference between Christianity and Judaism, and "both cannot be right in their claims about the true god," p. 475.

[21] *Ibid.*, pp. 15 and 31-36.

[handwritten margin note: St. Maximos the Confessor / Scripture / Church's / Scripture is The Lamp / Church is the lamp stand]

St. Maximos the Confessor once compared the mutual relationship between Scripture and Church by using the image of a lamp on a lamp stand, the lamp being Scripture and the lamp stand the Church.[22] Modern studies of the biblical canon now recognize that the doctrinal discernment of the Church, in the form of the appeal to the "rule of faith," critically determined the ecclesial selection of canonical books as part of the larger process of the consolidation and unity of historic orthodoxy. The doctrinal sense of the Church, which applies equally to the final and normative interpretation as well as to the canonical collection of the Scriptures, was not intended to constrict the diversity and richness of interpretive methodologies and results. The exegetical pluralism and multiple uses of Scripture are abundantly evident in the ancient Christian tradition. Rather, the doctrinal appeal was decisive in instances of false interpretive departures from the received apostolic tradition, such as in Gnosticism and Arianism, and was intended to maintain a broad communal unity through normative teaching on essentials of the Christian faith.

However, the canonization of Scripture testifies as well to the authority of the Bible as the word of God by which the Church is judged and to which it is accountable. The Church fathers are united in advocating the supreme authority of Scripture as divine revelation. The christological and trinitarian controversies focused precisely on the proper interpretation of Scripture, which in the cases of St. Athanasios and the Cappadocians developed into contextual and grammatical exegesis – the central concern of modern historical-critical studies of the Bible. Today the authority of Scripture and its theological witness can be discerned in more subtle terms through scholarly study. Furthermore, the communal dimension still retains its

---

[22] The reference is derived from Jaroslav Pelikan, "'Council or Father or Scripture': The Concept of Authority in the Theology of Maximus the Confessor," in *The Heritage of the Early Church: Essays in Honor of Georges V. Florovsky*, ed. D. Neiman and M. Schatkin, appearing in the series *Orientalia Christiana Analecta*, Vol. 195 (Rome: Pontifical Institute, 1973), p. 281.

influence because all Christians have their ecclesial traditions and their doctrinal viewpoints. They can approach the Bible with "critical realism" which embraces in its inquiry the full spectrum of human studies, ancient and modern. While committed to the authority of Scripture and its critical study, all readers should recognize that what each perceives as the reality of truth goes beyond simply speculative syllogisms. It involves a communal perception and a communal commitment to what is true and right about the Bible and Christian life. Such a perspective invites irenic mutual witness and calls for candid dialogical encounter based on serious scholarly reflection and the grace of the Spirit.

3) A third major feature of an Orthodox approach to the Bible has to do with the existential, spiritual dimension. Among the many challenges students have presented to me over the years, the most revealing came in the form of this question: "Is not the spirituality of the New Testament, together with everything else, also worthy of study for us?" It certainly is. But it is a delicate matter in which the line between refreshing spiritual insights and pious platitudes may be too easily crossed. How is one to define the relationship between critical analysis and spiritual vision or, to use Ihor Sevcenko's image, between the caterpillar and the butterfly? Are faith and spirituality to be taught, or are they to be caught, or both? Biblical figures such as the prophet Isaiah and St. Paul claim direct revelatory experiences and vibrate with the renewing power of the Spirit. The Church fathers shared this biblical horizon of faith and directly appealed to the transformative power of the word of God read in the Spirit of God. The affinity and difference between letter and spirit seemed clear to them. In today's secularized culture, most shy away from the spiritual reading and the spiritual witness of the Bible as being intellectually uncertain and socially unhelpful. Many others revel in it and promote it with seemingly self-assured and fanatical disposition.

Yet the spiritual challenge of Scripture remains, and it is fundamental to both Scripture and everyday life. The American biblical scholar, M. Robert Mulholland, Jr., in his book *Shaped by the Word*,[23] exemplifies a welcome perspective on the transformative dimension of biblical study. Mulholland warns about being victims of contemporary education determined by an objectifying and functional culture that seeks to control and manipulate knowledge. He critiques a one-sided "informational" approach to the Bible that intends to master the text through critical analysis and humanistic evaluation. He proposes a "formational" approach as well, by which the biblical reader is open to God's transcendent presence and gracious action through receptive faith and inward love of God. Scripture is the record of the "presence, purpose, and power of God" amidst human conditions, a revelation of the divine word as "matrix or the context of both human brokenness and human wholeness." Mulholland appeals to the "iconographic nature" of Scripture, that is to say, Scripture as a verbal window into a new order of being in which the biblical authors participated and lived. To understand and experience anew the transformative power of Scripture requires, according to Mulholland, participation in the same reality established through Jesus and actualized by the Spirit.[24]

Mulholland strikes a genuine biblical and patristic note of spirituality. While neither devaluating nor being restricted by human speculative knowledge, the ultimate orientation is to the word of God which becomes a living word when the Spirit is present and active. According to St. Paul, what God has prepared for those who love him is revealed through the Spirit which searches everything (1 Cor 2:9-10). Centuries later, St. Symeon the New Theologian, an heir of evangelical spirituality, insisted that the key to spiritual knowledge is the grace of the Spirit given to faith. Beyond ordinary study of Scripture, its spiritual treasures are opened by the risen Christ through the power of the Spirit to those who live in faithful obedi-

---

[23] M. Robert Mulholland, Jr., *Shaped by the Word: The Power of Scripture in Spiritual Formation* (Nashville: The Upper Room, 1985).

[24] *Ibid.*, pp. 3, 21-23, 28, 42, 47-50, and 64-65.

ence and are granted a new birth.[25] This apostolic witness to the new creation in Christ has been attested in various degrees by countless men and women through the traditional devotional reading of Scripture. It has been experienced by prayerful Christians in worship where the liturgical recitation of the Bible and inspired proclamation of the good news actualize God's saving presence and power for the whole body of the Church. The same is worthy of reverent critical reflection and systematic explication by biblical scholarship which moves beyond historical and literary analysis to the truth the Bible itself celebrates and proclaims for the life of the world.

---

[25] See Appendix 2 and relevant pages on St. Symeon in Chapter Seven under the "Transformative Level."

Chapter One

The Nature
of Holy Scripture

The nature of Holy Scripture is defined by several important factors. Among them are the historical origins of
Scripture, the variety of its books and contents, its
theological subject matter, as well as the role and uses of
Scripture in the life of the Church. Orthodox scholars have written on these matters and related questions from a general theological perspective.[1] Their contributions have underscored significant aspects of the Bible such as its revealed character,

---

[1] A classic expression of the Orthodox theological position on Scripture is provided by the late Georges Florovsky, arguably the greatest Orthodox theologian of
the twentieth century, in several articles collected in *Bible, Church, Tradition: An
Eastern Orthodox View* (Belmont: Nordland, 1972). Substantial pieces in English
have also been written by Thomas Hopko, "The Bible in the Orthodox Church,"
SVTQ 14 (1-2, 1970), pp. 66-99; Savas Agouridis, *The Bible in the Greek Orthodox Church* (Athens, 1976), a reprint of an article first appearing in the 21st volume of the annual scholarly publication (Ἐπιστημονικὴ Ἐπετηρὶς) of the Theological School of the University of Athens (1976) which are not easily available;
and by the late Panagiotis Bratsiotis, Professor of Old Testament in Athens, Greece,
"The Authority of the Bible: An Orthodox Contribution," in *Biblical Authority
for Today*, ed. A. Richardson and W. Schweitzer (Philadelphia: Westminster, 1951),
pp. 17-29. Greek scholars such as Evangelos Antoniadis (1938) and Panagiotis
Trembelas (1938) have written extensively on the question of inspiration, but as
an abstract theological issue, without real engagement with the text of Scripture
and the diversity of its witness, where the substance of the question of revelation
and inspiration lies. The works on biblical interpretation and hermeneutics by
Orthodox scholars are taken up in Chapters Three and Six.

inspiration, authority, interpretation, and relationship to tradition. These issues will occupy our attention in various ways throughout the present work. Our purpose in this first chapter is to provide an initial statement on the nature of Scripture based on the principle that theological affirmations about such matters as biblical revelation and inspiration must be grounded in the actual contents, historical composition, as well as the canonical formation of the Bible. Thus the nature of Scripture is here examined in terms of (1) the origins of the Jewish and Christian Bibles; (2) the relationship between the Old and the New Testaments; and (3) the divine and human aspects of Holy Scripture.

The Jewish and Christian Bibles

I would say at least 1500 years, from Moses to St. John

Scripture constitutes an entire library of sacred books written over a period of about one thousand years, from the tenth century B.C. to the first century A.D.. The various biblical writings were composed in Hebrew and Greek, and some parts in Aramaic,[2] by mostly unknown authors who lived in particular historical contexts and addressed important issues of their religious communities. The first reference to an authoritative holy book, "the book of the law" (2 Kg 22:8), which modern scholars identify as being essentially the Book of Deuteronomy, connects its origins with the Temple and the priesthood at the time of King Josiah (640-609 B.C.). Another reference places a "book of the law of the Lord" (2 Chr 17:9) about two hundred years earlier at the time of Jehoshaphat, ruler of Judah (873-849 B.C.). Scholars conjecture that the written sources behind the earliest books of the Bible, namely Genesis and Exodus, may go back as far as the tenth century B.C. At the other end of the biblical library, the Book of Revelation was written most likely

---

[2] Parts of Daniel and Ezra are preserved in Aramaic, a Persian language, different from Hebrew. Aramaic, the language of Jesus, became the popular language of the Jews from the time of the Persian control of Palestine (538-332 B.C.), just as Greek later became the popular language of the ancient world after the conquests of Alexander the Great (356-323 B.C.) and during the expansion of the Roman Empire.

in the late first century A.D. during the persecution of Christians under the Roman emperor Domitian (81-96 A.D.). In this case the author clearly identifies himself as John, a Christian prophet, who wrote from exile on the island of Patmos and claimed explicit authority for this book of prophecy (Rev 1:1-11; 22:7-19).[3]

Most of the scriptural books, however, neither claimed nor possessed authority as sacred books at the time of their composition. Such authority was accorded to them over many generations, indeed centuries, within the respective religious communities of Jews and Christians. In these communities, primary religious authority was attributed to living persons, patriarchs, priests, prophets, apostles, and above all Jesus of Nazareth, who in their own witness spoke and acted on behalf of God. Readers of the Bible should take special note of the fact that the foundational nature of biblical revelation is personal, while its written expression is by comparison secondary. The great moments and acts in which God made himself known involved powerful, experiential events that changed the lives of concrete persons in the context of their specific communities. Before any accounts of them were written, these revelatory events and experiences were remembered, celebrated, interpreted, told and retold by word of mouth over long periods – in the case of the Old Testament for centuries and in the case of the New Testament for decades.

Thus, behind the written Scriptures lies the dynamic reality of the oral religious traditions of the Jewish and Christian peoples. These oral traditions, maintained and developed through worship, instruction, and custom, were kept alive by God's people, and sustained the identity of God's people, guiding their beliefs and practices. Eventually they were committed to writ-

---

[3] Christian tradition has specifically identified the author with the apostle John to whom tradition has attributed five New Testament books, including the Gospel of John, three Epistles, and the Book of Revelation. However, one must point out that this identification, as well as the authority of the Book of Revelation, has been disputed in ancient as well as modern times. On the question of the importance of authorship, see below in this same chapter.

O.T.
c. 950 – 150 BC
(850 years)

NT
c. 50 – 100 AD
(50 years)

ing through complex processes. The Hebrew Scriptures were written from about 950 B.C. to 150 B.C. and the New Testament books from about 50 A.D. to 100 A.D. In each case, the sacred literature recounted the original events in layers of interpretation – primary, secondary, and tertiary – within each faith community. A startling variety of books were produced, Genesis as well as Ecclesiastes, the Gospel of Mark as well as the Epistle of James. In some instances, notably that of the Apostle Paul, we encounter individual known authors who contributed significantly to the written biblical tradition. Yet all these books organically emerged from the life of Israel and of the Church, serving their concrete needs of worship, instruction, daily guidance, and self-identity. From this perspective we can appreciate the profound fact that the books of the Bible are, by their very nature, *books of faith* both in that they were fruits of the life of faith, as well as in that they fostered and still foster the life of faith.

Not only were the individual books products of the faith community but their gradual gathering into a sacred collection involved, as well, a dynamic process of reception and selection within the ongoing life and tradition of the Jewish and Christian faith communities. As central as the Bible eventually became for Judaism and Christianity, we should remember that "Abraham did not have a Bible, any more than Jesus or Paul had a New Testament."[4] Only slowly did books gain the status of sacred authority and came to play an important role in both reflecting and determining belief and practice. The biblical writings were selectively preserved and gradually gathered into sacred collections in the religious communities of the Jews and the Christians over many centuries. No other justification can be given for the respective Jewish and Christian Bibles except the choices of these religious communities themselves. When

---

[4] Frederick E. Greenspahn in his introduction to the book *Scripture in the Jewish and Christian Traditions: Authority, Interpretation, Relevance*, ed. by him (Nashville: Abingdon, 1982), p. 10.

you say Hebrew Bible you say Synagogue. When you say Christian Bible you say Church.[5] These sacred collections are called *canons* (from the Greek χανών, meaning "rule" or "standard"). The Jewish canon of the Bible was completed by the first or second century A.D. and the Christian canon of the Bible, which includes the Old and the New Testaments, by the end of the fourth century.[6]

During the first century A.D., and prior to the emergence of the New Testament as part of Holy Scripture, Jews and Christians largely shared the same sacred writings deriving from the Jewish tradition. Although they interpreted them differently, they referred to them by the same titles. The term *Bible* comes from the Greek, βίβλος or βιβλίον (meaning "record," "document," or "book") and was first used by Greek-speaking Jews to refer to the Hebrew Scriptures.[7] The etymological roots lie in an Egyptian word for the papyrus shrub and its bark used for writing in the ancient world since the sixth century B.C. The New Testament authors employ this terminology in a few instances to refer to individual writings such as the Book of Isaiah (Lk 3:4) or the five books of the Law attributed to Moses (Mk 12:26; Gal 3:10). Once, the term occurs in the plural βιβλία (2 Tim 4:13). The same terminology is also found among the Church fathers, though somewhat rarely, for the entire Christian Bible. The ex-

---

[5] K. Stendahl, "Method in the Study of Biblical Theology," in *The Bible in Modern Scholarship*, ed. J. Philip Hyatt (Nashville: Abingdon, 1965), p. 198.

[6] About twenty-two of the New Testament books had gained canonical authority by the end of the second century but the remainder were disputed until the fourth century and beyond. For an overview see the articles on "Canon" by James Sanders and Harry Gamble in *ABD*, Volume 1, ed. D. N. Freedman (New York: Doubleday, 1992), pp. 837-861. See further S. Z. Leiman, *The Canonization of Hebrew Scripture: The Talmudic and Midrashic Evidence* (Hamden: Archon Books, 1976); A. C. Sundberg, *The Old Testament of the Early Church* (Cambridge: Harvard University Press, 1964); and Bruce Metzger, *The Canon of the New Testament* (New York: Oxford University Press, 1987). A popular account of the formation of the New Testament in the ancient Church is *Why Is There a New Testament?*, by J. F. Kelly (Wilmington: Glazier, 1986).

[7] G. Schrenk, "Βίβλος," *ThDNT*, Volume 1, ed. G. Kittel, trans. G. W. Bromiley (Grand Rapids: Eerdmans, 1964), pp. 615-620.

pression "The Bible" (meaning "The Book") came to prevail in the Western Christian tradition.

γραφή

The more frequent term for the sacred books was *Scripture* (Greek γραφὴ) or the plural *Scriptures* (Greek γραφαί), deriving from the verb γράφω, meaning to carve, inscribe or write. Whereas the word βίβλος seems to imply a stress on the material on which something is written, the word γραφὴ places the emphasis on the act and content of writing.[8] The New Testament authors use this terminology numerous times to refer to particular passages or generally to the Scriptures (Mk 12:10; Lk 24:27; Acts 8:32, 35; Gal 3:8, 22; Rom 15:4). The apostle Paul calls them "holy scriptures" (ἅγιαι γραφαί, Rom 1:2) one time. The terms "Holy Scripture" and "Holy Scriptures" came to prevail in the universal Christian tradition as titles for the entire Bible of the Old and New Testaments.

The Jewish people, as was noted, wrote and collected their own Scriptures. In the Jewish community, the Hebrew Scriptures have been classified from ancient times according to three divisions, the Law, the Prophets, and the Writings. The *Law*, also called the Law of Moses or *Pentateuch* (from the Greek Πεντάτευχος, literally, "five-volume work"), consists of the first five books of the Bible traditionally attributed to Moses. The Hebrew title is *Torah*, usually translated as "Law." But the term carries far richer meanings in Hebrew, including divine law, instruction, revelation. Although their focal center is God's Law given on Mt. Sinai, the books of Moses have a larger scope embracing as well the account of creation, the patriarchal epics, and the story of the exodus of the Jewish people from Egypt. The *Prophets*, in Hebrew *Nevi'im* (literally, "announcers" or "mouthpieces" of God), comprise numerous books from Joshua to Malachi not arranged chronologically. These include the historical books of Joshua, Judges, Samuel, and Kings. In both the Jewish and Christian tradition Moses, Joshua, and Samuel are all regarded as prophets, inspired leaders and spokesmen on behalf of God. The third broad category of books, the *Writings*, in

---

[8] G. Schrenk, "Γραφή," *ThDNT*, Volume 1, pp. 751ff.

Hebrew *Kethuvim*, makes up a diverse collection of books from the Psalms to Chronicles which, include prayers and songs, didactic and philosophical meditations, historical and apocalyptic narratives. In the Jewish tradition the Bible is called *Tanakh*, an acronym based on the first letter of the Hebrew words for Law, Prophets, and Writings (TNK).[9] Jesus and St. Paul referred to the two major divisions, "The Law and the Prophets" (Mt 7:12; Rom 3:21). The three divisions are echoed in the words of the risen Christ who, on the way to Emmaus, explained "the law of Moses, the prophets, and the psalms" (Lk 24:44) to Cleopas and another unknown disciple. The list of books in the Jewish Bible, as selected and arranged by the rabbinic teachers perhaps at Jamnia[10] toward the end of the first century A.D., or more

Fig. 1. Tanakh: The Hebrew Scriptures

> **THE LAW**: Genesis, Exodus, Leviticus, Numbers, and Deuteronomy
>
> **THE PROPHETS**:
>
> *The Former Prophets*: Joshua, Judges, Samuel (1 and 2), and Kings (1 and 2)
>
> *The Latter Prophets*: Isaiah, Jeremiah, and Ezekiel
>
> *The Twelve Prophets*: Hosea, Joel, Amos, Obadiah, Jonah, Micah, Nahum, Habakkuk, Zephaniah, Haggai, Zechariah, and Malachi
>
> **THE WRITINGS**: Psalms, Proverbs, Job, Song of Solomon, Ruth, Lamentations, Ecclesiastes, Esther, Daniel, Ezra–Nehemiah, and Chronicles (1 and 2)

---

[9] See the new JPS translation according to the traditional Hebrew text *Tanakh, the Holy Scriptures: Torah, Nevi'im, Kethuvim* (Philadelphia: Jewish Publication Society, 1985).

[10] Rendered also as Jabneh or Yavneh, a city of disputed location in Palestine, which served as a center of the rabbinic leaders of Judaism following the destruction of Jerusalem by the Romans (70 A.D.). Scholars debate whether or not a rabbinic council at Jamnia actually defined the canon of the Hebrew Scriptures by specifying the Writings, the third division of the Hebrew Bible, and thus closing the Hebrew canon. See Jack P. Lewis, "Jamnia (Jabneh), Council of," *ABD*, Vol. 3, pp. 634-637.

[handwritten margin note: Jamnia is also called Jabneh or Yavneh]

likely during the second century, appears above (See Fig. 1, p. 21).

The early Christian community was made up of Jewish and Gentile members. Both saw themselves rooted in the Jewish heritage and claimed to be special heirs to it. The early Christians therefore retained the Hebrew Scriptures, what eventually came to be called "Old Testament" in the Christian tradition, as the only Bible they knew, with two important differences. The first was the adoption of the Greek translation of the Hebrew Scriptures called *Septuagint* (Latin *septuaginta* and Greek ἑβδομήκοντα meaning "seventy").[11] This term goes back to a tradition of Greek-speaking Jews of Alexandria about seventy or seventy-two Jewish elders who translated the Hebrew Scriptures into Greek some two or three centuries before Christ. The story is told in a Jewish work, *The Epistle of Aristeas*, written in Greek by an unknown Alexandrian Jew in pre-Christian times. Its intent is to affirm the authority of the Greek translation of the Hebrew Scriptures accomplished over generations by Greek-speaking Jews and serving their needs in the Greek city of Alexandria. This version of the Scripture is most quoted by the New Testament authors and became traditional in the ancient Church. It remains the official version of the Old Testament in the Orthodox Church.

The second difference is that the early Christians adopted a larger number of Jewish writings than the official list compiled by the rabbinic teachers at Jamnia or later. These additional books were in circulation from pre-Christian times in the Greek language among Greek-speaking Jews who regarded them as valuable. These books express the diverse beliefs, practices, and hopes of many Jews during the time of the Greek and Roman dominance of the ancient world. However, because they carried neither sufficient antiquity nor authority in the Jewish tradition, they were left out of the Hebrew canon by rabbinic lead-

---

[11] M. K. H. Peters, "Septuagint," *ABD*, Vol. 5, ed. N. Freedman, pp. 1093-1104; S. Jellicoe, *The Septuagint and Modern Study* (Oxford: Clarendon, 1968); and by the same, *Studies in the Septuagint: Origins, Recensions, and Interpretations* (New York: KTAV, 1974).

ers who intended to unite and consolidate Judaism after disastrous wars with Rome during the first and second centuries.

But the Christians esteemed these writings and preserved them. In the East, they became known as *Readable Books* (Ἀναγινωσκόμενα, literally, "readable") and in the West *Deuterocanonical* ("of secondary authority"). Although their precise number varies, these writings are still part of the Orthodox and Roman Catholic canons of the Old Testament. With the Reformation, Protestants adopted the Jewish canon and eliminated these books from the Bible. They designated them as *Apocrypha*, a pejorative word meaning "hidden books," a term which in the ancient Christian tradition was applied to still other books whose authority was rejected by the Church. These latter books, such as the Book of Jubilees, the Martyrdom of Isaiah, and the Assumption of Moses, were nevertheless preserved by Christians on account of historical and religious interests. They carry no canonical authority but certainly bear historical value because they attest to the beliefs and practices of their authors and their specific religious groups. These books are still designated as Apocrypha in the Orthodox Church, but are called *Pseudepigrapha* (literally, "falsely titled") by Protestants.[12] Thus, by and large, what Protestants call Pseudepigrapha the Orthodox call Apocrypha, and what Protestants call Apocrypha the Orthodox called Readable or Deuterocanonical. Many current Protestant Bibles, for reasons of ecumenical openness and scholarly interests, regularly feature the Readable Books as "The Apocrypha" or "The Apocrypha/ Deuterocanonical,"albeit as an appendix (see FIG. 2, p. 24).

In addition to the Readable/Deuterocanonical books, the Orthodox and Roman Catholic Bibles contain extensive passages in the canonical books of Esther and Daniel not found in the Hebrew version of these texts. Although traditionally these passages are part of the canonical books, the Protestants placed them among the "Apocrypha" according to their nomenclature and call them "Additions" to the Greek versions of Esther and Daniel.

---

[12] See James H. Charlesworth, *Old Testament Pseudepigrapha*, 2 vols. (New York: Doubleday, 1986).

FIG. 2. The Readable/Deuterocanonical Books

In the Orthodox Bible	*In the Roman Catholic Bible*
Tobit	Tobit
Judith	Judith
Maccabees 1-3	Maccabees 1-2
Wisdom of Solomon	Wisdom of Solomon
Wisdom of Sirach	Wisdom of Sirach
(also called Ecclesiasticus)	(also called Ecclesiasticus)
Baruch	Baruch
Epistle of Jeremiah	Epistle of Jeremiah
Esdras	———

In the case of Daniel, these passages include the Prayer of Azariah and the Song of the Three Youths, the story of Susanna, and the story of Bel and the Dragon. In the case of Esther, they include shorter passages too numerous to mention here.[13] The inclusive interests of the Eastern tradition extended to additional texts that are taken up in the Orthodox Bibles. Among them are the Prayer of Manasses and Psalm 151. The Slavonic version alone includes Esdras 2. The Greek version alone includes Maccabees 4 as an appendix.

In total, the Hebrew Scriptures contain thirty-eight books, Ezra and Nehemiah forming one book. The Jewish tradition developed and maintains its own numbering and sequential arrangement of these books.[14] The Protestant Old Testament numbers thirty-nine books separating the Books of Ezra and Nehemiah according to ancient Christian tradition. The Roman Catholic Old Testament, including seven Deuterocanonical Books and the Epistle of Jeremiah joined to Baruch, totals forty-

---

[13] See *The New Oxford Annotated Bible with the Apocryphal/Deuterocanonical Books*, ed. Bruce M. Metzger and Roland E. Murphy (New York: Oxford University Press, 1991), p. 41 of the Apocrypha.

[14] Nevertheless, the 1985 translation of the Hebrew Scriptures by the Jewish Publications Society, cited above, note 9, numbers thirty-nine books, separating Ezra and Nehemiah.

six books. The Orthodox Old Testament maintains the most inclusive canon of the ancient Church which embraces, together with the ten Readable Books, forty-nine books. In addition, a few other writings mentioned above, such as the Prayer of Manasses and Psalm 151, are accorded some value within the Orthodox tradition.

It should be noted, as well, that the sequence of the scriptural books varies in the Protestant, Catholic, and Orthodox Bibles, something easily ascertained by any reader comparing current editions of the Bible from these traditions.[15] Two significant differences deserve the reader's attention. One is that the Orthodox and Catholic Bibles integrate the Readable and Deuterocanonical books within their respective Old Testament canons, whereas the Protestant Bibles put them in an appendix. This fact indicates a remaining difference of views regarding the canonical authority of these books. The second is that the official Orthodox Old Testament continues to be the Greek *Septuagint* version, whereas the current Protestant and Catholic Bibles are translations of the Hebrew original called the *Masoretic* text.[16] Finally, readers of the Bible should be aware that the "Apocrypha" of the New Testament are entirely different books, outside of the New Testament canon, which were written mostly during the second century A.D. and later.[17]

[15] Compare, for example, the Protestant New Revised Version, which enjoys wide ecumenical use and the Catholic New American Bible. The Orthodox have no English translations of the Bible and therefore one must consult Orthodox editions in other traditional Orthodox languages. The available English translation of the Septuagint published by Bagster and Sons features a slightly different sequence as well. *The Orthodox Study Bible*, produced in a popular rather than scholarly vein, and published by Thomas Nelson (1993), is not, of course, a new translation but uses the New King James Version.

[16] The original Hebrew text of the Old Testament preserved by Jewish scholars known as Masoretes. "Masorah" means tradition and "Masoretes" refers to scholars whose task was to preserve the tradition governing the production of copies of the Hebrew Bible throughout the centuries. An extant such copy is the famous Aleppo Codex, dating from the late first millenium.

[17] The apocrypha of the New Testament in English translation may be found in Wilhelm Schneemelcher, *New Testament Apocrypha*, Vols. 1-2, rev. ed. R. M. Wilson (Louisville: Westminster, 1990 and 1992). For the Gnostic writings discov-

The Old and the New Testaments

The terminology "Old Testament" and "New Testament" emerged among Christians during the first century and was applied to the two parts of the Christian Bible by the end of the second century. The key word *testament*, derived from the Latin *testamentum*, translates the Greek διαθήκη and the Hebrew *berith*. The English and modern Greek words are no longer quite appropriate. Contemporary readers usually take the word "testament" to mean a document for the disposition of an estate, as in the last will and testament. However, the correct meaning from the Hebrew word is *covenant*, meaning a bond, agreement, or alliance between two partners. The meaning of covenant in the biblical perspective is the sacred bond between God and his people, established by God's saving action and freely offered to his people as a permanent relationship of mutual love and fidelity. The "Old Covenant" is founded on God's deliverance of Israel from Egypt and his gift of the Law on Mt. Sinai. The "New Covenant" is grounded in the sacrifice of Christ – God's supreme act of salvation as a renewal of the covenant with his people (Mk 14:24; 1 Cor 11:25; Heb 8:8, 13; Jer 31:31-32).

The first to coin the expression παλαιὰ διαθήκη ("old covenant") in conscious contrast to καινὴ διαθήκη ("new covenant") was St. Paul in 2 Cor. 3:6, 14. However, as the context clearly indicates, the apostle had in view the Exodus story of Moses and the Sinai Covenant and not yet the entire Hebrew Scriptures as "Old Testament." The expressions "Old Testament" and "New Testament" were not applied to the sacred books until the end of the second century. For the apostle Paul and the early Christians the "new covenant" was neither a book nor a collection of books but rather the dynamic reality of the new bond between God and Christian believers based on the person and saving work of Christ.

---

ered in Egypt some fifty years ago, see James M. Robinson, *The Nag Hammadi Library in English* (San Fransisco: Harper & Row, 1989). Some scholars hold that the Gnostic *Gospel of Thomas* was composed during the second half of the first century at the time of, or even earlier than, the four canonical gospels.

The writing of letters, gospels, and other books by the apostles and their followers occurred during the first century in various regions of the Mediterranean world. Their gradual collection as authoritative books of the Christian tradition took place primarily during the second century. This complex process is known as the formation of the New Testament canon occurring in parallel with the formation of the Old Testament canon. In both cases the process continued for several centuries with considerable diversity and disputes over the selection of books based on tradition, authorship, and content.

The works of St. Irenaios, Tertullian, and a document called the Muratorian Canon attest that by the end of the second century Christians widely acknowledged twenty-two of the twenty-seven books of the New Testament as belonging to the new library of sacred books of the universal Church. For many generations the contested books continued to be 2 Peter, Jude, 2 and 3 John, the Book of Revelation, and to a somewhat lesser degree Hebrews and James. It was near the end of the second century that the appellation παλαιὰ διαθήκη ("Old Testament") came to be applied to the Hebrew Scriptures, first by Melito, bishop of Sardis, in Asia Minor.[18] One can suppose that the counterpart καινὴ διαθήκη (New Testament), applied to the new collection of Christian sacred books, was also in currency at that time, but extant references occur somewhat later in third-century authors such as Clement of Alexandria and Origen.

The so-called "closing" of the New Testament canon is usually dated with St. Athanasios the Great (367) who lists all the twenty-seven books of the New Testament.[19] The number

---

[18] Extant fragment in Eusebius, *Ecclesiastical History* 4.26. A translation of this fragment may be found in F. Sadowski, S.S.P., ed., *The Church Fathers on the Bible: Selected Readings* (New York: Alba House, 1987), pp. 26-27.

[19] In the 39th Festal Letter of St. Athanasios written on the occasion of Easter. For a translation, see *Nicene and Post-Nicene Fathers, Vol. 4, Athanasius: Select Works and Letters*, ed. Ph. Schaff (Grand Rapids: Eerdmans, n.d.), p. 552. With regard to the Old Testament, St. Athanasios differentiates between on the one hand the thirty-nine canonical books, which he enumerates as twenty-two (i.e., the number of the Jewish alphabet) according to the Jewish tradition and on the other hand the Readable books of which he lists only five: Wisdom of Solomon, Wis-

twenty-seven is, nevertheless, not absolute, not a matter of dogma. The ancient Syriac Church selected only twenty-two books for its New Testament without causing division. The Ethiopian Church embraced more than thirty. St. John of Damascus in the eighth century listed twenty-eight books.[20] Should one of the lost letters of St. Paul be discovered in the future, which is, of course, an extremely remote possibility, no sound reason could prevent it from inclusion. The "closing of the canon" is a firm but not rigid principle in the Orthodox Church because the classic Christian tradition never dogmatized the exact number of scriptural books and always valued many other writings and liturgical texts in addition to the canonical collection of the Scriptures.

The relationship between the Old and New Testaments, as that between Christianity and Judaism, is complex.[21] The foundational starting point is the statement of Jesus that he came not to abolish the Law and the Prophets but to fulfill them (Mt 5:17). Christ's work was a *renewal and completion*, not a rejection and abolishment of the Jewish heritage. Jesus lived fully

---

dom of Sirach, Esther, Judith, and Tobit. In the New Testament period he distinguishes between the twenty-seven canonical books and two others, the *Didache* and the *Shepherd*, which are recommended for reading.

[20] *An Exact Exposition of the Orthodox Faith*, Book 4.17 "Concerning Scripture." See *Saint John of Damascus: Writings*, trans. Frederic H. Chase, Jr., in *The Fathers of the Church*, Vol. 37 (Washington: The Catholic University of America Press, 1958), p. 376. This brief chapter appears as Appendix 1 of the present work. Readers may be startled that among the New Testament books St. John includes the Canons of the Holy Apostles attributed to Clement of Rome, a second-century work highly esteemed by ancient tradition. With regard to the Old Testament, St. John, as St. Athanasios before him, also lists the thirty-nine canonical books (i.e., twenty-two, according to the Jewish tradition) and distinguishes them from the Readable books of which he knows only Esdra, Esther, Wisdom of Solomon, and Wisdom of Sirach. The Church fathers exhibit great diversity pertaining to the Readable books.

[21] On a theological level, see the discussion by international scholars in *The Old Testament and Christian Faith: A Theological Discussion*, ed. B. W. Anderson (New York: Harper & Row, 1963) and more recently Paul J. Achtemeier and Elizabeth Achtemeier, *The Old Testament Roots of our Faith* (Peabody: Hendrickson, 1994). On an exegetical level, see among others E. Earle Ellis, *Prophecy & Hermeneutic in Early Christianity* (Grand Rapids: Baker Books, 1993).

within the traditions of his people. He accepted the authority of the Hebrew Scriptures and pointed to the ten commandments as a way to eternal life (Mt 19:16-19). However, Jesus, by his authority as well as his example, opened a new perspective on the Scriptures and the Jewish tradition. The new perspective is summed up by his reinterpretation of the Mosaic Law (Mt 5:21-48) and his teaching of unconditional love and forgiveness as the highest principles of God's kingdom beyond legal strictures (Mk 2:1-28).

In the light of Christ's resurrection and the guidance of the Holy Spirit, St. Paul and other New Testament authors built on this perspective. For them, the center of revelation was no longer the Law of Moses, but Christ in whom the resounding "Yes" of God's promises found fulfillment (2 Cor 1:10). They established Christ and the gospel as the criteria for the use and interpretation of the Old Testament. Above all, they read it as a book of prophecy foreshadowing the ministry of Jesus, the new covenant, and the inclusion of believing Gentiles into the people of God. While they accepted the authority of the traditional Jewish Scriptures, they also developed new positions of truth and conduct. Just as Jesus had set aside some written and oral traditions of the Law, such as the granting of divorce and the ritual washing of hands (Mt 5:31-32; Mk 7:1-23), so also St. Paul and the early Church put aside certain significant aspects of the Law, notably circumcision and the food laws as requirements for Gentile Christians (Gal 2:11-21; Rom 10:4; Acts 15:1-21). Yet for all Christians, the Hebrew Scriptures remained the inspired word of God written for their instruction and encouragement(Rom 15:4-5; 1 Cor 10:11) and profitable for correction and training in righteousness (2 Tim 3:16).

It is true that some later Christian authors held in varying degrees disparaging views of the Jewish legacy. The unknown author of the Letter to the Hebrews referred to the old covenant as obsolete and completely ineffectual (Heb 7:18; 8:13; 10:1-10). The author of the *Epistle of Barnabas* (9.4) claimed that circumcision commanded by God was never meant to be physical but only spiritual. The Christian heretic Marcion in the second century rejected the Old Testament altogether. By reason of his theological schema opposing "Law" and "Gospel" Martin Luther regrettably injected negative perceptions of the Old Testament and the Jewish heritage in some traditions of Protestantism. For example, a famous Lutheran biblical scholar once assessed the Old Testament as "a history of sin."

Over against such views it must be affirmed that the Old Testament is an essential record of revelation and an integral part of the Christian Bible. The Law of Moses, though no longer a criterion of salvation for Christians, is God's revealed Law, holy, good, and spiritual according to St. Paul (Rom 7:12-14). The great apostle never thought that either Jews or Jewish Christians should cease observing God's Law, only that the Law could no longer be imposed on Gentile Christians as people of God under the new dispensation of Christ and the gospel. He fully acknowledged the gifts of the Jewish heritage (Rom 9:1-5). While he believed that Christ alone was God's unique servant to both Jews and Gentiles (Rom 15:8-9), he categorically rejected the notion that God had abandoned the unbelieving Jews (Rom 11:1, 11, 29). With his apostolic authority, he warned Gentile Christians not to look with proudful contempt toward the Jewish people because they are still God's beloved people despite their state of disobedience as regards Christ (Rom 11:13-29). The destiny of the Jewish people, according to Paul, is best left in God's care and inscrutable wisdom (Rom 11:30-36).

In Orthodox perspective, the "Old" in the Old Testament implies no diminution of its revelatory character. The Church fathers, in their theological interpretation of the Old Testament found in certain passages, such as the account of the visitation of the three angels to Abraham and Sarah (Gen 18), intimations of the mystery of the Holy Trinity. As St. Paul had earlier perceived the eternal Christ at work in the Hebrew Scriptures (1 Cor 10:4), so did the Church fathers behold Christ as the agent of revelation in the Old as well as the New Testaments, for example when speaking to Moses from the burning bush

(Ex 3). The Holy Spirit descended upon the prophets and was active in Israel. Abraham, Moses, and the prophets were "friends of God" receiving direct revelations. The glory of God shone on the face of Moses (Ex 34:30; 2 Cor 3:7). The righteous figures of the Old Testament from Adam to Job, from Abraham to Moses, from Elijah to the Maccabean martyrs, are honored as saints in the Orthodox Church with specific feastdays dedicated to them. Readings from the Old Testament are integral to the worship of the Church. The hymnology and liturgical prayers are filled with the language of the Old Testament and references to God's savings actions on behalf of his people. In Orthodox iconography, a famous icon of the Resurrection depicts the risen Christ bursting the gates of hell and lifting up by each hand Adam and Eve surrounded by other righteous figures of Israel.

Has the Church then wholly coopted the Hebrew Scriptures as its own and taken them away from the Jews? Christians have no doubt been tempted to draw such an inference. But this plainly contradicts the apostolic authority of St. Paul who declared that "the gifts and the calling of God are irrevocable" (Rom 11:29). St. Paul took it for granted that the Jewish people are under God's care and would continue to live by the divine covenant given to them until the "mystery" of their unbelief was resolved by God himself (Rom 11:25-36). The Hebrew Scriptures are a gift to both Jews and Christians. From their own perspectives, both Jews and Christians understand themselves and claim to be the people of God faithful to their respective covenants. Although they read the Scriptures in a different light, the Jews from the standpoint of the Law and the Christians from the standpoint of Christ, Christians and Jews can serve in mutual respect as God's witnesses to one another and to the world according to their own calling. Christians are to be grateful sharers grafted on to the rich "olive tree" of the Jewish heritage that they "might glorify God for his mercy" (Rom 11:16-24; 15:9). If they call the Hebrew Scriptures "Old Testament," it is not to devalue its revelatory significance. Rather, it is to affirm their own understanding of the gracious acts of the living God, the Father of Jesus Christ, and to bear witness to their own experience of the new covenant in Christ which fulfills the first covenant.

Divine and Human Aspects

We call the Bible "Holy Scripture." Its sacred character derives not only from its role in the life and worship of the community of faith, Church or Synagogue, but also from its intrinsic nature and claims as witness to the revelation of God. The term *revelation* (from the Greek ἀποκάλυψις, Rev 1:1) denotes "uncovering," "disclosure," and "communication" of something hidden or previously unknown. The fundamental claim of Scripture, rooted in direct experience of God by privileged witnesses, is that the true God and Lord of the universe has chosen to make himself known to human beings in various ways, especially through actions and words. The living God, though searched for in shadowy ways from time immemorial, would have remained essentially unknown apart from his own acts of self-disclosure and communication toward humanity.

Scripture is called "the oracles of God" (τὰ λόγια τοῦ Θεοῦ, Rom 3:2) and the *word of God* (λόγος Θεοῦ, Lk 8:21; Jn 10:35; cf. Rom 3:2) because it communicates the knowledge God has chosen to make known through inspired authors. Words are means of communication through which we give shape to our deep thoughts, articulate them, and are thus able to communicate with others. Ideally, words are vehicles of truth. They seek to interpret reality and to bring the meaning of life to full light. It is no small matter to consider that Scripture in profound ways bears testimony to the treasures of God's thought, that is to say, insights and truths about the ultimate meaning of the whole of reality. From a religious rather than a scientific standpoint, that is exactly what Scripture claims to do. And it tells us that God's word, living and active, strikes with spiritual power, like a two-edged sword, piercing one's innermost being (Heb 4:12; Eph 6:17).

What does God desire to communicate through the testimony of Scripture? What central aspects sum up the religious and theological essence of the Bible as God's "communication book?" The Church fathers taught, and modern scholarship has confirmed, that readers should be attentive to the σκοπός, the comprehensive aim or purpose of Scripture, so that its parts can be seen in terms of the whole and the whole in terms of its parts.[22] From a holistic perspective, Scripture provides knowledge about God and his dealings with humanity in three significant and related ways.

First, the Bible bears testimony to *God's saving activity* in history, a process which has been called sacred history or the history of salvation. Some believers often understand this notion in a somewhat naive way, identifying the entire biblical story with literal history. However, the Bible was not written as technical history. The actual course of events and the dynamics of human interactions were far more complex than the story the Bible tells. This view does not deny any factual basis to the Bible, but only emphasizes that the narrative of Scripture represents the interpreted experience and religious memory of God's people over many generations. God's saving activity involves the whole range of human struggles to which the Bible honestly attests. At the core of this struggle are significant moments of God's revelation to key figures such as Abraham, Moses, the prophets, John the Baptist, Peter, Paul, and many others. God's saving activity is also defined by great acts of deliverance as understood, interpreted, and celebrated among God's people. The Bible calls these divine acts the "wonders" (τὰ θαυμάσια, Ex 3:20 LXX) or the "great deeds" (τὰ μεγαλεῖα, Acts 2:11) of God, such as the Exodus, the giving of the Law at Sinai, the entry into the Promised Land, Christ's incarnation, death and resurrection, and the gift of the Spirit on Pentecost.

---

[22] For a presentation of the patristic understanding of Scripture, see Chapter Four. The all-governing σκοπὸς of Scripture was Christ according to the Church fathers as well as, later, the Reformers Luther and Calvin. See Brevard S. Childs, *Biblical Theology of the Old and New Testaments* (Minneapolis: Fortress, 1993), pp. 44 and 49.

These moments of revelation and acts of deliverance, culminating in the person and ministry of Jesus, constitute the bedrock of divine revelation and the essence of the Bible as God's saving message.

Second, the Scriptures communicate *God's truth and wisdom* about creation and humanity, sin and salvation, moral right and wrong, heaven and hell. The chief truth and commandment is to acknowledge and worship the one, living God (Ex 20:1-6). "Let justice roll down like waters" (Am 5:24), the prophet Amos cried out on behalf of God, calling for social justice. Jesus taught: "Strive first for the kingdom of God and his righteousness" (Mt 6:33). St. Paul envisioned that "the creation itself will be set free from bondage to decay and will obtain the freedom of the glory of the children of God" (Rom 8:21). Knowledge about these matters is conveyed, again, from religious and theological, not scientific and strictly historical perspectives. It is mediated through a rich diversity of description of events and examples of conduct, narration of stories and collected teachings of wisdom, dreams and oracles, commandments and exhortations, psalms and prayers. It comes to us with varying degrees of clarity and accuracy through human experience and human words that often require careful interpretation. Nevertheless, Scripture in its overall σκοπός, whether by narrative or instruction, gives abiding testimony to God's saving truth which it views as light and life (Ps. 119:105).

Third and most importantly, Scripture communicates knowledge about the *mystery of the living God himself* – who he is and what his attributes are. Ancient peoples believed in all sorts of deities and paid homage to them in myriad ways. It is erroneous to claim that they all worshiped the same god by different names and in various ways. While the Bible attests to the truth that there is but one true God, human beings have nevertheless created countless of idols of material and conceptual gods throughout history. Holy Scripture proclaims the "true" God precisely in deliberate contrast and opposition to the "false" gods of paganism.[23] The true God is the living God of Abraham, Isaac, and Jacob, who guided his people in history and most fully revealed himself in the Son and the Spirit as a Triadic God (Mt 28:19; 2 Cor 13:13). He is the "living" God because he is the Lord, *Yahweh* ("I Am Who I Am," Ex 3:14), a personal God who, moved by love, lives and acts among his people with grace and truth. Not all pages of the Bible present God's character with equal clarity. But the total witness of Scripture proclaims and exalts the true God, the King of glory, a moral Lord, who commands justice and righteousness and who rules with love and mercy. Moreover, he desires to share his life – he yearns for covenantal fidelity and intimate communion with personal beings created in his image and likeness. In the end, the Bible points not to itself but to God. Its supreme testimony and greatest challenge to readers is the invitation to an intimate encounter and personal life with God.

It is also important to underscore that Scripture as God's communication is primarily addressed to God's people who nurture communal knowledge of God. God chose to make himself known to concrete persons such as Abraham and Sarah, Moses and Miriam, Paul and Lydia. His saving acts and words called forth a response and established relationships between God and such persons as well as between such persons and others who received their message. Those who answered the call sealed their relationship with God and with one another in mutual faith and loving obedience. Likewise God's great acts of deliverance were directed to the people of Israel and to the followers of Jesus. Their response was integral to the corporate covenant between God and his people. We can say that God's saving acts and words created these personal bonds and established the community of God's people itself. Holy Scripture emerged as "bones of bones and flesh of flesh" from the life of the faith community. As a book of faith and a book of the Church, Scripture constitutes the word of God not in the abstract but the

---

[23] A point strongly made by N. T. Wright, *The New Testament and the People of God*, pp. 467-476.

The Book of The Church

word of God addressed to his people. Corporate knowledge of the living God is the dominant theme of the Bible. God's word and those who receive it, Holy Scripture and the people of God, belong inseparably together. It is in this communal faith context that the words of Scripture become the "living word" of the living God in worship, preaching, teaching, guidance, and mission.[24]

Thus, the essence of the religious value and theological content of Holy Scripture as divine revelation is summed up by its testimony to God's saving activity, God's saving truth, and God's personal character. Scripture is the word of God insofar as it communicates to us knowledge about these crucial matters. However, such knowledge about God and his purposes is conveyed through human beings who spoke and wrote in human languages, Hebrew, Greek, and Aramaic. How is one then to understand the relationship between God's word and the human words in which the Bible is written? In what sense is the Bible the word of God? God neither has nor needs a physical mouth to make known his will. Did he perhaps miraculously create sounds to be heard as Hebrew, Aramaic, or Greek words by human subjects? Did he touch the minds of persons to convey his will, who subsequently communicated his messages to others in their own ordinary language and frame of reference? Or both? What about the interpretations of original revelations by later generations enshrined in the written biblical tradition? To what degree do the words of Scripture represent actual words of God? How does one begin to comprehend more precisely the truth that the Bible is the word of God in human words? The way one answers these questions determines one's view of Scripture, of inspiration, and of revelation. It also discloses where one stands in the spectrum of biblical interpre-

---

[24] It goes without saying that the faith community, which holds Scripture as its own sacred treasure, is the final interpretive authority of the Bible as God's word addressed to his people. Apart from this communal religious context, the Bible is reduced to a historical book, a book containing descriptions of experiences, beliefs, and customs of ancient peoples, which is a peculiar perspective of modern scholarly study of the Bible as we shall see in later chapters.

[handwritten marginal notes at top: "There is fundamentalism and radical fundamentalism then there is liberalism and radical liberalism then eschew all and be Orthodox!"]

tation from fundamentalism to radical liberalism.

[margin: "The record of revelation"]

In the Orthodox perspective, Holy Scripture is the *record* of revelation rather than direct revelation itself. To read about creation in Genesis is not the same as being present at creation. The prophet Isaiah personally beheld the Lord enthroned in glory, but in Isaiah 6 we have an account of that revelation, not the awesome revelation itself. The apostles and other devoted followers of Jesus experienced the outpouring of the Holy Spirit on Pentecost but in Acts 2 we meet a written description of that event, not the event itself. To be sure, the record of revelation is inspired, sacred, and canonical, but nevertheless it is still a record written by concrete human authors and in particular human languages.

[margin: "The Word of God in human words"]

Georges Florovsky has written that "the Bible is intrinsically historical … [in it] we hear not only the voice of God, but also the voice of man … Herein lies the miracle and mystery of the Bible, that it is the Word of God in human idiom."[25] The voice of God and the many voices of human beings combine in the single text of Scripture. No word of God is recorded except in human words. Divine revelation occurred neither in a vacuum nor as pure gold untouched by human contingency. God utilized ordinary human agents with their limitations of language and knowledge to communicate aspects of his will and purposes to limited subjects. The great thinker Origen called the Bible God's "baby talk" to humanity. St. John Chrysostom perceived Scripture as an expression of divine "condescension" (συγκατάβασις).[26] This view of Scripture presupposes a dynamic understanding of revelation and inspiration involving a process of personal divine-human interaction.

[margin: "Origen 'God's baby talk'", "Chrysostom συγκατάβασις 'condescension'"]

The most striking parallel to the twofold nature of Scripture is – by way only of analogy rather than by strict correspondence

[25] G. Florovsky, "Revelation and Interpretation" in the first volume of his collected works *Bible, Church, Tradition: An Eastern Orthodox View*, pp. 17-36. This article first appeared in *Biblical Authority for Today*, ed. A. Richardson and W. Schweitzer pp. 163-180.

[26] See R. C. Hill, "St. John Chrysostom and the Incarnation of the Word in Scripture," *CTR* 14 (1, 1980), pp. 34-38.

Analogy to the Christ and the two natures of Christ and the two the Bible

The divine and human Aspects of the verbal icon of Christ

— Jesus Christ who is himself called the incarnate Word of God (Jn 1:1,14). Although he was the eternal Logos and Son, the incarnate Christ was seen and touched; he spoke and acted in fully human ways, including the experience of hunger, frustration, and fear; yet he was without sin (Heb 4:15; 5:7). Just as the mystery of the one Christ is expressed in his divine and human natures, so also the mystery of Holy Scripture, the verbal icon of Christ, unites divine and human aspects. The divine aspects are to be found in Scripture's *saving message* about God, humanity, the gospel, the Church, grace and works, as well as the hope of the coming kingdom. This saving message is not merely an announcement of abstract concepts but a present reality as God's word which, when proclaimed and received by faith, becomes a living and transforming word through the power of the Spirit. The human aspects are to be found in the specific human languages of the Bible, the different kinds of literary forms and skills of the biblical authors and editors, as well as in their cultural and conceptual limitations which are intrinsic to all human endeavors.

It is not possible neatly to separate the divine and human elements of Scripture. The reader must engage the biblical witness in its totality and distinguish between central claims pertaining to salvation and subsidiary matters of history, chronology, language, and culture. That Jesus of Nazareth is the Christ and risen Lord is a truth of far greater magnitude than the historical question of the origin and development of christological titles. The hope of the resurrection of the dead and of the coming kingdom is far more important than the exact nature of these events as reported in various biblical books. To affirm that St. Paul experienced a true theophany of the risen Christ is one thing, to recognize that we have differing descriptions of this experience in Galatians and Acts is another. The Bible exhibits a tremendous variety in details as, for example, in the double accounts of the genealogies of Jesus, the Beatitudes, and the Lord's Prayer in the Gospels of Matthew and Luke. Questions can also be raised about cultural values and traditions reflected in Scripture pertaining to the institution of slavery, the role of women and children, and other social conventions. Where the line should ultimately be drawn and when it must be drawn between the saving truth of Scripture and its human expressions, especially in instances of major or controversial issues, becomes a matter of theological and normative interpretation in the life of the Church. Such issues, which have caused crises in Church history, raise questions that can be resolved not by expert interpretation alone but by the total ecclesial sense of what is God's will according to the spiritual receptivity of God's people.

In light of the above, therefore, the concept of the Bible as the word of God pertains primarily to the saving message of Scripture and cannot be applied literally to the exact words of each biblical verse. The latter view would virtually render the Bible a kind of massive computer printout of the mind of God, a gross misconception. Such understanding would entail insuperable difficulties especially concerning the scientific inadequacies and historical discrepancies in Scripture, which would inevitably be attributed to God. Moreover, from a theological viewpoint, the mystery of the living God cannot be strictly identified with the letter of Scripture. God is both revealed and hidden because he transcends human language and understanding. Accordingly, sufficient allowance must be made for the human factor in the reception of revelation and the composition of the biblical writings. Each author must be granted one's own personality, cultural framework, conceptual understanding, literary skills, and spiritual insight as an active contributor to the divine-human interaction. This position may be described as a dynamic view of the inspiration of Scripture.[27]

---

[27] An excellent example of the dynamic view of inspiration is Gregory of Nyssa's understanding of biblical revelatory language as being functional and accommodated to human capacities and circumstances. For him it is "blasphemous and absurd" to think that God actually spoke words in the act of creation (for, if so, to whom and in what language?). Gregory states that God did not speak Hebrew or any other language when communicating with such figures as Moses and the prophets. Rather, God communicated his will to "the pure intellect of those holy men, according to the measure of grace

a personal and dynamic mechanistic inspiration

rather than verbal concept

Orthodox theology holds to a personal and dynamic, rather than mechanistic and verbal, concept of inspiration. God did not merely dictate words or propositions to passive authors, but rather he impacted personally their whole beings, allowing them actively to comprehend, interpret, and convey his will to others according to the limitations of their understanding and language. It is important to note that the inspiration of the Holy Spirit embraces a far deeper and broader process than the composition of single books. Inspiration involves the entire community of faith, the life of a particular author, the composition of particular books, as well as their gradual gathering into a sacred collection. While all Scripture is "God-breathed" (θεόπνευστος, 2 Tim 3:16), it is not equally so, because of the variability of human receptivity. The inspirational character of the Book of Isaiah cannot be compared to that of the Book of Ecclesiastes, nor the inspirational character of the Gospel of John to that of the Epistle of Jude. Those who emphasize the literal authority of Scripture, often conservative and fundamentalist Protestants, debate the concept of *inerrancy.* They advocate essentially a Bible without error and are thus compelled to provide artificial defensive justifications.[28] Many seem to bypass the historical complexities and to attribute to Scripture an absolute character that properly belongs only to God, thus seemingly lapsing into a

inerrancy

---

of which they were partakers." They in turn communicated God's will in their own language and in forms adequate even to "the childishness of those who were being brought to the knowledge of God." See his work *Answer to Eunomius' Second Book,* trans. by M. Day, *Nicene and Post-Nicene Fathers, Vol. 5, Gregory of Nyssa: Dogmatic Treatises, etc.* (Grand Rapids: Eerdmans, n.d.), p. 276. I owe this reference to Peter Chamberas.

[28] The so-called "battle of the Bible" among Protestants has featured a wide spectrum of views concerning inerrancy as analyzed by Gabriel Fackre, "Evangelical Hermeneutics: Commonality and Diversity," *Int* 43(1989), pp. 117-129. For a balanced discussion see R. R. Nicole and J. Ramsey Michaels, eds., *Inerrancy and Common Sense* (Grand Rapids: Baker, 1980); D. A. Carson and J. D. Woodbridge, eds., *Scripture and Truth* (Grand Rapids: Zondervan, 1983); Clark H. Pinnock, *The Scripture Principle* (New York: Harper & Row, 1984); and D. G. Bloesch, *Holy Scripture: Revelation, Inspiration & Interpretation* (Downers Grove: InterVarsity, 1994).

kind of bibliolatry. The Roman Catholic view of inspiration may be expressed by the term *infallibility*, following the etymological sense that Scripture "does not fail" for the essential saving purposes for which it was given by God.[29] In the Orthodox tradition, perhaps the most appropiate expression is the *sufficiency* (αὐτάρκεια) of Scripture, an expression used by St. Athanasios to affirm the fullness of saving truth provided by Scripture.[30]

The question of *authorship* of scriptural books exemplifies the differing implications between dynamic and rigid views of inspiration. Those who incline toward a dictational view of revelation and inspiration are also concerned about securing the traditional authorship of the biblical writings. Those who hold to a dynamic view of inspiration are less anxious about authorship because they see God's guidance over the whole process,

---

[29] For a Roman Catholic perspective on Scripture see the Pontifical Biblical Commission's "The Interpretation of the Bible in the Church," *Or* 23 (29, 1994), pp. 498-524; the sections on "Hermeneutics" and "Church Pronouncements" in *NJBC*, ed. R. E. Brown and others (Englewood Cliffs: Prentice Hall, 1990); Bruce Vawter, *Biblical Inspiration* (Philadelphia: Westminster, 1972); Yves Congar, *The Revelation of God*, trans. by A. Manson and L. C. Sheppard (New York: Herder, 1968); Stanley B. Marrow, *The Words of Jesus in Our Gospels: A Catholic Response to Fundamentalism* (New York: Paulist, 1979); and the essays by Avery Dulles and Bruce Vawter in *Scripture in the Jewish and Christian Traditons: Authority, Interpretation, Relevance*, ed. F. E. Greenspahn.

[30] St. Athanasios, Κατὰ τῶν Εἰδώλων, in the prologue: αὐτάρκεις μὲν γάρ εἰσιν αἱ ἅγιαι καὶ θεόπνευσται Γραφαὶ πρὸς τὴν τῆς ἀληθείας ἀπαγγελίαν J. P. Migne, *P. G.* 25.1A. ["The sacred and inspired Scriptures are sufficient to declare the truth"]. The translation is from the series *Nicene and Post-Nicene Fathers*, Vol. 4, *Athanasius: Selected Works and Letters* (Grand Rapids: Eerdmans, 1975), p. 4. See also St. Athanasios, *The Life of Anthony*, chapter 16, where Athanasios uses the expression ἱκαναὶ αἱ Γραφαὶ to make the same point. Of course the term "sufficiency" is not to be taken in the sense that Scripture can stand by itself or interpret itself, for it is a book of the Church and its reading unavoidably involves selection and various levels of interpretation and application. For Orthodox perspectives on Scripture see Florovosky's article cited above and also P. Bratsiotis, "The Authority of the Bible: An Orthodox Contribution," in *Biblical Authority for Today*, ed. A. Richardson and W. Schweitzer; Thomas Hopko, "The Bible in the Orthodox Church"; Savas Agouridis, *The Bible in the Greek Orthodox Church*, and John Breck, "Orthodoxy and the Bible Today," in *The Legacy of St. Vladimir*, ed. John Breck and others (Crestwood: St. Vladimir's Seminary Press, 1990), pp. 141-157.

from the original moments and events of revelation to the formation of the biblical canon. Similar inferences may be drawn from differing perspectives on the relationship of the Bible to the believing community from which it came. Those who attribute to the Scriptures an absolute authority apart from or above the believing community may passionately defend authorship by eyewitnesses. In so doing, they desire to uphold the veracity of the Bible which must stand "alone," as if heaven opened to convey specific propositional statements and truths to individual authors. Those who recognize the dynamic relationship between Bible and believing community are less worried about traditional authorship because they view the whole life of the faith community as the ultimate context of inspiration and of sufficient teaching for salvation.

From an Orthodox perspective, the question of authorship is important but not critical. The ultimate theological criterion of truth is the life of the Church. In the Orthodox tradition, there are numerous valuable patristic writings, hymns, prayers, and other liturgical texts either by unknown or disputed authors over whom patristic and liturgical scholars debate without great anxiety about their findings' impact on the life of the Church. In the ancient Church, the authorship of a number of New Testament books, such as the Epistle to the Hebrews and the Book of Revelation, had already been freely debated for several centuries. It need not, therefore, be a cause of spiritual or theological confusion that modern scholars, for historical and literary reasons, continue this debate and even enlarge upon it. Such debate becomes pernicious only in cases where scholars, or other uninformed readers of the Bible who are conditioned by fundamentalist presuppositions, think that either the saving message of the canonical Scriptures or the theological value of ecclesial tradition are undermined by questions raised about the traditional authorship of the biblical writings. Whatever the historical complexities for or against the traditional attribution of authorship – and sound theology allows freedom for balanced historical research – the Church has embraced a variety of writings in its sacred canon and thus affirmed their value as multiple testimonies to God and his saving message. The essential value of the biblical documents lies in their theological content rather than in the historical circumstances of their composition.

Chapter Two

The Authority and Uses of Holy Scripture

We have invoked the analogy of the incarnation as the key paradigm for the right understanding of the nature of Holy Scripture, that is, Scripture as the word of God communicated in human words. The Bible has been affirmed to be, simultaneously, a book of God and a book of the Church. It is a book of God as it bears witness to the self-revelation of God through his redemptive acts and saving will. It is a book of the Church as it is the written and collected deposit of the living faith and developing traditions first of Israel and then of the Church in all their historical contingencies. To do justice to the intrinsic nature of Holy Scripture, these two elements, the divine and the human, like two threads inextricably interwoven and interpenetrating, must always be held together, whatever other implications are drawn from the historical and theological interpretations of Scripture.

Biblical authority, too, is incarnational. The authority of the Scripture, grounded as it is in the very nature of Scripture, involves two inseparable but distinct aspects. In its theological value and saving message, the Bible is the word of God which inherently bears God's authority. In its historical composition and canonical formation, the Bible is the word of Israel, and then the word of the Church, which carries the communal authority of the respective traditions of faith. Divine revelation, as noted, does not occur in a vacuum, but is always received revelation. It involves concrete human beings who must exercise insightful recognition, communicable interpretation, as well as practical application of God's saving word. In this sense, the divine authority of Scripture, the written repository of God's word, is integrally bound up with the authority of the religious community and its tradition, which constitute the living contexts of the reception and transmission of revelation.[1] The traditional uses of Scripture, such as liturgical, didactic, and doctrinal, presuppose this double-faceted authority of the Bible. How one exactly defines and assesses the interrelationship of the authority of Scripture, tradition, and Church is, of course, a rather delicate and crucial matter to which considerable attention will be devoted throughout this work.[2]

In modern times, the growth of the systematic and analytic studies of Scripture associated with Western universities over the last several centuries has produced a new situation that is both creative and disruptive. The development of scientific biblical criticism has gradually separated Holy Scripture from the religious community and placed it in what has been viewed as the "objective" setting of the scholar's study and the academic classroom. Along with undeniably brilliant achievements, the academic study of Scripture has also yielded negative results, including the questioning of divine authority as well as the traditional uses of the Bible. It is common knowledge that biblical critics today, especially those teaching in secular colleges and universities, routinely view and analyze the biblical writings not as Holy Scripture but as historical documents having primarily literary and cultural value. In view of the contemporary situation, it is neither possible, nor desirable, to conduct serious study of the Bible apart from engagement with prevailing biblical scholarship. Accordingly, a balanced perspective on the issue of the authority of Scripture requires consider-

---

[1] For the interplay between divine word and tradition in various religious communities, see *Holy Book and Holy Tradition*, ed. F. F. Bruce and E. G. Rupp (Grand Rapids: Eerdmans, 1968), and *Scripture in the Jewish and Christian Traditions*, ed. Frederick E. Greenspahn.

[2] In addition to this chapter, see especially the three hermeneutical chapters.

ation of the following issues: (1) the relationship between Scripture and tradition; (2) the traditional ecclesial uses of Scripture; and (3) the nature of the academic study of the Bible.

Scripture and Tradition

For centuries, Christians have thought of Scripture and tradition as distinct entities, harmonious or not. Scripture constituted the total number of authoritative books according to the canonical list of the religious community. Tradition was made up of everything else – including writings, teachings, liturgies, creeds, practices, and customs – outside of the biblical canon. The Reformation emphasis on the authority of the Bible (*sola Scriptura*) created a tension, and even opposition, between Scripture and tradition. The Catholic response was to affirm the authority of tradition as a "second source" of revelation. Up until recent times Orthodox theologians, influenced by the debate, also spoke of Scripture and tradition as "two sources" of divine revelation.

However, biblical criticism in the twentieth century has shed strikingly fresh light and has revolutionized the conceptualization of this issue. Analytic historical and literary studies have amply demonstrated an organic bond between Scripture, tradition, and the faith community. We have already noted that, prior to the formation of the Jewish and Christian Bibles, Jews and Christians lived and worshiped according to the dynamics of their respective ongoing traditions. Before the authority of the written word ever came to be, there was the authority of communal leaders, priests, prophets, apostles, and teachers who communicated and interpreted God's word with the living voice. Prior to the collection of the scriptural books into a canon, and yet reflected in the canon, there was the dynamic reality of the religious community in which oral teachings, the writing and editing of texts, and the fluid use and transmission of oral and written traditions were at work according to the changing circumstances and needs of the people of God.

[handwritten marginal notes: Protestant: Scripture vs. Tradition; Catholic: Scripture and Tradition as second source; Orthodox: Scripture and Tradition as two sources]

The result was that, through close historical study, scholars recognized the all-embracing reality of the faith community behind Holy Scripture and the all-powerful influence of tradition in its formation. Tradition as a living reality in which the life of faith was nurtured not only preceded and shaped Scripture, it also followed Scripture as the authoritative context for the reception, interpretation, and transmission of the word of God. A new slogan arose among scholars in conscious contrast to the Reformation principle of *sola Scriptura: sola traditio* (tradition alone)! It was also recognized, nevertheless, that the dynamics of community and tradition involved significant changes and new starts along the way. Without such new possibilities one would be at a loss to explain creative developments in the history of Judaism, not the least of which was the emergence of Christianity.

Several examples from the Old and New Testaments will illustrate the organic interplay between Scripture and tradition. Old Testament scholars have long observed that the first communal recognition of an authoritative book in the history of Israel was that of the Book of Deuteronomy, the pivotal document for the religious reformation under the devout King Josiah (2 Kings 22-23, *ca.* 620 B.C.). This "scroll of the Law" (2 Kings 22:8), the only book explicitly attributed to Moses (Deut 31:9), and which quite likely gave the title "Law" (*Torah*) to the entire Pentateuch, marks the beginning of the Jewish biblical canon, as well as an "archimedean point"[3] in Jewish religious history. Deuteronomy not only served as "the word of the Lord" (2 Kings 22:15) that authorized the Josianic centralization and reinterpretation of worship with lasting impact on all Jewish life. It also functioned as "the cornerstone of the eventual canon...with influence backward to Genesis and forward through the rest of the whole canon, whether MT or LXX."[4] However, the Book of Deuteronomy could function in

---

[3] The expression is by Moshe Weinfeld, "Deuteronomy, Book of," *ABD*, Vol. 2, p. 174.

[4] So James A. Sanders, "Canon, Hebrew Bible" in *ABD*, Vol. 1, p. 847. Sanders, who distinguishes between canon as authorizing function within the tradition

this authoritative fashion within the community only because of the antecedent function of authoritative traditions long at work within the same community. This phenomenon of *intertextuality*, that is, texts and traditions building on earlier texts and traditions, demonstrates the intimate interplay between the formation of Scripture and the living tradition of the community in which authoritative revelation is received, applied, and commended to later generations.

A second example of the interplay of Scripture and tradition from the Old Testament is the case of the prophets who claimed direct revelation from God and proclaimed the word of the Lord with the characteristic warrant: "Thus says the Lord!" In spite of the divine authorization to which the prophets appealed, many were persecuted and rejected in their own time by kings, priests, and false prophets. But the larger communal tradition vindicated them and canonized their oracles as part of Holy Scripture. Jeremiah, who lived at the time of Josiah and other kings, exemplifies the interaction between prophetic ministry and the historical vicissitudes of God's people. Jeremiah fully supported the reforms of Josiah, yet sharply condemned mere formal trust in "the Temple of the Lord" (Jer 7:4) as political security against threatening enemies (Jer 7). Kings and priests persecuted him on account of his oracles of judgment misconstrued as lack of support for the nation. In the end, a group took him captive to Egypt where, according to a tradition, Jeremiah suffered martyrdom. His divinely inspired oracles were nonetheless preserved by his scribe Baruch and, probably, other later editors who gave final shape to the Book of Jeremiah. In similar ways the oracles of other prophets survived and the prophetic writings came gradually to be revered in the Jewish tradition. Yet, as late as the time of Jesus, the "conservative" Sadducees, the highpriestly leaders of Judaism and keepers of the Temple,

---

and canon as final authorizing shape of Scripture also within tradition, is perhaps the foremost exponent of the closeness of canonization and the living tradition of the ongoing community. See further his books *From Sacred Story to Sacred Text* (Philadelphia: Fortress, 1987) and *Canon and Community* (Philadelphia: Fortress, 1984).

acknowledged as authoritative only the five books of Moses. Notwithstanding the many years of usage in the community, it took several more generations, and perhaps official initiatives by rabbinic leaders at Jamnia or later, before the prophetic books gained full canonical status for the Jewish community as a whole.

When we turn to the New Testament, similar parallels can be found regarding the mutuality between divine word and tradition, together with decisive expressions of renewal and creativity within the tradition.[5] It is well known that Jesus wrote nothing. He addressed his message to people in the vernacular Aramaic. Filled with the Spirit, he challenged his contemporaries with the call for the renewal of Judaism. His teachings circulated by word of mouth for a generation before written gospels appeared. The Synoptic Gospels, which are historically closest to Jesus, are written in Greek. These, in turn, are dependent on earlier Christian traditions and texts about the deeds and words of Jesus, which were translated into Greek and were used for the needs of the Christian congregations (Lk 1:1-4). We have no substantive historical or theological access to the incarnate Lord and his ministry except through these written records of faith that embody the oral and written traditions of the early Christians. In other words, as the form critics have taught us, despite some of the radical conjectures of these critics and their resulting notoriety, the authoritative words and deeds of Jesus have been mediated through the dynamics of the Christian community and its ongoing stream of tradition.[6] As written

---

[5] Some further reflections on these matters may be found in my article "Tradition in the New Testament," *GOTR* 15 (1, 1970), pp. 7-21.

[6] A comprehensive view of form criticism can be gained from Martin Dibelius, *From Tradition to Gospel*, trans. B. L. Woolf (New York: Scribners, n.d.); Rudolf Bultmann and Karl Kundsin, *Form Criticism*, trans. F. C. Grant (New York: Harper & Row, 1962); Klaus Koch, *The Growth of the Biblical Tradition: the Form-Critical Method*, trans. S. M. Cupitt (New York: Scribner's, 1969); and Edgar V. McKnight, *What is Form Criticism?* (Philadelphia: Fortress, 1969). The notoriety of form critics, especially that of Rudolf Bultmann, arose from the radical opinion that very little or nothing can be known about the actual words and views of Jesus because the early Christian tradition substantially changed the original reports and created new ones. This opinion, still nurtured in large measure by the Jesus Seminar today, has never been accepted by the

tradition, the Gospels themselves were esteemed and used in worship and teaching among various congregations long before they attained universal canonical status in the ancient Church by the end of the second century.

A whole new community arose around the person and work of Jesus, a community which itself generated its own traditions rightly called *apostolic*. Apostolic broadly connotes the traditions of liturgy, preaching, teaching, and practice of the early Christian congregations centered on the testimony and leadership of the Twelve, St. Paul, their chief associates, and numerous others involved in early Christian ministries (Acts 6:1-6; 1 Cor 15:5-11; Rom 16). Most telling is the case of the apostle Paul, a crucial and controversial figure during the painful process of symbiosis and separation between nascent Christianity and contemporary Judaism. St. Paul reflects in a particularly personal and dramatic way the creative struggle between faithfulness to the received religious heritage and openness to decisive new developments at God's beckoning.[7] Especially by his advocacy of the inclusion of Gentiles into the people of God as part of the new humanity in Christ, he epitomizes another "archimedean point" in the Jewish religious tradition from which to view the interactive dynamics of Scripture, tradition, and creative developments.

A Hebrew of Hebrews, a Pharisee blameless under the Law, and a zealous promoter of Jewish traditions, the apostle Paul knowingly and courageously set aside his former prerogatives, as he wrote, in order to know Jesus Christ his Lord and to proclaim the gospel to the nations (Phil 3:4-11; Gal 1:13-17).

---

majority of biblical scholars. See volume two of the present work, under form criticism.

[7] See Theodore Stylianopoulos, "Faith and Culture in Saint Paul: Continuity and Discontinuity," in *Rightly Teaching the Word of Your Truth: Studies in Honor of Archbishop Iakovos*, ed. Nomikos Michael Vaporis (Brookline: Holy Cross Orthodox Press, 1995), pp. 39-52, and by the same, "Faithfulness to the Roots and Commitment toward the Future: An Orthodox View," in *Orthodox Christians and Jews on Community and Renewal: The Third Academic Meeting between Orthodoxy and Judaism*, ed. Malcolm Lowe and published in *Immanuel* 26/27 (1994), pp. 142-159.

Nevertheless, whatever the creative implications of his call and conversion, the Apostle profoundly viewed the new situation in Christ not as a sectarian break from Judaism, much less a new religion, but one that was in deep continuity and essential fulfillment of the Jewish tradition. The God who sent forth his Son (Gal 4:4; 2 Cor 5:19), and who earmarked Paul as an apostle to the nations (Gal 1:15-16), is the God of Abraham, Isaac, and Jacob. Jesus, the Messiah/Christ, the Son of God and sharer of the divine glory (Phil 3:6-11; 1 Cor 2:8), is the final fulfillment of the Jewish tradition, "for all the promises of God find their Yes in him" (2 Cor 2:20; cf. Rom 9:4-5; 15:8-9). The Holy Scriptures are none other than the received Hebrew Scriptures that bear testimony to the new age of salvation (Rom 3:21; 2 Cor 6:1-2). The young Christian congregations that have taken root in various places of the Roman Empire constitute the "Church of God" (1 Cor 1:2; Gal 1:13; 1 Thess 1:1). The inclusion of the believing Gentiles into the people of God is a "grafting" on to the rich olive tree of Judaism (Rom 11:17), that is, a full integration into and in complete continuity with Jewish holy tradition according to God's plan (Rom 9:24-29; 11:32ff.).

On the other hand, the discontinuity between St. Paul's position and the contemporary Jewish tradition could not be more striking and controversial, particularly with respect to the Mosaic Law, the center of Jewish life. On the authority of God's call occurring through the personal "revelation of Christ" (Gal 1:12, 15; 1 Cor 9:1), the apostle Paul was utterly convinced that the Law as a criterion of salvation had come to an end (Rom 10:4; Gal 3:23-29). He may appeal to the ethical commandments of the Decalogue (Rom 14:8-10; 1 Cor 7:19) and draw lessons from the history of salvation (1 Cor 10:11). But as a matter of principle he is an adamant advocate of the justification of Christian Gentiles apart from the Law as a whole, especially the ritual Law governing circumcision, kosher foods, religious festivals, and the like (Rom 2:28-29; 3:21; Gal 2:3, 14-16; 4:9-10; 5:1-6). For him, the new center of life and thought was no longer the Mosaic Law but Jesus Christ. The energizing and guiding power was the Spirit (Rom 8:9-17; 1 Cor. 2:10-16; Gal 4:6). The decisive "word of the Lord" was now the one gospel of Christ on account of which St. Paul has become "all things to all people" (1 Cor 9:19-23; Gal 1:6-9). When one considers how this former strict Pharisee came to accommodate himself "under the Law of Christ" (ἔννομος Χριστοῦ, 1 Cor 9:21) to the ritually unclean Gentiles and their habits, including qualified acceptance of the eating of idol meats (1 Cor 10:25-33), one can appreciate the astonishing nature of the gospel's creative implications.

On the question of authority, St. Paul is a telling example of the dynamic interplay between divine word and tradition as well as between inspired leadership and community.[8] His writings testify that his call and authorization came directly from God in the manner of the prophet Isaiah whose language he cited (Gal 1:15). The gospel he proclaimed was not a mere human word but the word of God (Gal 1:11-12; 1 Thess 2:13). On the authority of his apostleship, and as one who possessed the "mind of Christ" (1 Cor 2:16), he set aside decisive Jewish traditions and became the transmitter of new definitive traditions, such as the Lord's Supper and the gospel, to both of which he refers with the explicit language of tradition (1 Cor 11:23; 15:1ff.). His personal union with Christ and consequent sense of speaking on Christ's behalf were such that, on the question of divorce, he could appeal to the authoritative teaching of Jesus prohibiting divorce, and then rather in passing qualify it by allowing separation but not remarriage (1 Cor 7:10-11).

Yet, St. Paul was not only an authoritative recipient of revelation but also its interpreter in dialogical relationship with the Jewish and Christian communities. Apart from what he viewed as questions of principle, and these were not always crystal clear, he was ever ready to be a Jew to the Jews and a Greek to the Greeks (1 Cor 9:20ff.). Two key features of his letters are persuasion and dialogical exposition in which he sometimes expresses his "opinion" (1 Cor 7:25) and in other instances leaves

---

[8] An insightful and practical book on this subject is by Helen Doohan, *Leadership in Paul* (Wilmington: Michael Glazier, 1984).

matters to the individual discernment of each Christian (Rom 14:5, 22-23). Above all, he knew that his own call was operative within God's larger call of the entire community, which corporately offered the "Amen" and over which the Apostle was not to be a dictator (2 Cor 1:20-24). His congregations were in fact the "seal" of his apostolic commission (1 Cor 9:2; 1 Thess 2:19-20; 3:8). It is no surprise that for the sake of the unity of the Church, although he vehemently disagreed with the demand of Jewish Christians to impose circumcision on Gentiles, he nevertheless consented to go up to Jerusalem and put the issue before the communal authority of the Apostolic Council (Gal 2:1ff.; Acts 15:1ff.).

The reception of St. Paul's writings in the ancient Church equally demonstrates the authoritative role of the wider community and its tradition. His Epistles circulated early among various Christian congregations (Col 4:16). They were the first group of apostolic writings to be collected and widely read, but not without misunderstandings (2 Pt 3:15-16; cf. Jas 2:20-24). During the second century, the apostle Paul became the hero of Marcion and other Gnostics who distorted his message and used his witness to undermine the developing great Church. The authority of Paul and his letters came into question, which may explain St. Justin Martyr's odd silence regarding Paul as late as the middle of the second century. Nevertheless, through the influence of church leaders and their local churches, such as St. Clement of Rome, St. Ignatios of Antioch, St. Polycarp of Smyrna, and St. Irenaios of Lyons, who all used and esteemed his writings, St. Paul's letters gradually gained universal authority in the Christian tradition. It is on the basis of their use in the tradition that, quite beyond what the Apostle could have anticipated, they eventually achieved full canonicity and became part of the Christian Bible.

What conclusions can one draw concerning the relationship between Scripture, tradition, and community? On the one hand, we must not excessively stress the authority of the Church and tradition in a way that would silence the intrinsic authority of

Scripture as the word of God. Orthodox theologians, sensitive to Reformation claims and concerned to counter them, have sometimes advocated the authority of Church and tradition "over" Scripture. For example, Panagiotis Bratsiotis strained his cogent thesis regarding the unity of Church, Bible, and tradition by claiming that the Bible derives its validity from the Church.[9] Such a claim erroneously misses the critical factor of the initiative of God behind all revelation, that is to say, the power and authority of the divine word given through prophets and apostles, indeed through Jesus himself. Even if one would argue that the Scriptures as the written word of God are part of sacred tradition, taking shape and deriving from the life of the Church, nevertheless the very fact of a biblical canon clearly implies recognition of the unique authority of what is received as divine revelation and thus the superior authority of the Bible in the general tradition. This is in complete harmony with the views of the Church fathers for whom Holy Scripture carried unquestioned and supreme authority as divine truth having God himself as its true author.[10] Without losing sight of the closeness between tradition and Scripture, it is essential therefore to acknowledge the authority of Scripture for tradition. In the words of Orthodox theologian Thomas Hopko:

> Once the Bible has been constituted as the scripture of the Church, it becomes its main written authority, within the Church and not over or apart from it. Everything in the Church is judged by the Bible. Nothing in the Church may contradict it. Everything in the Church must be bib-

---

[9] P. Bratsiotis, "The Authority of the Bible: An Orthodox Contribution," in A. Richardson and W. Schweitzer, eds., *Biblical Authority for Today*, p. 21. Bratsiotis was a respected Old Testament scholar at the University of Athens, Greece.

[10] Bruce Vawter, "The Bible in the Roman Catholic Church," in *Scripture in Jewish and Christian Traditions*, ed. Frederick E. Greenspahn, p. 117, points out that the Church fathers would not have been uncomfortable with the notion of *sola Scriptura* as such; only that they viewed Scripture within a learned ecclesial tradition. See below, chapter four, the section on the authority of Scripture and the Church fathers.

lical; for the Church, in order to be the Church, must be wholly expressive of the Bible; or more accurately, it must be wholly faithful to and expressive of that reality to which the Bible is itself the scriptural witness.[11]

On the other hand, we must not emphasize the authority of the Bible "over" the Church in ways that minimize the interactive authority of tradition and community in the origins, growth, and canonization of Scripture. For example, some would claim that the biblical "canon grew and was not 'made'" because it involved a gradual process in the tradition.[12] Yet it cannot be denied that selective choices about specific books had to be "made" along the way by Christian leaders, local churches, and eventually councils. In support of biblical authority, others would claim that the preaching of the gospel "founded the church,"[13] that is to say, the "self-authenticating" word of God, and in parallel the biblical books, "imposed" themselves upon the church.[14] But the mutual relationship between divine word, oral traditions, texts, canon, and community constitutes a seamless

---

[11] Thomas Hopko, *The Bible in the Orthodox Church*, pp. 66-67.

[12] So Wilhelm Schneemelcher in his introductory piece on the New Testament canon in Edgar Hennecke, *New Testament Apocrypha*, Vol. 1, p. 36. The English editor and translator is R. McL. Wilson, while the translator of Schneemelcher's contribution is George Ogg. Schneemelcher registers what he regards as a "decisive" point made earlier by A. Jülicher but nevertheless affirms that "the canon is certainly a work of the Church" and that "the authority of the theologians and bishops in the formation of the canon ought not to be underestimated," *ibid.*

[13] So Eduard Lohse, *The Formation of the New Testament*, trans. M. Eugene Boring (Nashville: Abingdon, 1981), p. 26. This is a very sound work, but at times reflects traditional Protestant accents. Lohse speaks of "the proclamation of earliest Christianity that founded the church." One would ask: Is there a time when the Church did not exist but only Christianity?

[14] Bruce M. Metzger in his piece introducing the New Testament in *The New Oxford Annotated Bible: The New Revised Standard Version*, p. vi. See further B. M. Metzger, *The Canon of the New Testament*. Metzger holds that the "intuitive insight" or discernment of the word of God by individuals in the tradition implies imposition of the word and the canon on the Church. However, this line of argument leads to the proverbial false alternative about which is first, the chicken or the egg. As has been repeatedly noted, revelation is always received revelation, the two elements, the divine and the human, belonging inextricably together. It is a

part of the same dynamic life of faith, a pulsating tradition which is responsive and propulsive, not merely passive and receptive. To speak of the Church as "being born from the hearing of the Word," or "to give priority over the church in the order of revelation," without further qualification, is to speak "inexactly" and on the basis of an "anachronism…predicated…on the [old] distinction between scripture and tradition."[15] The "one source" of revelation in the context of community is the Spirit itself, the primary bearer and creator of tradition.[16] Divine word and community, Bible and Church, cannot be played off against one another for they are both constitutive products of the same Spirit; just as there could be no Church without gospel, so also there could be no gospel without Church.

Finally, many would continue to advocate the unrelieved principle of *sola Scriptura* over against the Church and tradition. However this position is no longer historically or theologically tenable as a number of Evangelicals themselves have come to acknowledge.[17] Historical studies have shown what Harry Y. Gamble calls "an organic relationship" between Scripture and tradition.[18] J. N. D. Kelly and Henry Chadwick, among many others, have shown that tradition in the early Church signalled the whole salvific life of the Church, including liturgy,

---

question, theologically, in what sense God "imposes" (forces?) positive acceptance of his word on unreceptive subjects, although he certainly imposes his judgment.

[15] James Barr, *Holy Scripture: Canon, Authority, Criticism* (Philadelphia: Westminster, 1983), p. 28. Throughout his work, Barr emphasizes that the whole biblical tradition from oral word to final canon is thoroughly communal.

[16] This view, which is rooted in the biblical and patristic traditions, has been highlighted long ago by the Catholic theologian Johann Adam Möhler and has been repeated in various forms by both Catholic and Orthodox theologians such as Yves Congar, Henri de Lubac, Vladimir Lossky, and Georges Florovsky. See, recently, Avery Dulles, "Tradition and Creativity in Theology," *FT* 28 (Nov. 1992), pp. 20-27.

[17] For example, Clark H. Pinnock, *The Scripture Principle*, pp. 80-81, 150, and 218, and Donald G. Bloesch, *Holy Scripture*, pp. 12-13, 154-156. Especially Pinnock underlines that the Bible is a book of the Church, from which the Holy Spirit did not withdraw after the formation of the canon (p. 163), and that tradition and community provide controls in the interpretation of Scripture (p. 217).

[18] Harry Y. Gamble, "Canon: The New Testament," in *ABD*, Vol. 1, p. 859.

catechesis, evangelism, church order, and practice identified as apostolic.[19] It was in this stream of tradition that the New Testament had its genesis, with no sense of tension between oral and written traditions, or between Scripture and tradition. The scriptural books possessed authority because they were part of the tradition, that is by reason of their acceptance and usage in local churches. Against the Gnostics who generated numerous apocryphal books, the catholic Church in the second century appealed to orthodox doctrine, the "rule of faith," as a criterion of biblical canonicity. Subsequent to the Gnostic threat, when the Bible gained a supreme authority according to the Church fathers, its significance and value were nonetheless always integrally linked with the Church's continuous life and worship, and never apart from the Church's ongoing living tradition.

Recent studies on the biblical canon by such scholars as James A. Sanders,[20] James Barr,[21] and Harry Y. Gamble,[22] have underscored the indispensable and authoritative role of tradition and community in the making of the Bible. Gamble, in particular, accentuates the historical moorings of the biblical canon, rather than simply the creative power of some abstract, free-floating "word of God" behind Scripture. Notably absent as a criterion of canonicity is the appeal to inspiration because the whole life of the Church in all its traditions and functions was viewed as inspired and guided by the Spirit. For Gamble, the chief determinants of the formation of the New Testament canon are to be found in the historical origins of the Church's faith and the traditional usage of the New Testament books in the Church's worship and teaching.

---

[19] See J. N. D. Kelly, *Early Christian Doctrines* (New York: Harper & Brothers, 1960), pp. 29-51, a section he entitles "Tradition and Scripture" reversing the terms to reflect his thesis; and Henry Chadwick, "The Bible and the Greek Fathers," in *The Church's Use of the Bible: Past and Present*, ed. E. E. Nineham (London: SPCK, 1963), pp. 25-39.

[20] See above, note 4.

[21] James Barr, *Holy Scripture: Canon, Authority, Criticism.*

[22] See his article in the *ADB* cited above and his book *The New Testament Canon* (Philadelphia: Fortress, 1985).

Gamble isolates four criteria of canonicity: apostolicity, catholicity, orthodoxy, and traditional use.[23] A document was regarded as apostolic if its derivation was linked to an apostle or the times of the apostles, according to traditional views of authorship. To be catholic, it had to be known and relevant to the larger Church. To be orthodox, it had to agree with what the Church understood as correct teaching, which assumes that right doctrine could be known apart from Scripture and that Scripture had to be measured against authoritative, but unwritten, tradition. According to Gamble, the most operative criterion, even apart from the intrinsic value of a biblical writing, was traditional usage, especially among the great ecclesiastical centers of Christian antiquity. Gamble summarizes the interrelationship of Scripture and tradition as follows:

> The history of the canon shows that the contents of the canon were largely determined by ecclesiastical tradition (traditional usage, traditional ideas of authorship, and the appeal to traditional teaching), such that to acknowledge the authority of the canon is to acknowledge the authority of the tradition which gave rise to it. This point is now freely conceded by Protestant scholars....Thus it can be said that tradition precedes Scripture, is presumed by Scripture, and persists in Scripture....For these reasons it has become impossible any longer to juxtapose Scripture and tradition as alternatives. Rather, they stand in an organic relationship which precludes the exaltation of either against the other as theological authority.[24]

However, granted the organic mutuality of Scripture and tradition, it is also rather significant to observe that the community and its ongoing tradition exercised a certain functional precedence insofar as they acted as the critical interpretive agents in the whole process of the genesis, canonization, and application of Scripture. Just as revelation is never apart from a

---

[23] The references to Gamble are based on his contribution on the canon in *ABD*, Vol. 1, pp. 857-859.

[24] *Ibid.*, pp. 858-859.

Revelation is never abstracted text is from a human context word and the divine word is never disembodied

human context, so also the divine word is never disembodied, that is, apart from human understanding and communication. The role of interpretation before, during, and after the Bible – and thus a certain authoritative and controlling role of the community and the living tradition – is equally evident in both Christianity and Judaism. Jacob Neusner has cogently pointed out the function of the oral Law and the rabbinic tradition in giving voice to an otherwise silent sacred text.[25] Neusner considers it misleading to view Rabbinic Judaism as merely the end result of "an exegetical process or the organic unfolding of Scripture."[26] He insists that the rabbinic sages, through a conscious ideology and collected body of regulations outside of Scripture, also exercised a "mastery over" the holy writing so that it would speak with certainty and clarity to the community. In this sense, these ancient scholars made it speak "with their voice, in their idiom, and in their behalf."[27] According to Neusner:

> By controlling the Scripture both as sacred artifact and as intelligible text, sages guaranteed that it would always refer to their concerns and interests, that it would always validate and justify – but never contradict – their *halakhah* and the religious ideology that undergirded it. [28]

In parallel fashion, Christian thinkers and leaders in the ancient Church formulated a whole interpretive tradition in their active reception and diverse use of the Christian Bible according to the needs of the community. The Christian Bible emerged together with this interpretive tradition over against Judaism, Gnosticism, and Montanism. The canonical Bible was, by nature, an interpreted Bible as defined and understood by the wider apostolic and patristic exegetical tradition. The very life and identity of the ancient Church was based on what was affirmed to be a common and universal tradition of faith,

---

[25] Jacob Neusner, *Rabbinic Judaism: Structure and System* (Minneapolis: Fortress, 1995), especially pp. 31-43.

[26] *Ibid.*, p. 34.

[27] *Ibid.*, p. 43.

[28] *Ibid.*, p. 42.

liturgy, biblical canon, credal confession, church order, and practice. Whatever groups significantly disagreed with the growing catholic tradition simply went their own way as separate communities.

The point is not that the catholic tradition lacked freedom and variety – the opposite is true – but that the variety developed within a framework of unity according to the doctrinal sense of the Church signalled by the appeal to the "rule of faith" or "canon of truth." The later Ecumenical Councils, the doctrinal decrees of which were anchored on both Scripture and tradition, underlined the operative authority of the Church in interpreting Scripture and promulgating normative conciliar confessions of faith on crucial but disputed matters. In this perspective the gradual formation of the Christian Bible as the norm of Christian life and thought was integrally connected to a diverse but coherent exegetical tradition guided by the practice and fundamental credal insights of the universal Church. This double achievement, the formation of the biblical canon and the wider interpretive tradition which accompanied it, while allowing for ample creativity and rich variety, produced a classic unity between Scripture, tradition, and Church, and thus established a broad normative standard for all Christian generations.[29]

Ecclesial Uses of Scripture

We have affirmed the Bible as an ecclesial sacred text, that is, a text read and heard with living faith and prayerful attentiveness by believers. Holy Scripture has always been used in various but related ways to serve specific needs in the life of the Church, chiefly worship, preaching, teaching, meditation, practical guidance, and the articulation of doctrinal truth. In earlier epochs, of course, many people could neither read nor buy costly manuscripts, that is, texts written by hand. They could only hear the narrative of Scripture inliturgical recitation and see it depicted in sacred art. God's saving word was conveyed through

---

[29] See further, Theodore Stylianopoulos, "Scriptural Authority (Eastern Orthodoxy)," *ABD*, Vol. 5, pp. 1021-1023.

the reading and interpretation of Scripture in the corporate life of the Church and in monastic communities. Thus, exposure to the whole story of the Bible and its saving witness was primarily a corporate experience.[30] What follows is an account of the various uses and applications of Scripture in the life of the Church. It is intended to establish a basic perspective and not to present a complete statement on any of the ecclesial uses of the Bible.

1. LITURGICAL USE

The *liturgical* use is primary for several reasons. The liturgy is the main gathering of God's people for the celebration, remembrance, and renewal of the community's life with God.[31] Most of the biblical writings were written to be read aloud at such gatherings (Col 4:16; Rev 1:3), which were for prayer and worship, and not only for reading. In such context, the Scriptures were heard and interpreted as the word of God. A creative relationship also exists between worship and Scripture in that liturgical language has influenced the composition of biblical writings and in that the Bible has in turn powerfully impacted the forms and language of worship.[32] The Orthodox tradition

---

Hauerwas

[30] In contrast, after the Reformation, the emphasis on the authority of private interpretation placed Scripture in the hands of the individual and led to an ongoing process of separation and fragmentation, the bane of Protestantism, now accentuated by modern individualism. Among others, Stanley Hauerwas, a Protestant theologian, has sharply challenged the assumed "right" of each Christian to interpret the Bible. See his book *Unleashing the Scripture: Freeing the Bible from Captivity to America* (Nashville: Abingdon, 1993). This is not at all to suggest, however, that private devotional study of the Bible is wrong or to be discouraged, because the Bible belongs to the whole Church and to every member of God's people, not only to priest, monk, or theologian.

[31] Philip Rousseau, *Basil of Caesarea* (Berkeley: University of California Press, 1994), pp. 127-131, provides an excellent view of the patristic conviction that the liturgical context actualizes saving truth and that worship brings an understanding of its own as believers encounter the message of the text, assent to the all-sufficient truth of the gospel, and offer their public confession of faith in harmony with the apostolic tradition.

[32] Jean Daniélou, *The Bible and the Liturgy* (North Bend: University of Notre Dame Press, 1956); Ralph P. Martin, *Worship in the Early Church* (Grand Rapids: Eerdmans, 1974); C. Jones, G. Wainwright, and E. Yarnold, eds., *The Study of Liturgy* (New York: Oxford University Press, 1978); and P. F. Bradshaw, *The Search for the Origins of Christian Worship* (New York: Oxford University Press, 1992).

with its immense treasures of hymnological books, liturgical services, and calendar of feasts, exemplifies a thoroughly biblical character which has been insufficiently studied.[33] Above all, corporate worship constitutes the Church's grateful response to God's gracious actions, a doxological celebration of God's holy presence and renewal of life. The sheer liturgical recitation of Scripture, read meaningfully and with living faith, becomes a powerful hearing of God's word energized by God's Spirit, a transforming experience for the gathered community.[34]

As central and crucial as the liturgical use of Scripture is, however, it cannot be allowed to absorb the other uses of the Bible, each of which has its own integrity and purpose. This is an admonition that Orthodox theologians especially need to heed.[35] To emphasize that all things have their beginning and end in liturgy is an excessive generality. God's saving acts and words occur and are experienced outside of worship as well. Abraham was called as an idolater. Moses was shepherding his flock. Paul was persecuting Christians. There are other important things to do besides worship. God and his word are also served through preaching and teaching, pastoral work and mission, social justice and philanthropy, beyond specifically liturgical contexts.

---

[33] The major feasts of the ecclesial calendar are an ἀνάμνησις or liturgical actualization of the good news of Christ's ministry including his incarnation, birth, baptism, transfiguration, triumphal entry, death on the cross, resurrection, ascension and the gift of the Spirit, with hundreds of hymns proclaiming and celebrating the meaning of these events. The periods of the Great Lent, Holy Week, and Easter to Pentecost are likewise rich in biblical content. The eight-week cycle of hymns of the Παρακλητική, especially for Saturday Vespers and Sunday Mattins, is an astonishing liturgical proclamation of the gospel. The prayers of the services constantly refer to God's great acts of deliverance in Scripture.

[34] This dimension is emphasized by John Breck, *The Power of the Word in the Worshiping Church* (Crestwood: St. Vladimir's Seminary Press, 1986).

[35] Because of the weight and importance of the liturgical tradition, there is an Orthodox "cultic pull" toward a kind of "liturgicalism" or "eucharisticism." Orthodox theologians have seen the liturgy as the hermeneutical key to all questions. However, it is doubtful that there is a single key to all the dimensions of Christian life and thought such as moral choices, discussion of doctrinal truth, governing order, and of course personal faith, prayer, and corporate worship. For a discussion of hermenutics, see below the relevant chapters.

Liturgy should, but does not necessarily of itself lead, to effective preaching, teaching, mission, and social responsibility, ministries that require their own faithful commitment, insight, and skills.

2. *HOMILETICAL USE*

The *homiletical* use of the Bible finds its integrity in the meaning and function of the *kerygma* or proclamation of God's saving message.[36] While closely related to liturgy, God's word can and should be proclaimed in life's many contexts. Although the liturgical recitation of Scripture itself resounds with God's saving message, the specific integrity of proclamation is that there is a *faithful proclaimer* as well as a message to be proclaimed. The proclaimer is one in whom God's word has already been actualized and through the proclaimer it seeks to be actualized anew by the Spirit's power working in the hearts of others. Effective proclamation presupposes a dynamic experience of God's word and leads to an awakening and nurturing of faith. Preaching at its best energizes worship and makes the liturgy a more powerful experience. However, proclamation can, in appropiate ways, occur not only in the solemnity of corporate worship but also in any human circumstance as casual as a visit between neighbors. Preaching should not be excessively overbearing, didactic, moralistic, or politically ideological, but must do justice to the freedom and power of God's word, mediating God's presence, love, and forgiveness.

3. *CATECHETICAL USE*

The *catechetical* use of Scripture concentrates on biblical teaching for the edification of God's people.[37] Along with proclamation of God's saving message, there is also *didache* ("teaching," Mt 7:28; Rom 6:17; 1 Cor 14:6) intended for

---

[36] Among many useful works on biblical preaching, see Anthony Coniaris, *Preaching the Word of God* (Brookline: Holy Cross Orthodox Press, 1983); J. M. Reese, *Preaching God's Burning Word* (Collegeville: Liturgical Press, 1975); H. W. Robinson, *Biblical Preaching* (Grand Rapids: Baker, 1980); John Burke, *Gospel Power* (New York: Alba House, 1978); and *Preaching in the Patristic Age*, ed. D. G. Hunter (Mahwah: Paulist Press, 1989).

[37] Helpful handbooks include Dick Murray, *Teaching the Bible to Adults and Youth* (Nashville: Abingdon, 1987); and Michael E. Williams, *The Storyteller's Companion to the Bible*, 5 vols. (Nashville: Abingdon, 1991-1994).

ethical instruction and practical guidance. In Scripture itself, books such as the prophetic writings, the Gospels, and St. Paul's letters, contain both proclamation and teaching. Others, such as the Book of Proverbs and the Epistle of James, offer largely moral instruction. In the Christian tradition, as much as the Jewish, teaching is a divinely commanded ministry of religious training involving discipline, learning, guiding, and correction. The Church fathers who wrote biblical commentaries and preached didactic homilies attributed great value to κατήχησις ("teaching" or "instruction"). They envisioned the Bible to be the textbook for Christian παιδεία ("training" or "education") and Christ the supreme παιδαγωγὸς ("instructor" or "educator") of humanity.[38] Effective biblical teaching presupposes living faith and evangelical spirit, else it risks becoming tedious and lifeless.

4. DEVOTIONAL USE

The *devotional* use is the reading of Scripture during prayer and meditation, both an ancient and modern exercise of piety in both Judaism and Christianity.[39] Psalm 119 is a magnificent celebration of God's Law as song of joy and lamp of truth for the psalmist's pilgrimage of life. An ancient Christian monastic *Evagrios* expressed similar sentiments when he said, "May the sun on rising find you with a Bible in your hand."[40] In monasticism, where whole scriptural books were and are memorized and recited by heart, the reading of Scripture has been a pillar of piety.

---

[38] Werner Jaeger, *Early Christianity and Greek Paideia*, pp. 66-102.

[39] Paul Evdokimov, "*Lectio Divina:* Reading the Bible," in his *Struggle With God*, trans. Sister Gertrude, S.P. (Glen Rock: Paulist Press, 1966), pp. 189-193; D. Burton-Christie, *The Word in the Desert: Scripture and the Quest for Holiness in Early Christianity* (New York: Oxford University Press, 1993). For contemporary devotional use, see Thomas Hopko, *Reading the Bible* (New York: Religious Education Department, Orthodox Church of America, 1970); Theodore Stylianopoulos, *Bread for Life: Reading the Bible* (Brookline: Department of Religious Education, Greek Orthodox Archdiocese of North and South America, 1980); and Kallistos Ware, "How to Read the Bible," *The Orthodox Study Bible*, ed. Peter E. Gillquist and others (Nashville: Thomas Nelson, 1993), pp. 762-770.

[40] Paul Evdokimov, *Struggle With God*, p. 189. The saying is by Evagrios, a fourth-century ascetic of the Egyptian wilderness.

Among God's people, countless men and women have been both inspired and strengthened in their life of faith through prayerful reading of God's word. Moments of prayer are moments of personal revelation. In the context of prayer, God's written word can strike with piercing illumination to convict and purify the heart. Far from the classroom and formal theological studies, ordinary people have experienced God's presence and power through the devotional study of the Scriptures in ways more profound than many theologians and scholars adept at biblical analysis. The Church fathers urge all believers to apply themselves to the daily reading of Scripture, approaching God's written word as they would the sacramental Word in the eucharist. For the Church fathers, the devotional reading of Scripture marks a personal encounter with God – a time in which God intervenes, speaks, guides, and draws the believer into his life in the company of the angels and the saints.

The *doctrinal* use of the Bible arose in theological controversies and the necessary defense of the Christian faith. The New Testament itself gives evidence of such disputes and the rejection of false teaching through credal formulations (1 Cor 8:5-6; Col 1:15ff.; 1 Jn 4:2-3). In subsequent centuries, numerous theological controversies emerged over the nature of God, creation, the Old Testament, Christ, the Holy Spirit and other issues. Church leaders and theologians faced mighty struggles in interpreting and formulating more clearly the conceptual contours of Christian truth in contrast to Judaism, Gnosticism, and later heresies, such as Arianism. The correct interpretation of the Scriptures was at the heart of these debates as shown by the works of St. Justin Martyr, St. Irenaios, St. Athanasios, and the Cappadocians. Theological writings and creeds were composed to formulate in a normative way the intellectual content of faith and thus also to define more clearly the identity of the Church itself. The Ecumenical Councils functioned as the highest ecclesial authority for the normative promulgation of Christian truth.[41] The harvest of this long and

---

[41] See Mark Santer, "Scripture and the Councils," *Sobornost* 7 (2, 1975), pp. 99-111 and Constantine Scouteris, "Holy Scripture and Councils," *ibid.*, pp. 111-116.

painful process was the Nicene Creed which is an interpretive summary of Scripture's major themes and, as well, an abiding testimony to the classic heritage of Christian doctrine.[42]

Academic Study of Scripture

By academic study we mean the formal and systematic study of Scripture at the level of universities, colleges, and theological schools which have flourished in Western Europe, North America, and now all over the world.[43] Such study presumes to be scientific in that it is conducted on the basis of a system of standards and methods developed by a long-standing academic tradition in the liberal arts and humanities. This academic tradition deserves careful consideration not only for its impressive accomplishments, but also for its disruptive effects pertaining to all traditional approaches to the Bible. The liberal tradition of biblical studies, complex and diverse as it is, consti-

---

[42] In view of the doctrinal confusion or rather chaos in contemporary times, the World Council of Churches has done well to put the Nicene Creed at the center of a substantive project toward doctrinal consensus as a basis for Christian unity. See *Confessing the One Faith: An Ecumenical Explication of the Apostolic Faith as it is Confessed in the Nicene-Constantinopolitan Creed (381),* Faith and Order Paper No. 153 (Geneva: WCC Publications, 1991), and also Hans-Georg Link, ed., *The Roots of Our Commmon Faith: Faith in the Scriptures and in the Early Church,* Faith and Order Paper No. 119 (Geneva: World Council of Churches, 1984).

[43] For a simple and positive account of the rise of academic biblical research, see Luis Alonso Schoekel, *Understanding Biblical Research,* trans. Peter J. McCord (New York: Herder and Herder, 1968). A comprehensive perspective on the various methods is provided by the following: Daniel J. Harrington, *Interpreting the New Testament: A Practical Guide* (Wilmington: Glazier, 1979); Bruce Chilton, *Beginning New Testament Study* (Grand Rapids: Eerdmans, 1986); Christopher Tuckett, *Reading the New Testament: Methods of Interpretation* (Philadelphia: Fortress, 1987); I. Howard Marshall, ed., *New Testament Interpretation: Essays on Principles and Methods* (Grand Rapids: Eerdmans, 1977); S. Neil and T. Wright, *The Interpretation of the New Testament 1881-1986* (Oxford: Oxford Univ. Press, 1988); and E. J. Epp and G. W. MacRae, S.J., eds., *The New Testament and Its Modern Interpreters* (Philadelphia: Fortress, 1989). For basic bibliographies, see D. J. Harrington, S.J., *The New Testament: A Bibliography* (Wilmington: Glazier, 1985) and D. A. Carson, *New Testament Commentary Survey* (Grand Rapids: Baker Books, 1993).

tutes in fact a new tradition and represents a new community, that is, a community of scholars with their own interests and presuppositions which go beyond particular methodologies. The ideology of academic scholarship has often yielded radical judgments about the authority of Scripture as traditionally held by all Christians. Moreover, the dominance of scholarship has imperceptibly given rise to an intimidating supposition that only scholars can truly know the Bible, a notion as arrogant as it is foolish. The following sketch of biblical criticism is amplified by a more extensive assessment of contemporary biblical scholarship in Chapter Five.

AMEN!

The prevailing academic study of the Bible, conducted as scientific scholarship on the basis of historical and literary criticism, is a product of the modern world. It is closely linked with the birthpangs of modern Western civilization marked by the Reformation, the religious wars, the rise of science, intellectual reaction to rigid forms of both Catholicism and Protestantism, and with the embrace of reason as the primary way to truth and human progress.[44] Given the elements of freedom from church authority and of the use of autonomous reason, biblical criticism could first develop only within the Protestant world, yet not without bitter acrimony and further cross-sectional divisions among Protestants into liberal, conservative or evangelical, and fundamentalist camps.[45] From the beginning, biblical criticism advocated a detached, rational reading of the Bible, "like any other book," and fostered a

---

[44] See the articles on "Biblical Criticism" by J. C. O'Neill and W. Baird in *ABD*, Vol. 1, pp. 725-736, as well as G. H. Reventlow, *The Authority of the Bible and the Rise of the Modern World.*

[45] The story from a conservative Protestant standpoint is told by M. A. Noll, *Between Faith and Criticism: Evangelicals, Scholarship, and the Bible in America* (Grand Rapids: Eerdmans, 1991). For a liberal view, see James Barr, *The Bible in the Modern World* (New York: Harper & Row, 1973). An excellent comparative overview of the approaches to Scripture by the Reformers as well as contemporary conservative and liberal Protestants is provided by David H. Kelsey, "Protestant Attitudes Regarding Methods of Biblical Interpretation," *Scripture in the Jewish and Christian Traditions: Authority, Interpretation, Relevance*, ed. F. E. Greenspahn pp. 133-161.

hostility toward traditional Christian beliefs. It sought to discover the "pure natural religion" of Jesus over against the distorted religion about Christ created by the Church and its doctrines, which had presumably caused controversies and wars. Central teachings of the New Testament, such as the deity of Jesus as Son of God and the miracles recorded in the Bible, including Jesus' resurrection, were viewed with marked skepticism. These and similar ideas, hostile to traditional Christianity, can be traced back to the English rationalists such as John Locke (1632-1704) and the German G. E. Lessing (1729-1781). They were developed and refined in various ways by numerous German scholars such as J. S. Sempler (1725-1791), F. C. Baur (1792-1860), J. Wellhausen (1844-1918), A. Harnack (1851-1930), R. Bultmann (1884-1976), and still surface today through the work of the American Robert Funk who is the driving force behind the radical "Jesus Seminar."[46]

Biblical criticism did not advance in linear fashion but through diverse dynamics and various schools such as the Tübingen, the "history of religions," and the Bultmannian. Nor have all liberal biblical critics been radicals. As biblical criticism gained acceptability in mainstream Protestantism, the hostile edge of the earlier critics was tempered, subtly hidden, or even justified in the name of scientific research. Some mainline Protestant scholars have themselves raised their voices in criticism of biblical criticism in its technical, historical, and philosophical extremes.[47]

---

[46] The chief work of the Jesus Seminar to date is *The Five Gospels: The Search for the Authentic Words of Jesus* (New York: Macmillan, 1993), ed. by R. W. Funk and others, a work that finds little authentic material in the Gospels. While high "scientific scholarship" is claimed, members of the Jesus Seminar do all they can to achieve wide publicity for their radical views with the deliberate purpose, so some explicitly state, to remove the doctrinal underpinnings and thereby the prejudices of traditional Christianity. For a severe critique of the Jesus Seminar by a mainstream scholar, see R. B. Hays, "The Corrected Jesus," *FT* 43 (May 1994), pp. 43-48, who finally refers to the methodology and conclusions of the Jesus Seminar as a "reprehensible deception," p. 47.

[47] F. Hahn, *Historical Investigation and New Testament Faith*, trans. R. Maddox and ed. E. Krentz (Philadelphia: Fortress, 1983); Peter Stuhlmacher, *Historical Criticism and Theological Interpretation of Scripture*; Walter Wink, *The Bible in*

The field as a whole, granted its brilliant historico-philological findings, has been marked by rationalist ideology and a distinct strain of Enlightenment radicalism. As William Baird puts it, "the history of NT criticism from the end of the 18th century through the first two thirds of the 20th is largely a recital of the Enlightenment themes with variations."[48]

It is not surprising that biblical criticism did not readily find receptive ground within the Roman Catholic Church.[49] Although one of the earliest pioneers was the French Oratorian priest R. Simon (1638-1712), a convert from Protestantism, Catholic biblical studies remained defensive until the second half of the twentieth century. Two great Catholic scholars appeared in the early twentieth century, M. J. Lagrange and A. Loisy. Lagrange, who was founder of the Biblical School in Jerusalem and the journal *Revue Biblique*, convincingly demonstrated that critical biblical research could be conducted without necessary opposition to faith and Church. Loisy, a gifted philologist and exegete, fell into critical extremism and was excommunicated (1908) as a leader of the Modernist heresy. Earlier, the Pontifical Biblical

---

Human Transformation; Martin Hengel, "Historical Methods and the Theological Interpretation of the New Testament," in his *Acts and the History of Earliest Christianity*, transl. by John Bowden (Philadelphia : Fortress, 1979), pp. 127-136. Eta Linnemann, a scholar who describes herself as "a Bultmannian turned evangelical" has written *Historical Criticism of the Bible: Methodology or Ideology?* trans. R. W. Yarbrough (Grand Rapids: Baker, 1990). From a conservative Lutheran viewpoint, see Gerhard Maier, *The End of the Historical-Critical Method*, trans. E. W. Leverenz and R. F. Norden (St. Louis: Concordia, 1974). A recent mainline critique of liberal theology and charges of heresy come from Paul C. McGlasson, *Another Gospel* (Grand Rapids: Baker, 1994) with a supporting foreword by Brevard Childs.

[48] "New Testament Criticism," in *ABD*, Vol. 1, p. 731.

[49] A perspective on biblical criticism within the Roman Catholic Church can be gained from L. A. Schoekel, *Understanding Biblical Research*; R. E. Brown, "Our New Approach to the Bible," in his *New Testament Essays* (Garden City: Image Books, 1965), pp. 21-35; J. J. Collins and J. D. Crossan, eds., *The Biblical Heritage In Modern Catholic Scholarship* (Wilmington: Glazier, 1986); R. B. Robinson, *Roman Catholic Exegesis Since Divino Afflante Spiritu: Hermeneutical Implications* (Atlanta: Scholars Press, 1988); and G. P. Fogarty, *American Catholic Biblical Scholarship* (San Franscisco: Harper & Row, 1989).

Commission (1902) had been established to keep a watchful eye on biblical exegetes.

The cloud over Roman Catholic biblical scholars was not lifted until the papal encyclical *Divino Afflante Spiritu* (1943), the charter of the modern Catholic historical-critical study of Scripture. On the basis of that document and by the encouraging guidance of the Biblical Commission, Catholic biblical scholarship has come to full maturity during the last fifty years through the work of numerous scholars such as the French P. Benoit and J. Daniélou, the Belgians L. Cerfaux and A. Descamps, the Germans J. Schmid and R. Schnackenburg, and the Americans R. Brown and J. A. Fitzmyer. These scholars have shown that front-line critical biblical studies can be conducted apart from philosophical biases and extreme positions. However, tensions between liberal and conservative scholars, as well as doubts and attacks on biblical criticism, continue to exist within the Roman Catholic Church, not least because of the radical tendencies of some scholars.[50]

In the Orthodox Church, critical biblical studies are still largely derivative due to the absence of many universities in Orthodox countries and the consequent lack of long-standing academic traditions for the advancement of all disciplines. In Russia, the tremendous intellectual ferment centered around numerous academies and the promise of an amazing revival in arts and sciences in dialogue with European developments were tragically cut short by the Bolshevik Revolution (1917).[51] Greece,

---

[50] A critique from the conservative Catholic side is by G. A. Kelly, *The New Biblical Theorists: Raymond E. Brown and Beyond* (Ann Arbor: Servant Books, 1983). R. E. Brown himself has devoted much effort to answering conservative critics and establishing a "centrist position" over against both conservatives and liberals, for example, in his works *The Critical Meaning of the Bible* (New York: Paulist, 1981) and *Biblical Exegesis and Church Doctrine* (New York: Paulist, 1985). See also the contributions of Brown and Cardinal Ratzinger in *Biblical Interpretation in Crisis: The Ratzinger Conference on Bible and Church*, ed. R. J. Neuhaus (Grand Rapids: Eerdmans, 1989).

[51] For an account of the intellectual ferment in Russia at the turn of the twentieth century, see Nicolas Zernov, *The Russian Religious Renaissance of the Twentieth*

after four centuries of Ottoman rule, gained political independence in the early nineteenth century and was the only Orthodox country aside from Cyprus to escape Communist rule in the twentieth. In Greece, with the establishment of two national universities in Athens (1837) and Thessalonike (1926), the foundations were set for systematic studies in all areas, including theology, with relative freedom of inquiry and apart from direct ecclesiastical supervision.

In biblical studies, a number of scholars emerged, most of them trained in Germany, such as E. Zolotas, N. Damalas, E. Antoniadis, V. Vellas, P. Bratsiotis, V. Ioannidis, and S. Agouridis, who collectively have produced substantial critical work within Orthodox theological parameters.[52] The future growth of Orthodox biblical studies cannot occur apart from an overall assessment of their labors.[53] Orthodox biblical scholars

Orthodox Biblical Critics (handwritten marginal note)

Century (London: Darton, Longman & Todd, 1963). See also P. Valliere, "The Liberal Tradition in Russian Orthodox Theology," *The Legacy of St. Vladimir*, ed. J. Breck and others, pp. 93-106.

[52] See John Karavidopoulos, "Οἱ Βιβλικὲς σπουδὲς στὴν Ἑλλάδα" *DelBibMel* 4 (July-December, 1985), pp. 73-87, and in German "Das Studium des Neuen Testaments in der griechisch-orthodoxen Kirche in Vergangenheit und Gegenwart," *BTZ* 3 (1, 1986), pp. 2-10. In particular, S. Agouridis has been a prolific author and energizing force among contemporary Greek biblical scholars who pursue systematic work through a biblical society and the journal Δελτίον Βιβλικῶν Μελετῶν, under the supervision of Agouridis. For a bibliography on the substantial ouput of Greek biblical scholars, writing primarily in modern Greek, see this journal and the following bibliographical tools: John Karavidopoulos, Ἑλληνικὴ Βιβλικὴ Βιβλιογραφία 1961–1975 (Θεσσαλονίκη, 1975) and Ch. S. Tzogas and P. S. Papaevangelou, Ἑλληνικὴ Θεολογικὴ Βιβλιογραφία τῆς Τελευταίας Ἑκατονταετίας 1860–1960 (1963). In English see R. Pietarinen, *A Bibliography of Major Orthodox Periodicals in English* (Joensuu, Finland: University of Joensuu, 1987), pp. 10-13.

[53] In this regard a programmatic essay is by Savas Agouridis, "Ἡ Ἑρμηνεία τῶν Ἁγίων Γραφῶν καὶ ἡ Νεοελληνικὴ Θεολογικὴ Πραγματικότης," *Th* 56 (3, 1985), pp. 504-518, reprinted in his collections of articles "Ἀράγε γινώσκεις ἃ ἀναγινώσκεις";Ἑρμηνευτικὲς καὶ ἱστορικὲς Μελέτες (Ἀθῆνα: Ἔκδοση Ζωῆς, 1989), pp. 11-26, in which he places Greek biblical studies in the context of the socio-political dynamics of modern Greece as a small state struggling to develop amidst the cross-currents of Byzantine traditionalism and western Enlightenment. According to Agouridis, Greek biblical studies have been underdeveloped because,

in Greece and elsewhere are seeking to clarify the nature and role of critical biblical studies within the Orthodox Church in terms of three focal issues: a) the historical-critical method; b) the patristic exegetical tradition; and c) the liturgical dimension as a hermeneutical perspective.[54] Substantive progress in these areas and ecclesiastical support for academic research can provide hope for the next level of growth in Orthodox biblical studies in the spirit of a "Neopatristic synthesis" proposed long ago by Georges Florovsky.[55]

Scientific biblical research, whether carried out within Protestant, Catholic, or Orthodox circles carries a double

---

in an uncertain and defensive social context, biblical scholarship a) retreated into safe academics, b) was intimidated by Byzantine traditionalism falsely claiming the spirit of the great Church fathers, and c) did not work toward a renewal integrating Scripture and the Church's worship as a compelling contribution to modern Greek life.

[54] See the article "Biblical Studies in Orthodox Theology" by S. Agouridis and responses by V. Kesich and T. Stylianopoulos in *GOTR* 17 (1, 1972), pp. 51-85. Further on biblical criticism, see G. P. Fedotov, "Orthodoxy and Historical Criticism," in *The Church of God*, ed. E. L. Mascall (London: SPCK, 1934), pp. 91-104; V. Vellas, "Κριτικὴ τῆς Βίβλου καὶ Ἐκκλησιαστικὴ Αὐθεντία," Ἐπιστημονικὴ Ἐπετηρὶς Θεολογικῆς Σχολῆς Ἀθηνῶν (Ἀθῆνα, 1937), pp. 150-160; G. Florovsky, "The Pattern of Historical Interpretation," *ATR* 50 (2, 1968), pp. 144-145; T. Stylianopoulos, "Historical Studies and Orthodox Theology," *GOTR* 12 (3, 1967), pp. 394-419; P. Vasileiadis, "Βιβλικὴ Κριτικὴ καὶ Ὀρθοδοξία," Ἐπιστημονικὴ Ἐπετηρίδα Θεολογικῆς Σχολῆς Θεσσαλονίκης, (Θεσσαλονίκη,1980), pp. 337-377; V. Kesich, *The Gospel Image of Christ* (Crestwood: St. Vladimir's Seminary Press, 1991); and S. Agouridis, «Ἡ ἐφαρμογὴ νέων μεθόδων στὴ μελέτη τῶν ἁγίων Γραφῶν,» *DeltBibMel* 4 (January-June, 1985), pp. 5-23, reprinted in *Ἀρά γε γινώσκεις*, pp. 27-45. On the patristic exegetical heritage, a first volume has appeared of a magisterial three volume work by John Panagopoulos of Athens University, entitled *Ἡ Ἑρμηνεία τῆς Ἁγίας Γραφῆς στὴν Ἐκκλησία τῶν Πατέρων*, Vol.1, (Athens: Akritas, 1991).

[55] G. Florovsky, "The Ethos of the Orthodox Church," *Orthodoxy: A Faith and Order Dialogue* (Geneva: World Council of Churches, 1960), p. 45, who explains that the "Patristic synthesis" must be anchored on a personal and corporate life in Christ. The appeal to the Church fathers is not merely an appeal to antiquity but to truth testified by the apostolic tradition of the Church on which patristic theology is based. This truth becomes living truth for the Church and believer only by the grace of the Holy Spirit.

burden. On the one hand, it has the task of objective study of the biblical writings in their own historical and communal settings in order to provide fresh access to the original intentions and voices of their authors as they perceived and expressed the word of God in all its cultural contingency and theological depth. In this regard, academic research has produced an astonishing array of tools and riches for biblical study. It has also demonstrated amazing success in clarifying innumerable literary, historical, and theological issues, including the crucial issue of the relationship of Scripture and tradition discussed earlier in this chapter. Balanced academic study of the Bible, no less than similar study of the classic Christian tradition, holds, in part, the promise of renewal for the churches and contemporary society in ways that transcend divisive differences through a positive and holistic understanding of creation, humanity, and life.

However, the serious shortcomings of the academic use of Scripture must be recognized as well. The spirit of modern biblical criticism and modern Western theology in general, although it does not necessarily have to be so, is derived neither from Scripture nor the classic Christian tradition, which are based on prayer and ecclesial life, but primarily from Renaissance humanism and Enlightenment philosophy. Biblical scholarship has often rendered itself irrelevant to the life of both Church and society by a gravitational pull toward historical, philological, and technical preoccupations. Worse, when lapsing into hypercriticism or falling captive to philosophical presuppositions, biblical criticism has tended to consume its own subject matter, the substance and value of Scripture, until there is virtually nothing left. In obvious accommodation to culture, the upshot has been the wide promotion of skepticism toward the very authority of Holy Scripture, a treatment of the Bible as a kind of cultural monument from which to glean supporting references for desirable goals and one-sided ideologies. J. Christiaan Beker, a mainline Protestant biblical scholar, critiques the prevailing biblical studies with these words:

A visit to any recent conference of the guild of biblical scholars will demonstrate the extent to which we have cast aside the issue of the normative biblical authority. Indeed, we have substituted the notion of the Bible as an archaeological-historical deposit for one of the Bible as an authoritative *viva vox* (living voice) for the community of faith. And thus the authority of the Bible is among us at best an incidental authority, becoming authoritative when and if it conforms in some of its expressions to what we consider to be helpful guidelines for our present situation.[56]

In view of this state of affairs, it is no surprise that biblical critics have provoked charges of outright heresy and have caused deep alienation first among Protestants and then, to a lesser degree, among Catholics as well. Some prominent Protestant biblical scholars, notably Brevard S. Childs,[57] have labored hard to recover the sense of biblical authority so necessary to the vitality of the Church. Without rejecting the achievements of scholarship, and certainly without going back to a pre-critical stage, Childs has drawn attention to the canonical nature as well as the theological witness of Scripture. Most Roman Catholic biblical scholars have succeeded in conducting critical research while remaining faithful to their doctrinal tradition. The primary example is Raymond E. Brown who has written on the most sensitive subjects, including the virgin birth, the divinity of Christ, and the Petrine authority.[58] Taking on literalists on

---

[56] J. Christiaan Beker, *The New Testament: A Thematic Introduction* (Minneapolis: Fortress, 1994), p. 135.

[57] In addition to his book *Biblical Theology of the Old Testament* cited above, see also his previous works *The New Testament as Canon: An Introduction* (Philadelphia: Fortress, 1984) and *Introduction to the Old Testament as Scripture* (Philadelphia: Fortress, 1979).

[58] Raymond E. Brown, *Jesus: God and Man* (Milwaukee: Bruce Publishing Company, 1967); *The Virginal Conception and Bodily Resurrection of Jesus* (New York: Paulist, 1973); *Peter in the New Testament*, coedited with others (Minneapolis: Augsburg/Paulist, 1973); and *Mary in the New Testament*, coedited with others (New York: Paulist, 1978).

the one hand and radicals on the other,[59] Brown has ably shown through his many works and commentaries that freedom of research is not compromised by faithfulness to classic Christian doctrine. He has defended critical studies and has carved out what he calls a "centrist position" on principle that historical critical methodology can be kept distinct from extraneous philosophical ideological assumptions.[60]

In the case of Orthodox scholars, strong ecclesial and doctrinal anchors have largely spared the Orthodox from turmoil. In Orthodoxy, patristic and doctrinal interests hold sway, while the gradually increasing number of biblical scholars enjoy relative freedom to do their work. As they strive for the growth of biblical studies in their own tradition, Orthodox biblical scholars are still learning from their Western colleagues but they ought to be cautious about repeating their errors. They are wise to take cognizance as well of Evangelical scholarship with which they share considerable theological ground. Evangelical scholars present not only a sharpened critique of liberal biblical criticism,[61] but also positive contributions in contemporary biblical research.[62] In this manner, Orthodox biblical scholars may keep in perspective the wider world of the modern academic study of Scripture in order both to welcome its contributions as well as to guard against its shortcomings. The erudite legacy of the great

---

[59] See especially Raymond E. Brown, *The Critical Meaning of the Bible* and *Biblical Exegesis and Church Doctrine.*

[60] A more recent defense of the critical method by Brown may be found in his article "The Contribution of Historical Biblical Criticism to Ecumenical Church Discussion" in *Biblical Interpretation in Crisis: The Ratzinger Conference on Bible and Church*, pp. 24-49, which includes an interesting exchange of ideas with Cardinal Ratzinger.

[61] See, for example, Clark H. Pinnock, *The Scripture Principle*; Mark A. Noll, *Between Faith and Criticism*; D. A. Carson and John D. Woodbridge, eds., *Scripture and Truth*, and by the latter as coeditors *Hermeneutics, Authority, and Canon* (Grand Rapids: Zondervan, 1986).

[62] Especially impressive and fair-minded is the work of Gordon D. Fee, for example, his *Gospel and Spirit* cited above and a recent monumental work *God's Empowering Presence: The Holy Spirit in the Letters of Paul* (Peabody: Hendrickson, 1994).

Church fathers and the spirit of freedom within the Orthodox tradition provide hopeful foundations for the continued advancement of Orthodox biblical scholarship.

Chapter Three
Hermeneutics: Faith, Reason, and Church

Defining Terms

W hat has been discussed in the previous chapters concerning the nature and uses of Holy Scripture inevitably raises the question of interpretation. How is Scripture to be read and interpreted? Given its divine and human aspects, as well as the different ways in which it has been received and used, how can the reader be sure that the true meaning of Scripture is grasped? When a preacher, teacher, or priest speaks on a biblical text or subject, how can we know if the teaching or homily is based on sound interpretation? What role should biblical scholars play in the ecclesial use of Scripture? How is the fact of their diverse opinions to be faced? Cannot the average Christian simply read the Bible and apply it to life in various ways as many Christians actually do? Cannot the Bible have, after all, more than one meaning for different people?

When such questions are raised, one enters into the realm of *hermeneutics*, a discipline that entails its own complex factors. The task of hermeneutics – to reflect on the what, how, and why of biblical interpretation – can quickly turn quite abstract in that it involves many dimensions, including philosophical theories of knowledge and linguistics.[1] The technical term comes

---

[1] An overview of hermeneutics is offered by B. C. Lategan, "Hermeneutics," *ABD*, Vol. 3, pp. 149-155; by R. E. Brown and S. M. Schneiders, "Hermeneutics," *NJBC*, pp. 1146-1165; and by the Pontifical Biblical Commission's "The Interpretation of the Bible in the Church" in *Origins* as noted above. In the literature at

from the Greek word ἑρμηνεία, which can be translated "interpretation," "explanation," or "translation." Etymologically, it derives from the name Ἑρμῆς (Hermes), the messenger and spokesman of the gods in ancient Greek mythology. As Hermes was a carrier of messages, so ἑρμηνεία is the act and process by which meaning is perceived and conveyed. A biblical author, as any author, is already an interpreter and deeply involved in the process of the communication of meaning. The author's interpretive understanding is, in varying degrees of clarity and fullness, enshrined in what the author writes. Later readers come to the text and, again in varying degrees of clarity and fullness, seek to grasp and articulate the text's (not necessarily or exactly the author's) meaning for themselves and others. One can imagine the complexities that arise in this whole process in terms of language, history, psychology, philosophy, theology, and spirituality! Scholars talk about the "hermeneutical question" or the "hermeneutical problem," and often refer to the subject with the plural "hermeneutics" or the singular "hermeneutic."

What follows is a simplified presentation of biblical hermeneutics based on an Orthodox patristic perspective (see Chapter Four) and involving the key dimensions of faith, reason, and Church.[2] Our overall hermeneutical position may be

least five foci in the discussion about hermeneutics may be distinguished: a) an explanation of the various current methodologies of biblical criticism as in *Reading the New Testament: Methods of Interpretation* by C. Tuckett; b) a history of exegetical methods from antiquity to the present as in *The Study and Use of the Bible* by J. Rogerson and others (Grand Rapids: Eerdmans, 1988); c) a theological discussion of revelation, inspiration, and the comparative authority of Bible and Church as in D. G. Bloesch, *Holy Scripture: Revelation, Inspiration & Interpretation*; d) a philosophico-linguistic discussion of theories of understanding as in R. E. Palmer, *Hermeneutics: Interpretation Theory in Schleiermacher, Dilthey, Heidegger, and Gadamer* (Evanston: Northwestern University Press, 1969) culminating in the work of Paul Ricoeur and David Tracy; and e) a consideration of the approaches of the new literary criticism as in *Interpreting the Bible: A Popular Introduction to Hermeneutics* by T. J. Keegan, O.P. (New York: Paulist, 1985). One finds of course various combinations of these perspectives.

[2] A number of handbooks on the formal, historical, and theological aspects of hermeneutics have been written by Orthodox biblical scholars from V. Antoniadis (1921) to S. Agouridis (1979). In the narrow philosophical sense, an excellent

described as *dynamic conservatism* anchored on the following presuppositions: a) a high regard for the authority of Scripture, the Church, and classic Christian doctrine; b) the importance of prayer, worship, and spiritual life in the study of Scripture; c) an honest and responsible quest for truth based on the principle that the primary meaning of the biblical text is the one gained by critical, grammatical, and historical exegesis, and d) the final purpose of biblical exegesis is to illuminate the theological truths and ethical values of Scripture. More detailed treatment of the hermeneutical question is presented in Chapters Six and Seven.

First, certain fundamental distinctions may be helpful. Although the adjectives exegetical, interpretive, and hermeneutical are often used indiscriminately or in overlapping ways, more precise discussion requires clearer definitions. *Exegesis* (from the Greek verb ἐξηγέω, meaning literally "to lead out from" or "to take out from") has to do primarily with the original meaning of the text, that is, what its author conveys through the original language in a given style, grammatical structure, and historical context. Absolute objectivity in exegesis is an illusion, but relative objectivity is possible as already demonstrated by significant areas of consensus by scholars at the exegetical, descriptive level. The grammatical and historical contexts provide some

Exegesis

---

work is by P. Andriopoulos, *Τὸ πρόβλημα τοῦ «Ἱστορικοῦ Ἱησοῦ» ἐν τῇ συγχρόνῳ Ἑρμηνευτικῇ* (Athens, 1975). See also A. Ugolnik, "An Orthodox Hermeneutic in the West," *SVTQ* 27 (2, 1983), pp. 93-118; J. Breck, "Exegesis and Interpretation: Orthodox Reflections on the 'Hermeneutical Problem,'" *Ibid.*, pp. 75-92, and his book *The Power of the Word*; as well as M. Ford, "Seeing, But Not Perceiving: Crisis and Context in Biblical Studies," *SVTQ* 35 (2-3, 1991), pp. 107-125. The patristic dimension is most powerfully voiced by John Panagopoulos in his works, including recently an introduction to the New Testament (1994). One cannot say that the Orthodox have yet defined for themselves the hermeneutical question with sufficient clarity. The many aspects and factors of hermeneutics need to be both delineated and brought into some kind of integrative perspective. An effective way to do this is perhaps to distinguish more clearly between, and then again to relate, exegesis, interpretation, the relationship between faith and reason, the role of scholarship and its critical methods, as well as the practical life and authority of the Church.

objective criteria for a fairly accurate understanding of most scriptural passages.[3] Descriptive accounts of the overall thought of
scriptural books and authors, though they involve more vari-
ables and are therefore less secure, are also possible. While any
careful reader can come up with exegetical insights, trained scholars are best equipped to do systematic exegesis on a conscious
level and with appropriate tools. Ideally, exegesis is a descriptive
task in which the focus is on the text. As long as the exegete
pursues the original meaning, all the various literary and historical methods employed are welcome as heuristic and neutral
in principle. The main complexities in exegesis arise from:
a) insufficient evidence; b) arbitrary conjectures by exegetes; c)
excessive analysis of background; and d) unchecked biases by
interpreters, in which case exegesis becomes *eisegesis* (that is, putting the interpreter's own ideas into the text). The best way to
treat these difficulties is for the exegetes themselves to check one
another and to make sure they are doing descriptive exegesis,
seeking the original or plain meaning contextually conveyed by
the author's words.

Interpretation is, in principle, another level of dealing with
Scripture in which the text is viewed from the standpoint of its
value for the reader consciously or more often unconsciously. It
is a freer appreciation and application of a perceived meaning in
a text, usually based on the reader's own questions, selectivity,
interests, and values, interpreted as any person might interpret
any event, document, or work of art. The most sound interpretations are the ones genuinely grounded in the original, exegetical meaning of the text. However, interpreters are inevitably selective and often move beyond the author's frame of reference
into other possible meanings and applications of the text that
are enriching but can also be conflicting. Interpretation is primarily not a descriptive but evaluative task seeking to derive
useful or abiding truth from Scripture. Without drawing an
absolute distinction, which is impossible, descriptive exegesis
seeks what the Bible "meant" and evaluative interpretation seeks

---

[3] Raymond Brown, "Hermeneutics," in *NJBC*, p. 1152.

what the Bible "means."[4] For many believers, of course, what the Bible meant and what it means are essentially the same, especially pertaining to the events and truths of salvation.

However, it would be plainly obscurantist to affirm a literal six-day creation or that waters are stored above a solid heavenly vault just because the Bible describes the universe in this manner. For such knowledge, the sciences have advanced our understanding profoundly. Most would not attribute revelatory significance to the advice that one should drink a little wine (1 Tim 5:23), but some might do so pertaining to women's head coverings (1 Cor 11:5-10).[5] What about slavery and the lower status of women in the world of the Bible? What about demon possession and miracles? What about teachings such as that obedience to God brings unfailing prosperity and disobedience brings suffering which the Book of Job and life itself often disprove? Such issues make the task of evaluative interpretation as necessary as it is inevitable. It is also obvious that interpretation can be extremely controversial and divisive because of the conflicting presuppositions, values, and choices of the interpreters.

Hermeneutics has to do with reflection and explanation of the

---

[4] The strongest case for the distinction between "what it [the text] meant" and "what it means," that is, the descriptive and evaluative tasks in biblical study, is by Krister Stendahl, "Method in the Study of Biblical Theology," *The Bible in Modern Scholarship*, ed. J. Philip Hyatt, pp. 196-209, and "Biblical Theology, Contemporary," *IDB*, Vol. 1, ed. George A. Buttrick (New York: Abingdon, 1962), pp. 418-432. This methodological distinction is not to be trivialized as some kind of an hermeneutical "gimmick," something that Stendahl utterly rejects. It is an essential heuristic distinction (not absolute separation) to clarify the two related tasks and to show that the real hermeneutical problem, which must be squarely confronted, lies in the evaluative or normative task of biblical interpretation. According to Stendahl, the descriptive approach does not guarantee objectivity but only calls for constant checking toward objectivity, over against the equally constant tendency to surrender to one's preconceptions and prejudices, for the sake of the most clear understanding of the original text and the layers of interpretive traditions in Scripture and the patristic literature. The more precise the nuances of meaning at the descriptive level, the more clear (not necessarily easier) the challenge of the evaluative task becomes.

[5] These examples are taken from Gordon D. Fee, *Gospel and Spirit: Issues in New Testament Hermeneutics*, pp. 2-3, 5.

methods, principles, as well as presuppositions of both exegesis and interpretation – the theory of the whole art of biblical study. What was said above about exegesis and interpretation constitutes hermeneutical considerations. Hermeneutics embraces the whole process from the simplest grammatical observation on a text to the most profound meditation about the experience of God described in it. At the exegetical level, the hermeneutical task tends to be a formal and fairly neutral description of the tools and procedures of literary and historical methodology.[6] At the eclectic interpretive level, the hermeneutical task, the task of explicating evaluative understanding, becomes far more theologically demanding. At the level of linguistics and philosophical theories of communication, the task of conceptually analyzing how ultimate meaning is conveyed across cultural boundaries and diverse worldviews is even more formidable, perhaps philosophically impossible.[7] The most burning problem in hermeneutics is the proper *relationship between faith and reason* in examining the contents of Scripture and in assessing what elements of those contents are of abiding significance. The hermeneutical task is made clearer, although not easier, when exegesis and interpretation are methodologically (rather than ultimately) distinguished and the interpreter's own presuppositions are brought into the open for discussion and clarification.

---

[6] For example, O. Kaiser and W. G. Kümmel, *Exegetical Method: A Student's Handbook*, trans. E. V. N. Goetchius (New York: Seabury, 1963); J. H. Hayes, *Biblical Exegesis: A Beginner's Handbook* (Atlanta: John Knox, 1983); and G. D. Fee, *New Testament Exegesis: A Handbook for Students and Pastors* (Philadelphia: Westminster, 1983). However, a presentation of principles and methods can also in part contain heavy evaluative presuppositions, for example, pertaining to the role and application of form criticism, as in H. Conzelmann and A. Lindemann, *Interpreting the New Testament: An Introduction to the Principles and Methods of N. T. Exegesis*, trans. S. S. Schatzmann (Peabody: Hendrickson, 1988).

[7] See R. E. Palmer, *Hermeneutics: Interpretation Theory in Schleiermacher, Dilthey, Heidegger, and Gadamer* for an account of the grand hermeneutical theories in the modern era, which have been further advanced and refined by the works of Paul Ricoeur and David Tracy.

A Life Perspective

The hermeneutical question goes beyond the reading and study of the Bible. In life, everyone and everything is inescapably involved in a hermeneutical process, whether consciously or more often unconsciously. A person reading the Bible or the daily newspaper, an historian examining an ancient document or inscription, a scientist looking at a virus or a galaxy, a lover conversing with one's beloved; all these are engaged in hermeneutics. Personal life, history, science, literature, art, etc., have their distinctive hermeneutical aspects. How one might think about and relate all these areas is part of the larger hermeneutical question, coterminous with life itself. And insofar as this quest involves search for truth on which to anchor life decisions, it entails an intrinsic moral obligation, that is, it is to be pursued with integrity. Efforts to manipulate the evidence, or any other deception in research, trivialize the quest and commit a disservice to truth. Since life is a great mystery and human understanding is limited, the search for truth is best carried out with a sense of receptive openness and epistemological humility, in the hope that the intrinsic beauty and power of truth, wherever found, may win the day and attract human hearts. The process requires awareness of the presuppositions and limitations of one's own claims, as well as willingness to bring them into the light of discussion. These elements provide a basis for the respectful treatment of others for the sake of universal human dignity and avoidance of sheer polemics.

With regard to the right reading and correct understanding of Scripture, it must be remembered that the biblical authors dealt with the relations between God and people on the scale of life itself; they wrote not for the technical exegete, theologian, or preacher but for all.[8] They assumed that every reader or hearer of their words would understand the substance of their message about God, his saving action, and his moral demands. Their message and outlook centered not on technical exegesis of texts but on broad interpretation of life grounded in their experi-

---

[8] R. Brown, "Hermeneutics," in *NJBC*, p. 1151.

ences of God and the values of the faith community in which they lived.

For example, when dealing with the Old Testament, the New Testament authors were concerned less with exegesis and more with interpretation based on their experience of Christ and the early Church's understanding of his saving work. Looking for contextual exegesis, in the modern sense, among early interpreters, whether Jewish or Christian, would be a gross anachronism. It is at the level of interpretation, seeking the value and relevance of the Scriptures for the community of faith, that one can appreciate the appropriateness of allegorical and typological interpretations, which are found already in the New Testament itself (Mt 13:18-23, 36-43; Gal 4:21-31; 1Cor 10:1-11). The Church fathers, as well, in various homiletical and didactic ways, successfully exploited this kind of "interpretive exegesis" for the pastoral nurture of God's people. More markedly contextual and grammatical exegesis among the Church fathers, for example Athanasios and Basil, emerged especially in doctrinal debates in which accuracy of discourse was crucial.[9]

Most contemporary readers, whether Protestant, Catholic, or Orthodox, continue to use the Bible at this broad level of interpretation. They are less dependent on the technical exegesis of scholars and more on the interpretive traditions of their churches conveyed through worship, sermons, and catechesis.[10] The majority of preachers and teachers, as well, work at this level of interpretation. Since the saving message of Scripture is addressed to all, all enjoy the right of direct access to the Bible – to be challenged directly by God's word without the necessity of scholar as mediator between reader and God. Moreover, although there are degrees and levels of rational comprehension, all are capable

---

[9] In the case of Athanasios against Arianism and in the case of Basil against Eunomianism, see T. Stylianopoulos, "The Biblical Background of the Article on the Holy Spirit in the Constantinopolitan Creed," *Études théologiques 2: Le IIe Concile oecuménique* (Chambésy: Centre Orthodoxe, 1982), pp. 155-173, reprinted in T. Stylianopoulos, *The Good News of Christ: Essays on the Gospel, Sacraments and Spirit* (Brookline: Holy Cross Orthodox Press, 1991), pp. 168-195.

[10] R. Brown, "Hermeneutics," *NJBC*, p. 1163.

of understanding Scripture's essential religious and moral claims. Faith in a living God, the good news of his love and forgiveness in Christ, and his demands for holiness and righteousness are essentially open and comprehensible in various ways to all.

The life of faith, both of the Church and the believer, can never be ultimately dependent on scholarship. Actualization of the essential message of Scripture, which is to believe in what God has done for humanity and to live by his blessings and in his presence, is a personal matter that transcends professional theological knowledge and sophisticated hermeneutical theories. In fact, it can be the case, as noted earlier, that a believer in simplicity of faith and prayerful receptivity can derive more spiritual benefit from an uncritical reading of the Bible than an expert exegete or trained theologian with all his or her erudition and critical skills. To think otherwise is theologically invalid, historically false, and professionally presumptuous.

However, Church and scholarship, believer and scholar, need not be cast in opposition but in cooperation with one another. Scholars and scholarship have existed in Judaism and Christianity from earliest times and worked within the context and with the methods of their time. Contemporary scholars properly work with contemporary methods of exegesis and interpretation of the Scriptures.[11] Their contributions have been invaluable in literary, historical, as well as theological analysis of biblical books, themes, concepts, institutions, and of course exegetical details. Biblical scholarship, when it is positive and sympathetic to its subject matter, provides essential clarifications of issues and difficulties–for example on justification by faith, the roles of Peter and Mary in the New Testament, word and sacrament, etc.– issues of immense personal, ecclesiastical, and ecumenical implications.[12] The study, use, and application of Scripture by the

---

[11] See Chapter Five.

[12] See "English Roman Catholic–Methodist Dialogue: Justification–A Consensus Statement," *OC* 24 (3, 1988), pp. 270-273; J. Reumann, *'Righteousness' in the New Testament: 'Justification' in the United States Lutheran–Roman Catholic Dialogue* (Philadelphia: Fortress, 1982); R. E. Brown and others, eds., *Peter in the New Testament*; R. E. Brown and others, eds., *Mary in the New Testament*; E. R.

Church and the believer should be well-informed by such scholarly work even if they go beyond them.

While scholarly results may be beneficial for all, lay persons, teachers, preachers, theologians, as well as the Church, all these will be usually engaged with biblical scholarship to the degree that it is both useful for and appropriate to their own levels of function and responsibility.[13] The average person is simply refreshed by a drink of water, while the scientist can analyze water in terms of its hydrogen and oxygen atoms. Similarly, a child can drink the spiritual water of a scriptual story, while the exegete can analyze it in minute detail. The former has to do primarily with spiritual knowledge, that is, experiential knowledge based on faith and the grace of God. The latter has to do primarily with conceptual knowledge gained through reason and critical analysis.

The Dynamics of Faith, Reason, and Church

In the end, the greatest hermeneutical challenge lies in defining the proper relationship of faith and reason as applied to biblical exegesis and interpretation, all of which are ultimately inseparable. If exegesis ideally strives to draw out of a text what is there, it must converge on the essence of the text, namely, its theological claims about the saving action of God manifested in transformative experiences of concrete human beings.[14] Exegesis is invaluable in elucidating the historical background and

---

Carroll, "Mary in the Apostolic Church: Work in Progress," *OC* 25 (4, 1989), pp. 369-380; and G. Wainwright, "Word and Sacrament in the Churches' Responses to the Lima Text," *OC* 24 (4, 1988), pp. 304-327.

[13] R. Brown, "Hermeneutics," *NJBC*, p. 1164, wisely observes that "common sense dictates that all education be scaled to the ability of the audience, but this does not mean that elementary biblical instruction would be noncritical. It means that elementary instruction should be critical in an elementary way."

[14] This crucial point is made by H. Schlier, quoted by F. Hahn, *Historical Investigation and New Testament Faith: Two Essays*, p. 22. Schlier points out that "the goal of interpretation must be to appropriate God's claim, which is made with and in Scripture; for this claim, and nothing else, is the truth of Scripture." This position is consistent with the patristic concentration on the σκοπός, that is, the central aim or intention of Scripture, as the essence of interpretation.

intellectual nuances of those theological claims. However, exegesis of itself cannot, without the aid of faith, assent to the theological truth of the text. Much less can exegesis as a human achievement, that is, as refined rational activity to arrive at the most precise intellectual understanding of the text's theological truth, enter into the actual saving experience of God signalled by that theological truth. Thus, the essential salvific import of the biblical text is inaccessible to pure exegesis apart from the dynamics of faith and grace.

Similarly, at the level of evaluative interpretation, conceptual hermeneutical models proposed by brilliant theorists, from Schleiermacher to the most recent new literary critic, may be intellectually satisfying as theories of knowledge, that is, as paradigms for explicating the conditions in which human understanding and the communication of meaning occur. But these theoretical models cannot of themselves bring about the deep understanding of the biblical text in its theological value or release its spiritual power in the present. The greatest flaw in modern hermeneutical theories is in fact their one-sided focus on the fallen realm of human consciousness and cognition to the neglect of the classical biblical and patristic emphasis on the role of faith, purification of the heart, and the Holy Spirit in biblical study and interpretation

It is our position that the biblical text's full meaning and actualization of that meaning can only occur through the act of faith which assents to the text's truth claim and experiences the transforming power of that truth by the action of the Holy Spirit. From this perspective, the primary way to read, understand, and live by what the Bible's witness essentially offers is not through abstract dialectics but experiential faith. It is the horizon of vibrant faith, what the Church fathers call spiritual vision (θεωρία),[15] that provides access to spiritual knowledge, that is, knowledge as a gift of the Spirit. This constitutes true knowledge in the distinctive biblical sense, knowledge with personal

---

[15] On the concept of θεωρία, see Chapter Four under the section "Exegetical Methodology" of the Church fathers.

and existential depth, which implies intimate affinity with and spiritual sensibilities appropriate to the divine reality attested by the text. St. Cyril of Alexandria describes such knowledge as "inclusion in itself of the whole power of the mystery and a participation in the mystic blessing, whereby we are united to the living and life-giving word."[16] Accordingly, the study of Scripture for the appropriation of its spiritual value is a charismatic activity qualitatively determined by the life of faith.[17]

For example, when St. Paul writes that in the fullness of time God sent his Son to redeem humanity and also sent the Spirit of his Son into the hearts of believers by which they experientially know and affirm their filial standing before God (Gal 4:4-6), he is stating theological truths about God's saving activity and presence. There is no decisive way to understand and live these truths except by grace through faith. Similarly, when Christ declares that he is the true vine, his followers are the branches, and that he and his followers must live in a mutual, intimate communion of love (Jn 15:1-11), there is no way, to comprehend deeply and experience this spiritual reality except by grace through faith. So also Scripture's call to holiness, reconciliation, peace, and righteousness is actualized more fully through faithful living than correct conceptual knowledge of these terms gained by the work of trained exegetical experts.

According to St. Basil, words and concepts fall short in spiritual and theological matters. The interpretation of Scripture goes beyond the intricacies of logic to essential matters of the Church

---

[16] Quoted by Maurice F. Wiles, *The Spiritual Gospel: The Interpretation of the Fourth Gospel in the Early Church* (Cambridge: Cambridge University Press, 1960), p. 86. Wiles, pp. 84-86, points out the shared view of Scripture and the Church fathers concerning experiential knowledge of God by participation in the divine life.

[17] G. Florovsky, "The Ethos of the Orthodox Church," p. 41, expresses this patristic perspective as follows: "Apart from the life in Christ theology carries no conviction, and, if separated from the life of faith, theology may easily degenerate into empty dialectics.... Patristic theology was rooted in the decisive commitment of faith... 'Theology' is not an aim in itself. It is always but a way. Theology presents no more than an 'intellectual contour' of the revealed truth, a 'noetic' testimony to it. Only in an act of faith is this contour filled with living content."

and religious life. Since reason is darkened by the inner, fallen world of desires, reliance for true knowledge of God must be based on righteous actions, that is, genuine Christian living, guided by the essential facts and truths of the Christian tradition.[18]

However, is there not a significant role for reason in the reading and study of Scripture? Reason is a gift of God and should be used to its fullest extent, provided it recognizes its proper role and limits. For St. Gregory of Nyssa, reason was the "highest faculty" of the human being, the mark of the image of God.[19] Reason can search out and enrich our knowledge of St. Paul's full conceptual meaning of "Son of God," the fourth evangelist's image of Christ as the "true vine," as well as the inter-relationship of Scripture's spiritual and moral commands. Reason can seek out the σκοπός, the essential purpose of Scripture's witness, which is, as we have already observed, to proclaim God's saving activity in history, God's truths about life and salvation, and the saving experience of God to which Scripture attests and invites.

Reason can also seek to resolve or explain discrepancies in the Bible. Are we saved by faith and not works, according to Paul (Rom 3:28; Gal 2:16), or by faith and works, according to James (2:24)? What do we do with contradictory details in the reports of Christ's missionary instructions (Mk 6:8-9; Mt 10:10) and Paul's conversion (Acts 9:7; 22:9)? What about moral questions such as the obvious cultural acceptance of slavery and that slaves should obey their harsh as well as gentle masters (1 Pt 2:18)? Reason can deal with those issues and questions, not against faith but in cooperation with faith. Furthermore, reason can prevent faith from lapsing into simplistic literalism such as the notion of tearing out one's eyes when sinning through them (Mt 5:29) or the notion that God has actual hands because he created the heavens with his hands (Heb 1:10), or even the notion that God is a male because the Bible often refers to him as

[18] So Philip Rousseau, *Basil of Caesarea*, pp. 106-112, 117f.

[19] The Cappadocian fathers were defenders of rationality as much as they were guardians against its excesses. So Jaroslav Pelikan, *Christianity and Classical Culture* (New Haven: Yale University Press, 1993), p. 128.

Father. Reason can guide us to appreciate the human aspects of God's word and to read the Bible as a book of faith and religion, not a book of strict history and science.

Then what happens if, on rational grounds, radical questions are raised about whether we should accept the veracity of St. Paul's statement about the Son of God or the declaration of Christ, who himself wrote no gospel, that he is the true vine? The answer can only be that one must trust in the testimonies of Paul and the fourth evangelist who bear witness to the life and values of the larger community of faith which received these testimonies as true and included them in its Bible. Here we encounter the decisive importance of holy witnesses, the prophets, apostles, saints, and above all the Lord himself.[20] In other words, the faith of the believing reader or interpreter ultimately rests in the apostolic faith of the New Testament and the broader reality of the Church that put the New Testament together. Of course, one can on moral grounds inquire about and be persuaded by the ethical content of the life and teachings of Jesus, Paul, and the Church. For example, to claim an experience of God and teach love is one thing, and to make a similar claim and teach war is quite another. In the final analysis, the reader can only depend on the apostolic and ecclesial faith regarding the transcendent claims about Christ until such time that, by grace through faith, the reader himself or herself has an experience of the saving presence Christ – the ultimate personal persuasion for a reader or interpreter. Still, even such profound and decisive experiences never preclude the use of reason, but rather illuminate and guide it.

Therefore, while reason can analyze and elucidate many aspects of the Bible, it cannot of itself enter into the presence and power of the transcendent faith claims of Scripture and cannot

---

[20] According to Florovsky, "The Ethos of the Orthodox Church," p. 40, the appeal "following the Holy Fathers" is "not a reference to abstract tradition, to formulas and propositions. It is primarily an appeal to persons, *to holy witnesses.*" For Florovsky this applies, as well, to the apostles because the Church, being apostolic as well as patristic, is equally committed to the apostolic gospel as well as to the patristic doctrine.

therefore presume ultimately to evaluate them. It is amazing that, in their efforts to explicate the hermeneutical process of communication between Bible and modern reader, hermeneutical theorists have analyzed innumerable linguistic, historical, and philosophical elements, but have neglected the value of faith, prayer, and corporate Christian living as integral to the understanding and reception of the essential religious value of the Bible's witness. From an Orthodox perspective, according to St. Symeon the New Theologian, the spiritual reality of Scripture's teachings, and not merely their conceptual dimensions, is precisely what constitutes the treasures of the Bible disclosed as spiritual knowledge to the believer by Christ and the Spirit.[21] In the end, since God's truths and blessings are not separate from God as some kind of "eternal truths" or self-subsistent realities in the Platonic sense,[22] the existential perception of the treasures of Scripture involves, according to Symeon, nothing less than participation in the divine life, that is, personal knowledge of and mystical communion with Christ in the Spirit. In this vein, M. Robert Mulholland, Jr. invokes the Orthodox metaphor of the "iconographic nature" of Scripture. For him Scripture is "a verbal window" to a transcendent reality, the reality of God's holy and transforming presence experienced by encounter with the biblical text.[23] Luke T. Johnson puts the matter this way:

> The NT writings approach us as witnesses to and interpretations of specifically religious claims having to do with the experience of God as mediated through Jesus. They never claim, we notice, to mediate that experience themselves. It should go without saying, therefore, that the con-

[handwritten margin note: St. Symeon the New Theologian]

---

[21] On St. Symeon, see further Appendix 2.

[22] John Panagopoulos, *Εἰσαγωγὴ στὴν καινὴ Διαθήκη* (Athens: Akritas, 1994), pp. 433-434, emphasizes this important point that the Bible is not a deposit of definitive propositions of eternal truths but a witness to the transcendent mystery of God in his saving activity.

[23] M. R. Mulholland, Jr., *Shaped by the Word: The Power of Scripture in Spiritual Formation*, p. 64.

temporary reader cannot reach that experience by using the tools of anthropology, history, and literary criticism. But the contemporary reader can claim [i.e., by using critical tools] to come in contact with the witness and interpretation.[24]

But if reason stubbornly persists to ask radically skeptical questions, and if reason presumptuously assumes it can subject God's saving action and presence to rational scrutiny, then it oversteps its bounds in a foolish act of philosophical blindness. It becomes a destructive rather than constructive tool in its treatment of Scripture. When scholarship uses reason in this fashion, it creates, implicitly or explicitly, an ambiance of uncertainty about essential matters in the Bible, thus undermining its authority as God's word. The philosophical consequence is that the inability of rationalism to deal with ultimate reality, and above all with the mystery of God, is mistakenly viewed as a deficiency in the Christian verities. In such case, according to St. Gregory the Theologian, the limitations of reason are misconstrued as a weakness of Christian truth. Here are his incisive words:

> When we abandon faith to take the power of reason as our shield, when we use philosophical enquiry to destroy the credibility of the Spirit, then reason gives way in the face of the vastness of realities.... Give way it must... [being] the frail organ of human understanding. What happens then? The frailty of our reasoning looks like a frailty in our creed. Thus it is that as Paul too judges, smartness of argument is revealed as a nullifying of the Cross.[25]

The tragedy of the radical aspects of biblical criticism is that, while the critic sets out to clarify the biblical witness, he or she ends up "throwing out the baby with the bath water." To the degree that one commits oneself to philosophical rationalism toward revelation, that is, toward the faith claim of God's per-

---

[24] Luke T. Johnson, *The Writings of the New Testament: An Appreciation* (Philadelphia: Fortress, 1986), pp. 7-8.

[25] *Oration* 29.21, cited by Frederick W. Norris, *Faith Gives Fullness to Reasoning: The Five Theological Orations of Gregory Nazianzen*, p. v.

sonal self-disclosure to biblical figures and believers throughout the ages, to the same degree one will be inclined toward skepticism and atheism. Without the essential horizon of faith, biblical exegesis and interpretation, as well as hermeneutical reflection, take on then the specter of an immense intellectual chess game, which may be engrossing for those who are professionally engaged in it, but confusing and useless for those concerned with the challenges of real life.

But are there not issues of integrity of research and free scholarly discussion which may in good faith raise disturbing questions about the Bible? Are there not informed people of sincere faith who may hold diverse views and may sharply disagree about a number of important issues pertaining to the Scriptures? Are there not fervent believers who may claim religious experiences and, knowingly or unknowingly, misuse the Bible in various ways? Are we, then, to surrender our freedom of assent to an authoritative *magisterium*, ecclesial or scholarly, for a final and externally imposed interpretation of Scripture? All these are valid and serious questions. In what ways can these be addressed from the standpoint of hermeneutics?

First, it must be clearly stated that full freedom is granted to historical research according to professional standards based on the best available critical methodologies. Biblical criticism, in all its ancillary literary and historical methodologies, is free to work judiciously on the biblical material. On the one hand, a certain flexibility concerning the historicity of biblical accounts due to the paucity of evidence as well as to the unique nature of Scripture as a divine and human book is welcome. For example, the fact of the early Church's experience of the outpouring of the Spirit is far more important than whether or not the pentecostal gift occurred according to the details of Acts 2:1-13 or John 20:19-23. On the other hand, the professional guild itself, if it is to maintain credibility, bears responsibility for correcting excesses of skeptical historical judgment which at times reach preposterous dimensions for reasons of sensationalism and other personal predilections.[26] Parenthetically, too frequently scholars of great prominence have appeared hesitant in critiquing excesses of well-known colleagues and thus have unnecessarily permitted confusion to spread in the field and scandal in the Church. Nevertheless, faith and truth that cannot stand the scrutiny of serious historical examination are not worthy of the Bible, which honestly exposes the failings of its greatest heroes and yet calls for unwavering faith in God's saving presence and action.

Second, at the level of substantive evaluation of the theological and moral content of the Bible, things are different. At the descriptive, exegetical level, scholars are free in good faith to explore and debate all the nuances of the theological and moral ideas, let us say, of the apostle Paul. But when it comes to deciding the ultimate truth of Paul's experience and teaching, this is no longer a matter of historical, but philosophical judgment, which can neither prove nor disprove Paul's experiential convictions about God and the life of righteousness. It is deceptively pernicious to confuse historical and philosophical judgments. While any person has a right to a philosophical stance and to go his or her own way in life, the biblical scholar as biblical scholar should not in good conscience pose as a hidden philosopher, and skeptical philosopher at that, in his exegesis or interpretation.

Third, if the line between historical and philosophical judgments is clearly maintained, the biblical scholar is exegetically free in good faith to study even the most dogmatically sensitive teachings, for example, Paul's understanding of Jesus as Son of God and Lord.[27] One scholar may propose that Paul's

---

[26] A popular exposure of ungrounded extremists such as B. Thiering, A. N. Wilson, and J. Spong is by N. T. Wright, *Who Was Jesus?* (Grand Rapids: Eerdmans, 1992). These extremists, some of whom are avowed enemies of Christianity, and others radical-minded officials of liberal churches, misuse scholarly research and make shocking claims that confuse the uninformed. The cultivation of sound scholarship is the most effective way to defend against them.

[27] This is in agreement with the position of R. Brown in his several books and in his piece "Hermeneutics" in *NJBC*, pp. 1163-1164.

christological language entails a distinct subordinationist ring because, as is well known, the source and center of divine action for Paul is God the Father. Another scholar may agree but further point out that the great wonder of Paul's christology is not its partly subordinationist ring but its amazingly heightened development already in the first Christian generation. To the latter, Paul's christology may be only a short step away from later dogmatic formulations of the Church entirely consistent with Paul's christological understanding. Scholars can continue to discuss such questions in full awareness of the difference in historical contexts and of the implications of their discussion. One implication is that there is development in the formulation of doctrine. Another is that the Church's trinitarian and christological formulations are consistent with the witness of the New Testament. Still another is that they are not consistent, in which case a scholar can either convincingly make one's case to the Church – what are more compelling alternatives to Paul's christology or interpretations of it? – or risk reading oneself out of the Church according to the dictates of one's conscience.

(4) But fourth, what a scholar as scholar cannot do, is define the normative faith of the Church. At this deep level of life, we reach the communal grounding of hermeneutics, that is, the fact that the communication of meaning occurs and is ultimately validated by a community of faith. We all live in communities of faith, whether religious or secular. It is within some communal framework that most people exchange, enjoy, or tolerate degrees of variety and unity of ideas and beliefs. Even the Jesus Seminar is based on a community of faith, a group of scholars with their presuppositions, values, and agenda which are openly inimical to traditional Christianity. All Christians live within their own churches and traditions, but have significant cross-sectional similarities and differences. It is from a broad communal perspective that we work and read the Bible, despite our sincere efforts to be as objective as possible, which efforts that should never cease. Comparatively rare and admirable are the persons who have the courage to change communal setting for

purely theological reasons. While our communal grounding is inevitable, it is imperative that we carry on a public dialogue with integrity and mutual respect in the hope that intrinsic truth itself may be the primary criterion of persuasion and conduct.

Therefore, there is a crucial ecclesiological dimension to hermeneutics. Along with the hermeneutics of faith and the hermeneutics of reason and scholarship, we have the hermeneutics of the Church. Ideally these work together, both reinforcing and correcting each other. Personal faith enters into the realm of the direct experience of God to which Scripture testifies. Scholarship provides historical and theological analysis of the Bible. The Church holds to the canonical authority of Scripture, a book of the Church, to the witness of which it is accountable and which it must normatively interpret pertaining to theological and moral teaching. The entire trilogy of hermeneutics is interdependent and functions most effectively as an integral unity in which saints, scholars, and officials work together or combine these dimensions. Fervent faith, without scholarship and Church, may lead the believer to invidualist piety, obscurantism, even fanaticism. Analytic scholarship, without faith and Church, may lead the scholar to irrelevant academics and arbitrary revisions of Christianity. The institutional Church, without fervent faith and scholarship, may be inclined toward formalism and abuse of power.

The above model of hermeneutics applies to all Christians and their particular churches. All have the right and burden to assess their hermeneutical stance regarding the Bible, not only in terms of doctrine but also of life. The separated churches need to continue to discuss their differences in the light of ecumenical scholarship which holds tremendous promise as long as the gospel according to the apostolic tradition is taken seriously. In the Orthodox perspective, there can be no church unity apart from the apostolic tradition of classic Christianity anchored on Scripture. The Orthodox Church has no *magisterium*, its highest authority being councils, the decisions of which must be

received by the whole people of God.[28] The ultimate grounding
of truth is the life of the Church in which all members from
rank-and-file believers to bishops are witnesses and bear responsibility. All are privileged and accountable to follow the prophets, the apostles, and the Church fathers in their approach to the
mystery of God and the biblical word.

In a remarkable essay, Thomas F. Torrance has put his finger
on two definitive aspects of the Orthodox tradition as being
"fidelity to truth" and "respect for mystery."[29] These two aspects
can be viewed, as well, as key Orthodox hermeneutical modes
or perspectives. Torrance points out that the adjective "Orthodox" in classic Orthodoxy does not signify "some sort of regi-
mentation of the mind of the Church whereby truth is imposed
upon it from the outside, but rather to a basic orientation of the
Church to the truth of the Gospel" according to the apostolic
tradition.[30] "Orthodox" means "rightly related to the truth" –
fidelity to truth – the full truth of the gospel of God's saving
work through Christ in the Spirit, lived and celebrated in the
life of the Church. But there is also "respect for mystery" in that
doctrinal formulations, however essential, fall short of the
transcendent mystery of God.[31] What can be said about Scripture from a patristic viewpoint, Torrance states about church
doctrines: "They cannot be thought of as containing the truth
in themselves but rather as ways of directing us to the mystery
of Christ, and the mystery of the Trinity."[32] Othodoxy does not,
in principle, prohibit new formulations in the proclamation and

[28] K. Ware, "The Ecumenical Councils and the Conscience of the Church," in
Kanon: Jahrbuch der Gesellschaft für das Recht der Östkirchen (Wien: Herder, 1974),
pp. 217-233, provides an excellent account of the conciliar nature of the Church
as it seeks to live by the ultimate authority of truth, the truth of God. For an
explanation of the authoritative interpretation of the Bible by the Roman Catholic Church, including the magisterial authority of the Pope, see R. Brown,
"Hermeneutics," *NJBC*, p. 1163.

[29] Thomas F. Torrance, *The Relevance of Orthodoxy* (Stirling: Drummond Press,
n.d.), pp. 9-19.

[30] *Ibid.*, p. 10.

[31] *Ibid.*, pp. 10-11.

[32] *Ibid.*, p. 11.

teaching of the gospel as if God's truth were locked only in dog-
mas and the Bible. Scholars, teachers, and preachers are free to
use their creativity to the fullest as long as the gospel in its apostolic fullness is safeguarded with fidelity to truth and respect for
mystery. Their work and statements should be such that they, to
quote again Torrance, "instead of coming in between Christ and
our understanding, allow Christ in all His wonderful reality and
mystery to reveal Himself to us through them continually."[33]

---

[33] *Ibid.*, pp. 11-12.

Chapter Four
The Church Fathers and Holy Scripture

In our discussion of various aspects of Holy Scripture, as well as its use and interpretation in diverse hermeneutical contexts, a number of references have been made to the ideas and contributions of the Church fathers. It is well known that the Church fathers were devoted students of the Bible. They were above all biblical theologians and expositors. The authority and value of Scripture as the supreme record of divine revelation were for them both indisputable and massive. The Church fathers hold an authoritative position especially in the tradition and theology of the Orthodox Church. It is therefore essential that we examine the patristic legacy pertaining to biblical interpretation. The purpose of this chapter is to present a comprehensive picture of the exegetical work of the Church fathers in terms of the following topics: (1) the overall achievement of the patristic exegetical heritage; (2) the patristic view of the authority of Scripture; (3) the significance of the appeal to the Church fathers; and (4) an overview of the patristic methodology.

The Patristic Exegetical Heritage

In the last two generations, international scholars such as Werner Jaeger, Hans von Campenhausen, G. L. Prestige, F. L. Cross, G. W. H. Lampe, Henry Chadwick, J. Quasten, and P. Chrestou have amply documented the literary and theological achievement of the Church fathers. The work of these scholars has, on the one hand, redressed earlier erroneous views about the "hellenization" of Christianity in antiquity, and on the other, established the basis for a deeper and wider appreciation of the patristic legacy. From the side of biblical scholarship, the exegetical heritage of the Church fathers has also received extensive and positive attention by scholars such as J. Daniélou, K. H. Schelkle, R. P. C. Hanson, R. M. Grant, Rowan A. Greer, and more recently, John Panagopoulos. The ongoing study of patristic interpretation has resulted in numerous handbooks.[1] And from time to time, valuable essays on patristic approaches to Scripture have appeared in various places.[2]

Nevertheless, despite the rejuvenation of patristic studies in the twentieth century, a lingering cloud remains in the minds of biblical scholars about the exegetical work of the fathers. Merely

---

[1] R. M. Grant with David Tracy, *A Short History of the Interpretation of the Bible* (Philadelphia: Fortress, 1984); James L. Kugel and Rowan A. Greer, *Early Biblical Interpretation* (Philadelphia: Westminster, 1986); Joseph W. Trigg, *Biblical Interpretation: Message of the Fathers of the Church* (Wilmington: Glazier, 1988); Frank Sadowski, S.S.P., ed., *The Church Fathers on the Bible: Selected Readings*; K. Froehlich, *Biblical Interpretation in the Early Church* (Philadelphia: Fortress, 1984); and Bertrand de Margerie, S.J., *An Introduction to the History of Exegesis, Vol. 1: The Greek Fathers*, trans. Leonard Maluf (Petersham: Saint Bede's Publications, 1993).

[2] For example, Geoffrey W. Bromiley, "The Church Fathers and Holy Scripture," in *Scripture and Truth*, D. A. Carson and John D. Woodbridge, eds., pp. 199-220; J. Pelikan, "The 'Spiritual Sense' of Scripture: The Exegetical Basis for St. Basil's Doctrine of the Holy Spirit," in *Basil of Caesarea: Christian, Humanist, Ascetic*, Part I, ed. P. J. Fedwick (Toronto: Pontifical Institute, 1981), pp. 337-360; by the same, "'Council or Father or Scripture': The Concept of Authority in the Theology of Maximus Confessor," *The Heritage of the Early Church: Essays in Honor of Georges V. Florovsky*, ed. D. Neiman and M. Schatkin (Rome, 1973); Andrew Louth, "The Hermeneutical Question Approached through the Fathers," *Sob* 7 (7, 1978), pp. 541-549; Allan E. Johnson, "The Methods and Presuppositions of Patristic Exegesis in the Formation of Christian Personality," *Dial* 16 (3, 1977), pp. 186-190); and T. J. Towers, "The Value of the Fathers," *CQR*, July–September 1965, pp. 291- 302. See also the recent collection of studies by Metropolitan Demetrios Trakatellis Οἱ Πατέρες Ἑρμηνεύουν-Ἀπόψεις Πατερικῆς Βιβλικῆς Ἑρμηνείας (Athens: Apostolike Diakonia, 1996).

to hear that the Church fathers practiced "allegorical," "typological," and "spiritual" exegesis is enough to raise the suspicions of modern scholars inculcated in the critical-historical and literary methodologies. We may grant that allegorizing extremes and platonizing excesses can be found among ancient interpreters, notably Origen. It is also true that in literary and historical analysis, modern biblical studies are incomparably advanced. It would be as futile as it is anachronistic to look among the Church fathers for parallel critical discussions about the synoptic problem, the origins of christological titles, and other refined literary and historical problematics of current biblical studies. However, the impression is that most biblical scholars ignore the work of the fathers all too quickly. It is as if few biblical scholars have worked beyond the allegorical approach of Origen to the sober exegesis of Athanasios, Basil, and Cyril of Alexandria, who consistently rely on contextual and grammatical,[3] as well as theological and doctrinal understanding. Because of an overwhelming preoccupation with the historical method, modern biblical scholarship seems to have developed a professional deafness to the value of the patristic exegetical heritage. This is regrettable because interactive biblical and patristic studies can yield fruitful results especially in the area where the Church fathers were the strongest – in interpreting the theological witness of Scripture and making its saving message alive for the Church and society.

In recent years, the Greek biblical scholar John Panagopoulos has been engaged in systematic study of the scriptural output of the Greek fathers. The first volume of a projected three-volume work entitled Ἡ Ἑρμηνεία τῆς Ἁγίας Γραφῆς στὴν Ἐκκλησία τῶν Πατέρων has already appeared.[4] In this masterful study,

---

[3] Jaroslav Pelikan, *Christianity and Classical Culture*, p. 221, points out that the Cappadocians, trained in the literary, rhetorical, and grammatical methodologies of the hellenistic tradition, were skillful Greek philologists. In particular, Basil was "dedicated to the principle of taking the meaning 'in every phrase and in every syllable' of Scripture with the utmost seriousness."

[4] *The Interpretation of Holy Scripture in the Church of the Fathers.* The first volume covers the first three centuries and the Alexandrian tradition up through the fifth century to Cyril.

Panagopoulos argues that the fundamental misconception of modern biblical scholars about the patristic exegetical legacy is based on a narrow, absolutist view of historical-critical methodology and a failure to grasp the whole interpretive vision of the fathers. This essential patristic vision embraces a) the task of theology, b) the nature of biblical truth, and c) the life of the Church.[5] For the Church fathers, according to Panagopoulos, the basic problems of biblical interpretation neither arise from nor can be resolved by particular methodologies and the analysis of specific texts. Rather, they have to do with substantial issues about existential appropriation as well as intellectual comprehension of the central aim (σκοπός), character (χαρακτήρ), and mind (νοῦς) of Scripture pertaining to the great events of salvation. The challenge is not merely to interpret the written text but to comprehend and actualize God's purposes and gifts to which the text bears testimony. From this perspective, the contribution of the Church fathers as a whole is, as Panagopoulos demonstrates, nothing short of a grand theological and exegetical achievement. It integrates philological study, a realistic view of historical truth behind the witness of the Bible, existential response to God's gracious acts, and the actualization of the canonical Scriptures in the life of the worshiping Church.

Panagopoulos is not unaware of the distance between modern scholarship and the patristic tradition with regard to the practice of historical criticism and literary analysis. Trained in Germany, he has written several works on the basis of scholarly standards, including a critical study on Jesus entitled Ὁ Προφήτης ἀπὸ Ναζαρὲτ.[6] While aware of the differences in methodology and historical research, Panagopoulos

---

[5] Panagopoulos presents his thesis especially on pp. 33-58. A strong note of appreciation for the exegetical achievement of the Church fathers has recently come from Brevard S. Childs, *Biblical Theology of the Old and New Testaments,* pp. 31-39, who positively assesses not only the work of St. Irenaios but also of Origen ("the whipping boy' of critical exegesis," so Childs) observing that their exegetical work must properly be seen in the context of their entire theology.

[6] *The Prophet from Nazareth* (Athens: Parisianos, 1973).

assesses the permanent value of the patristic exegetical heritage in terms of the following themes summarized here.[7]

1) *The integral connection between Scripture and the person and work of Jesus Christ.* Scripture is a testimony to the incarnation: the mystery of Scripture and the mystery of Christ in their inseparable human and divine aspects must be approached historically and spiritually in a balanced, integrated way. The fullness of faith in Christ decisively determines the essence of interpretation and the soundness of the whole hermeneutical enterprise in terms of content and final value.

2) *Christocentric interpretation.* As the fulfillment of the Old Testament and the fullness of historical revelation, Christ is the chief aim and main subject (σκοπὸς) of Scripture and, therefore, the beginning, center, and end of biblical interpretation. In both biblical revelation and biblical interpretation the living Christ personally reveals himself as the ultimate interpreter by the power of the Spirit. In an important way, interpretation is a fruit of the personal revelation of Christ, the Word, to the interpreter.

3) *The organic relationship between Old and New Testaments.* Building on the foundations laid by the New Testament authors regarding God the Father, Christ, and the Church, the Church fathers established the unbroken unity of the Scriptures and, consequently, the unity of covenantal history over against both Judaism and Gnosticism which rejected either the new or the old dispensations.

4) *The unity of biblical interpretation and theology.* Authentic interpretation is theologizing, the pursuit of the essential purpose and meaning of God's redemptive plan and saving activity for humanity. Despite the value of words and grammar, biblical interpretation goes far beyond a philological exercise. It nurtures the theological consciousness of the Church by elucidating and articulating the spiritual depth of the salvific witness of Scripture, the essence of theology.

---

[7] Ἑρμηνεία τῆς Ἁγίας Γραφῆς, pp. 54-58.

5) *The unity of the biblical word and daily life.* The biblical word, as a word enlivened by the Spirit, is anchored on the historical events of revelation and is dynamically actualized in the life of the faithful. Despite admittedly excessive allegorizing seeking abstract and timeless ethical values, patristic exegesis is on the whole grounded in God's saving work viewed in a christocentric light. For example, the Exodus from Egypt is simultaneously a historical event, a prefiguration of the death and resurrection of Christ, as well as a call for a new exodus of the believer from the slavery of sin to the freedom of the grace of God.

6) *The integral connection of the biblical word with the sacramental life of the Church.* Interpretation in its chief aim, seeking the mystery of Christ's presence, is a prayerful, liturgical act. The great acts of biblical revelation are lived and celebrated in the Church's sacraments. The whole story of salvation and the power of the biblical word come alive in the liturgical remembrance (ἀνάμνησις) of the Church's worship.

7) *The open-endedness of exegetical methodology.* The Church fathers never narrowed biblical exegesis to the practice of strictly formal principles and methods. For them the question of method always remained open. Priority was given not to method but to the salvific content of the biblical witness. At stake is not merely the linguistic and conceptual understanding of the text but the dynamic actualization of its saving truth by the Spirit's power. To behold the mystery of Christ in Scripture is always a spiritual act.

8) *The error of evaluating patristic exegetical work by exclusively current scholarly criteria.* It is an anachronism to assess the exegetical work of the fathers exclusively by contemporary scholarly standards. The Church fathers used the scholarly methodologies of their time. Many of their specific interpretations appear exaggerated and superficial by modern scholarly criteria. However, significant elements of their exegetical insights are continuously discovered to be on par with the results of contemporary scholarship. Moreover, even extreme interpreta-

tions of patristic exegetes often reflect a spiritual vision grounded in sound ecclesial and theological tradition.

9) *Discernment of the critical issues of biblical hermeneutics.* The Church fathers recognized the burning issues of biblical hermeneutics such as the christological basis of biblical interpretation, the relationship between the Old and New Testaments, the nature of revelation and inspiration, the hermeneutical value of faith and tradition, the relationship between Scripture and the Church, and the actualization of the value of Scripture in personal and corporate life. Furthermore, having expert knowledge of contemporary philosophy and philology, the great fathers developed certain exegetical principles which anticipate essential elements of contemporary hermeneutics. These principles pertain to a) the idiomatic language of Scripture, b) the limitations of language and dialectic in seeking to comprehend and express the mystery of God, and c) the decisive importance of seeking the central exegetical aim or purpose (σκοπὸς) of the biblical text.

Panagopoulos' work is impressive in its scope and depth. Although at times he seems to accentuate his case in a spirit of assumed opposition to modern scholarship, he has abundantly succeeded in presenting the spiritual and theological value of the exegetical work of the fathers. What is needed is clarity in defining substantive areas of engagement between patristic studies and contemporary biblical scholarship. Interaction between the two fields holds considerable promise as long as the strengths and weaknesses of both are appropriately recognized. Modern biblical studies are strongest in literary and historical analysis. Patristic exegetical work is strongest in spiritual and theological interpretation. Engagement of the two perspectives entails exciting possibilities for continuing biblical research and the life of the Church.

The Authority of Scripture

The Church fathers everywhere exhibit a very high regard for the authority of Scripture as a book of God.[8] Justin Martyr in his *Dialogue with Trypho* frequently quotes the Old Testament with the formula "God speaks" or "God says," without reference to human authors. For John Chrysostom, Christ himself speaks through the apostle Paul because the Apostle possessed the mind of Christ (1 Cor 2:16). Patristic expositors frequently insist that every scriptural word, being inspired, deserves meticulous attention. God being its ultimate author, the whole Bible containing the Old and New Testaments is, according to the fathers, an organically unified entity with integral and substantial mutual relationships. In its entirety, Holy Scripture is the supreme treasure of revealed truth providing rich instruction and spiritual nourishment for the life and guidance of God's people.

The divine authority of Scripture assured its centrality in the ongoing life of the Church. St. Basil in Letter 22 presents an extensive description of the life of Christian perfection entirely derived from the New Testament. The role of Scripture in the formulation of the trinitarian and christological doctrine is well known. Patristic commentaries and homilies on Scripture abound. Holy Scripture is the focal source of patristic thought; this is evident not only in the exegetical works but in all the writings of the fathers. The Church fathers are first and foremost biblical theologians who viewed the Bible as both the book of God and the book of the Church. The brilliant platonist Origen himself was fundamentally a biblical theologian who, however fanciful in some of his interpretations, was committed to the historical revelation of God and was ready to submit his judgment to the authority of the universal Church.

However, the exaltation of the authority and centrality of Scripture in the patristic tradition did not lead to its absolutization as a kind of holy book delivered directly from heaven. It is true that, on the one hand, without the benefit of current critical awareness pertaining to the composition of the biblical writings, the Church fathers held a distinctly higher view

---

[8] On the patristic view of the authority of Scripture, see also Chapter Two.

of the divine authority and historical veracity of the Bible than
is usual among modern scholars and theologians. But, on the
other hand, the Church fathers did not reach a kind of
fundamentalist view of the Bible as found in Protestant orthodoxy. We may say that the fathers in their total witness were
indeed fundamental but never fundamentalist about the Bible,
acknowledging in significant ways its human as well as divine
character.

In the patristic perspective, the authority of Scripture is
qualified by several important considerations. Among them is
the awareness of the idiomatic language of Scripture which
cannot always be taken at face value. Based on grammatical and
syntactical meaning alone, many texts would yield unacceptable notions about God and his saving activity. For example,
according to Chrysostom, unbelief in Christ, though anticipated
by Scripture, is not predestined by the necessity to fulfill the
prophecy of Isaiah as literally stated by some texts (Jn 12:39-40;
cf. Mk 4:11-12). Chrysostom states that it was not because Isaiah
so spoke that the opponents of Jesus did not believe, but rather
that Isaiah so spoke because they were not about to believe. Isaiah
merely foresees and describes, but does not predetermine and
cause, unbelief. Chrysostom concludes that Scripture has
certain "idioms" (ἰδιώματα) and it is necessary to make allow-
ances for its laws (νόμοις...παραχωρεῖν).[9]

The Church fathers, as is well known, approached the Scriptures with a certain freedom and boldness. Their focus was on
the spirit rather than the letter of Scripture. Numerous examples
can be given of the patristic refusal to stay with the plain
teaching of Scripture when such teaching compromised the
overall understanding of God. Biblical texts that are predesti-
narian in grammatical meaning (Rom 8:29; 9:11,16-17)

---

[9] Homilies on the Gospel of John, 68.2. The best English translation is by Sister
Thomas Aquinas Goggin, S.C.H., *Saint John Chrysostom: Commentary on Saint
John the Apostle and Evangelist*, 2 vols. (New York: The Fathers of the Church, Inc.,
1957 and 1960), which supersedes the antiquated translation in the series *The
Nicene and Post-Nicene Fathers*. See also R. C. Hill, "St. John Chrysostom and the
Incarnation of the Word in Scripture," pp. 34-38.

cannot, according to the Church fathers, be taken at face value without leading to unacceptable deductions about God who is loving and just, and not arbitrary.[10] The Book of Revelation may teach a literal millennium (Rev. 20:4), and the Epistle to the Hebrews seems to prohibit the possibility of a second repentance after serious sin (Heb 10:26-27; 12:16-17). Although some early interpreters advocated such ideas, for example, the author of the *Shepherd of Hermas*, St. Justin, and St. Irenaios, these doctrines never became part of the normative teaching of the Church.

In a remarkable instance of freedom from biblical literalism, St. Isaac the Syrian, arguably the greatest mystic in the tradition of Eastern Christianity, intentionally demythologizes the image of hellfire.[11] Although he by no means rejects the reality of hell, he reinterprets it as a separation from and inability to participate in God's eternal love, a separation more painful according to him than any physical hell. For St. Isaac, hell did not exist prior to sin and its ultimate end is unknown. Hell is not a place of punishment created by God, but a spiritual mode of anguished suffering created by sinful creatures willfully separated from God. According to Isaac, sinners in this hell are not deprived of the love of God; only they suffer in the profound realization of having offended against love and of being unable to participate in it. Hell is none other than this bitter awareness of separation and regret, what St. Isaac calls the "scourge of love." Thus, the same divine love radiating towards all is bliss to the righteous but torment to sinners. Certainly the patristic tradition, known for its spiritual exegesis, cannot be

---

[10] According to the Cappadocians, God's freedom from fate and any deterministic necessity assured that "there could not be a fundamental opposition between divine providence and human free will," just as "there could not be a permanent contradiction between sound reason and correct faith." See J. Pelikan, *Christianity and Classical Culture*, p. 216.

[11] *The Ascetical Homilies of Saint Isaac the Syrian*, trans. Holy Transfiguration Monastery (Boston: Holy Transfiguration Monastery, 1984), Homily 27, p. 133 and Homily 28, p. 141. An earlier translation is by A. J. Wensinck, *Mystic Treatises by Isaak of Nineveh* (Wiesbaden: Martin Saendig, 1923), pp. 128 and 136. In another work on prayer, St. Isaac expresses this freedom of the spirit as follows: "It

charged with slavish literalism to an absolute holy word. In the end, as H. Chadwick has observed, the Church fathers knew that Christianity is not a religion of a book but of a Person.[12]

Another critical factor that qualified the patristic view of the authority of Scripture was the clear recognition of the necessity of its interpretation. Fathers and heretics did not question either the authority or the centrality of the Bible as such. The burning question concerned its correct interpretation, especially concerning doctrinal matters. As Mark Santer puts it, the sufficiency of Scripture pertaining to saving truth was qualified by its practical insufficiency.[13] Who had the right to interpret the Bible and on what basis? Over against the wild allegorizing of Valentinian gnostics, the great Origen himself was concerned about avoiding private, unrestricted fantasy. He offered these controlling interpretive principles: (1) take Scripture as a whole not piecemeal; (2) interpret obscure passages by comparing them with clear ones; (3) consult with other interpreters of the Church, especially revered predecessors; and (4) keep Christ as the key to the unity and interpretation of Scripture.[14]

The Appeal to the Fathers

Origen's advice to check with other biblical expositors developed into a standard appeal to previous interpreters in the tradition of the Church. Already St.Irenaios had used the writings of Justin Martyr and invoked the Church's rule of faith as a guiding interpretive principle. This was essentially an appeal to the developing doctrinal consensus of the living ecclesial

---

is a childish mentality which investigates and is concerned with the exact sequence of words, rather than setting its sights on their sense.... Altering the outward form of the words of the prayer which our Lord handed down makes no difference provided our prayer stems from its sense, and that the mind follows that sense," *The Syriac Fathers on Prayer and the Spiritual Life*, trans. S. Brock (Kalamazoo: Cistercian Publications, 1987), p. 288.

[12] H. Chadwick, "The Bible and the Greek Fathers," in *The Church's Use of the Bible*, p. 39.

[13] Mark Santer, "Scripture and the Councils," *Sob* 7 (2, 1975), pp. 109-110.

[14] From H. Chadwick, *Early Christian Thought and the Classical Tradition*, p. 39.

tradition on key disputed issues such as the nature of creation, the unity of the Old and New Testaments, grace and freedom of the will, and the Son's relationship to the Father.[15] Where wide controversy did not arise in the ancient Church, for example, pertaining to the Petrine authority attested by Mt 16:18, a surprising divergence of interpretations may be found from Tertullian to Chrysostom.[16] The patristic tradition amply shows that invoking the rule of faith and appealing to the authority of other interpreters were by no means restrictive to creativity by rigidly seeking a single interpretation for every biblical verse. Ancient interpreters enjoyed a variety of interpretations and displayed freedom in discussing exegetical options.

Rather, the appeal to revered interpreters expressed the concern for doctrinal integrity and signified the *ecclesial dimension* of biblical interpretation, a dimension which underscores that the Bible is above all a book of the Church. Scripture belongs to no one alone. Properly speaking, it belongs to the Church, the community of faith that produced the Scriptures and upholds their authority. While interpreters should pursue scholarly objectivity and debate, no interpreter can engage the Bible as Bible apart from the context of the Church and its exegetical tradition. The interpretation of Holy Scripture as Holy Scripture is, in the final analysis, a ministry of the Church. It is assumed that there is freedom of historical research and there are multiple approaches to and uses of Scripture according to particular contexts and purposes; however, the deep doctrinal sense of the classic tradition of the Church must not be ultimately violated.

---

[15] R. M. Grant, "The Appeal to the Early Fathers," *JTS* 11 (1, 1960), pp. 13-24, reprinted in R. M. Grant, *After the New Testament: Studies in Early Christian Literature and Theology* (Philadelphia: Fortress, 1967). For the wider scope, see J. Pelikan, *The Christian Tradition, Vol. 2: The Spirit of Eastern Christendom* (Chicago: University of Chicago Press, 1974), pp. 8-36 on "The Authority of the Fathers."

[16] Oscar Cullmann, *Peter: Disciple, Apostle, Martyr*, trans. F. V. Filson (New York: Meridian Books, 1964), pp. 158-162.

After the period of the great fathers up to Chrysostom, respect for the exegetical tradition gradually resulted in the collection of ἀνθολόγια (*florilegia*), chains of patristic interpretations on biblical passages.[17] It is often said that these collections indicate lack of creativity; there is some truth to this. Yet stifling rigidity was not the order of the day. These chains of exegetical traditions themselves both reflect and invite a variety of interpretations. Their intent was not to stifle creativity, but to benefit the faithful through exposure to the patristic heritage and to keep interpretation within the spirit of the Church's teaching. The agonizing trinitarian and christological controversies had raised the fear of heresy and division. The exegetical achievement of the patristic luminaries was esteemed and preserved as a basis for unity and truth.

As regards creativity, not every age can boast creative thinkers. When they do arise, as in the case of St. Photios the Great, one of the foremost intellectual figures of Byzantium, they display their gifts. St. Photios in his Ἀμφιλόχια (ca. 867 A.D.) takes up numerous difficult questions of Scripture. What is the meaning of being created in the image of God? What does it mean that God hardened Pharaoh's heart? Who were the brothers of Jesus? How do we deal with the obscurity (ἀσάφεια) of Scripture? In answering such questions, Photios exemplifies the skills of a philologist taking into account the Bible's idiom, the problems of translation from Hebrew to Greek, as well as errors in the transmission of manuscripts.[18]

From this angle, as well, one should evaluate the intent of Canon 19 of the Quinisext Council "in Trullo" (691), which admonishes Church leaders to preach and teach God's scriptural word not according to their own minds but following the fixed

---

[17] Modern editors of such series include J. Cramer, H. Lietzmann, K. Staab, J. Reuss, and others. Collections in English translation have been compiled by Johanna Manley, ed., *The Bible and the Holy Fathers for Orthodox: Daily Scripture Readings and Commentary* (Menlo Park: Monastery Books, 1990) and by the same, *Grace for Grace: The Psalter and the Holy Fathers* (Menlo Park: Monastery Books, 1992).

[18] The information on St. Photios is from an unpublished paper by my colleague, Nicholas P. Constas.

interpretations of the fathers.[19] A close reading of this canon clearly indicates its contextual concerns: 1) correct interpretaion in controversial matters; 2) possible lack of exegetical experience or skill by Church preachers; and 3) risk of departure from Church doctrine. The canon by no means precludes creative work, given skilled interpreters who remain within the Church's doctrinal heritage. In the Greek tradition, later fathers and saints such as Symeon the New Theologian (d. 1022), Nicholas Kabasilas (fourteenth century), and Kosmas Aitolos (d. 1779), show no hesitation in reading and interpreting Scripture directly without constant reference to the Church's earlier fathers, yet they remain faithful to the doctrinal conscience of the Church.

In the case of St. Symeon, we note a distinctly creative and charismatic interpreter within the tradition. On the basis of his direct reading of Scripture, especially the Gospel of John and the Letters of Paul, as well as his own mystical experiences, Symeon literally shook up the religious establishment of Constantinople and was exiled on account of it.[20] Appealing to the evidence of the New Testament St. Symeon insisted that all Christians, most especially clerics and theologians exercising leadership and teaching functions, must have an apostolic experience of salvation, indeed an adult renewal experience based on a baptism of the Holy Spirit, in order properly to fulfill their responsibilities. While controversial in his own times, he is acknowledged as one of the greatest theologian saints in the Orthodox tradition.

---

[19] H. R. Percival, ed., *The Seven Ecumenical Councils* in *The Nicene and Post-Nicene Fathers*, Vol. 14 (Grand Rapids: Eerdmans, 1991), pp. 374-375. Some one thousand years later, because of the Reformation and the dangers of Protestant missionary activity, Patriarch Jeremiah III, in an encyclical of 1723, prohibited Orthodox Christians from the very reading of Scripture! This cannot be considered a definitive Orthodox position but an emergency pastoral act to protect the faithful at a time when the Church lacked the freedom and means to educate its members.

[20] *Symeon the New Theologian: Discourses*, trans. C. J. deCatanzaro, published in the series *The Classics of Western Spirituality* (New York: Paulist, 1980). In this and some other cases the series is a misnomer. See especially discourses 13, 15-18, and 28-34. Further on St. Symeon, see Chapter Seven and Appendix 2.

Exegetical Methodology

Many studies have been written on the various approaches and methods of patristic interpretation, including grammatical exegesis, allegory, typology, and the concept of θεωρία ("spiritual insight" or "spiritual vision").[21] These methods and approaches must be seen in the light of their purposes and interrelationship in the total task of interpretation as an ecclesial ministry. *Allegorical* exegesis, practiced especially in Alexandria, sought a deeper spiritual meaning in the literal words of Scripture, usually in order to: 1) transcend difficulties in the biblical text; 2) provide a Christian interpretation of the Old Testament; or 3) offer a variety of edifying teachings within the framework of the doctrinal unity of the Church. Perhaps the most exaggerated example is the *Epistle of Barnabas*, a second century document possibly from Alexandria. For the unknown author of this work, the whole system of the Jewish ritual had no literal but only spiritual value. The command to fast from foods meant abstention from wickedness. Circumcision was intended as spiritual circumcision of the heart. Not to eat swine and other unclean animals and birds were prohibitions about not consorting with people who behaved in the manner of such creatures. The temple of true value was not the Jerusalem Temple but the temple of the heart alone.[22] Such allegorizing developed in a far more sophisticated fashion in Clement of Alexandria and Origen who distinguished several levels of interpretation without necessarily denying the literal and historical meaning of the biblical text.[23] These and other later interpreters used allegorical exegesis not only to overcome difficulties in Scrip-

---

[21] Among others, see R. P. C. Hanson, *Allegory and Event* (London: SCM Press, 1959); G. W. H. Lampe and K. J. Woollcombe, *Essays on Typology* (Naperville: Allenson, 1957); G. A. Barrois, *The Face of Christ in the Old Testament* (Crestwood: St. Vladimir's Seminary Press, 1974); and the study by Panagopoulos. See also the handbooks on patristic exegesis cited above, note 1.

[22] *Epistle of Barnabas* 3.3; 9.4-5; 10.1-4; 16.7. An English translation is by R. A. Kraft, *Barnabas and the Didache* in *The Apostolic Fathers: A New Translation and Commentary*, Vol. 3, ed. R. M. Grant (New York: Thomas Nelson, 1965).

[23] Later, among the Cappadocian fathers, Gregory of Nyssa was especially given

ture but also to celebrate the perceived mysteries of revelation and draw out their relevance for Christian nurture. The value of such interpretations, however fanciful at times, lies not in their accuracy as historical exegesis but in their usefulness for the edification of Christians within the doctrinal framework and the common life of the Church.

(2) Typology

Typological exegesis differs in that it does not seek a timeless spiritual meaning but engages the historical perspective according to the biblical pattern of promise and fulfillment. Practiced especially in the Antiochene tradition, it is a theological and historical method of affirming the unity of the Old and New Testaments, and how events and figures of the former were fulfilled in the latter. For example, the author of the Epistle to the Hebrews writes that the ritual of the Mosaic Law was but a "shadow" (σκιὰ) of the future "realities" (πράγματα) to come in Christ (Heb 10:1). In typological exegesis, the Old Testament "shadow" or prefigurement of something or someone is called τύπος or "type." Its fulfillment in an event or person of the New Testament is called ἀντίτυπον or "antitype," meaning reality. Among the early fathers, Justin Martyr features massive typological interpretation of the Old Testament in both substantial and trivial matters. For example, the Passover lamb of the Exodus (Ex 12) is a type fulfilled by Christ through his death on the cross.[24] But the twelve bells of the high priest's robe (Ex 39:25), as well, are a type fulfilled by the same number of apostles. The inclusion of Gentiles into the Church through faith in Christ was anticipated by the prophets but, equally, through such subtle details as the mention of two animals in Gen 49:11 and Zech 9:9 (a female donkey and its colt), which were types fulfilled by

---

to allegorization but never lost sight of the Bible's historical reality. In such interpretations, his technique was to "take the words allegorically, and so penetrate to the inner sense of history, yet without losing sight of the truths or its facts," as quoted by J. Pelikan, *Christianity and Classical Culture*, p. 226. Pelikan further points out that Gregory's brother, Basil, was in contrast a critic of allegorists and cites him saying, "for me grass is grass; plant, fish, wild beast, domestic animal – I take them all in the literal sense," *ibid.*

[24] *Dialogue with Trypho* 40.1.

Jewish and Gentile followers of Christ.[25]

Typological exegesis confirmed the Old Testament as a Christian book, affirmed the unity of the Bible, and also served as an effective polemic against Marcion and his followers who rejected the Old Testament altogether. Typology is closer to Scripture's own historical schema of promise and fulfillment, and was widely practiced among the Church fathers. Prominent Old Testament figures such as Jacob, Moses, and Joshua were viewed as types fulfilled by Christ. Events such as the Exodus, the crossing of the Red Sea, Israel's wandering in the wilderness, and the entry into the Promised Land, were understood as types fulfilled by events in the ministry of Christ and the life of the early Church. The prayers and hymnology of Eastern Christianity are replete with typological figures and images derived from the patristic exegetical heritage. The value of typological exegesis is to be found in connection with the theological interpretation of the Old Testament on the basis of Christ and the gospel, an inescapable issue for the Christian evaluation and reception of the Hebrew Scriptures.

Several important qualifications must be made about the use of allegory and typology by the Church fathers. First, these methodologies were interpretive tools used by both Greek and Jewish authors in pre-Christian antiquity. We also have significant examples of them in the New Testament itself (Mt 2:15; 13:18ff.; Jn 3:14-15; Heb 10:1).[26] The apostle Paul employs the very terminology of "allegory" and "type" in linking Old Testament persons and events to New Testament counterparts (Gal 4:22-27; 1 Cor 10:1-13; Rom 5:14). Such interpretations have apostolic origin and were not mere inventions of the Church

---

[25] See especially Justin Martyr, *Dialogue with Trypho* 40.1; 42.1; 53.1,4. Knowledge of the number of bells of the high priest's robe derives not from the Old Testament but from an oral Jewish tradition. Other typological interpretations include Moses outstretched arms as type of the cross of Christ (*Dial.* 90.4), Jacob as a type of Christ (140.1), his wives Leah and Rachel as types of Jews and Christians, respectively. A good translation is by A. L. Williams, *The Dialogue with Trypho* (London: SPCK, 1930).

[26] L. Goppelt, *Typos: The Typological Interpretation of the Old Testament in the New*, trans. D. H. Madvig (Grand Rapids: Eerdmans, 1982).

fathers. Rather, the later Christian interpreters followed and elaborated useful lines of interpretation already set in the New Testament.

Second, sharp distinctions can be drawn neither between allegory and typology nor, for that matter, between the Alexandrian and Antiochene exegetical traditions. The differences are a matter of emphasis, at times extreme, but never mutually exclusive. Both approaches are fundamentally metaphorical and symbolic, and both seek to derive the maximum spiritual and theological value from Scripture as a Christian book for doctrinal interests and pastoral edification. In the hands of the best interpreters, neither approach was intended to abandon the literal and historical basis of Scripture; nor was the Church ever prepared to do so. An Alexandrian such as Origen, given to allegorizing, was also a philologist, while an Antiochene such as John Chrysostom, practicing mainly literal-grammatical interpretation, was also capable of both typological and at times allegorical interpretations.

Third, the developing tradition among the great exegetes moves toward literal-grammatical interpretations as shown by the works of both the Alexandrians, such as Athanasios and Cyril, as well as the Antiochenes, such as John Chrysostom, Theodore of Mopsuestia, and Theodoret of Kyros. This movement was quite likely due to the inevitable need for precision of discourse in doctrinal controversies.[27] A comprehensive view of patristic writings seems to indicate that doctrinal discourse reflects contextual and grammatical exegesis, while homiletical or pastoral discourse may freely indulge in allegorical and typological interpretations. St. Basil the Great, who is consistently attentive to the literal-grammatical meaning of biblical texts, is arguably the best example of sober biblical interpreta-

---

[27] In certain key instances, such as the reference to the origins of personified wisdom in Prov 8:22 (created or uncreated?), Athanasios and the Cappadocians, probably dependent on Origen's philological work in the *Hexapla*, took recourse to the original Hebrew meaning as decisive in their dogmatic interpretive disputes with the Arians and Eunomians. See J. Pelikan, *Christianity and Culture*, pp. 222-224.

tion in both pastoral as well as doctrinal writings.[28]

Fourth, whatever the specific methodological approaches used by the Church fathers, one must keep in view Panagopoulos' caveat that methodology was for them secondary to the substance of the scriptural witness. While the question of method could remain open, the more essential concern was how to do justice to God's saving activity as attested by Scripture, and how existentially to appropriate the soteriological value of the sacred writings.

It is clear, then, that the modern interpreter must look for the essential strength of the Church fathers which consists in their biblical theology and their hermeneutical perspective or φρόνημα ("spirit" or "mindset"). The definitive traits of this hermeneutical perspective may be summed up as: 1) a strong view of the authority of Scripture and the basic historicity of the saving events; 2) concentration on the theological and salvific message of the Bible ultimately centered on Christ; 3) interpretation based on contextual reading of the part in the light of the whole, seeking the σκοπὸς of the text; 4) philosophical sobriety about the capacity of philological analysis to control or define the mystery of God; 5) commitment to the doctrinal sense of the Church; 6) acknowledgment of biblical interpretation as a ministry of the Church; and 7) recognition of the interpreter's own personal stance of faith as essential to authentic interpretation.

The last of the above points has to do with the patristic understanding of θεωρία (literally, "vision of God").[29] This technical term may be translated "spiritual insight," "spiritual vision," or "spiritual receptivity." It is not simply a concept but above all an experience. It does not only refer to fine discern-

---

[28] J. Pelikan, "The 'Spiritual Sense' of Scripture: The Exegetical Basis for St. Basil's Doctrine of the Holy Spirit," pp. 337-360. See also above, n. 23.

[29] For discussion of this elusive term, see K. Froehlich, pp. 85-88; John Breck, "Theoria and Orthodox Hermeneutics," *SVTQ* 20 (4, 1976), pp. 195-219 and chapter 2 of his book *The Power of the Word*; Andrew Louth, *The Origins of the Christian Mystical Tradition: From Plato to Denys* (Oxford: Clarendon, 1981); by the same, *Discerning the Mystery: An Essay on the Nature of Theology* (Oxford: Clarendon, 1983); K. Ware, "Ways of Prayer and Contemplation: Eastern," *Chris-

ment of the theological teachings of Scripture but also to the spiritual stance of the interpreter guided by the Holy Spirit. Broadly speaking, θεωρία pertains to the whole of Christian life and understanding transformed and inspired by the Holy Spirit. It is the crown of a life of repentance, forgiveness, cleansing from sin, purity of heart, prayer, and love. It may be described as a prayerful sense of awe and wonder in the presence of God, his creation, the great acts of salvation, the Bible, and all things. In the dynamic state of θεωρία, the beholder may be deeply stirred by a green leaf as much as by a brilliant star; by a simple act of human kindness as much as by a great truth in the biblical narrative.

In the reading of Scripture, θεωρία is experienced like a ray of light accompanying one's understanding of the text according to St. Isaac the Syrian,[30] or a sudden awareness of the Lord's presence while pondering something in the Scriptures according to St. Ambrose.[31] St. Symeon the New Theologian has written an entire discourse entitled *On Spiritual Knowledge,* an excellent example of the spiritual reading of Scripture.[32] Θεωρία is a gift of the Spirit which does not impede reason, but rather enriches it by infusing it with insight into what really matters in

---

tian Spirituality: Origins to the Twelfth Century, ed. B. McGinn and others, (New York: Crossroad, 1987), pp. 399-402; and Panagopoulos, Ἑρμηνεία τῆς Ἁγίας Γραφῆς, pp. 42-43.

[30] Holy Transfiguration Monastery, *The Ascetical Homilies,* Homily 1, p. 6, where St. Isaac writes: "Those who in their way of life are led by divine grace to be enlightened are always aware of something like a noetic ray running between the lines ... and the soul that has a share of the Spirit, on hearing a phrase that has spiritual power hidden within, ardently draws out its content for itself"; and in A. J. Wensinck, *Mystic Treatises,* p. 4.

[31] G. Weidenfeld, ed., *St. Ambrose: Select Works and Letters* (New York, 1900), pp. 8-9. St. Ambrose writes: "If the soul desires it, if it longs, if it prays ... reaching out undividedly to the Word, suddenly it seems to hear the voice of him whom it does not see, and recognizes the fragrance of his divinity in the depths of its being.... Does it not happen that when we are pondering something in Scripture ... suddenly the highest mysteries appear to us."

[32] *Symeon the New Theologian: The Discourses,* pp. 261-266, reproduced as Appendix 2 in this volume.

the Bible and by conveying to the reader the saving power of that which matters. It is a state of dynamic inspiration, a moment of illumination, an act of personal revelation in which the written word becomes the living word of God and its value is existentially actualized in the life of the interpreter by the grace of the Holy Spirit.

This patristic model of charismatic interpretation would be hopelessly romantic and superficial unless placed in the context of the struggles of self, Church, and history. The Church fathers knew of neither cheap grace nor cheap scholarship. The struggles to overcome personal sin through genuine repentance and to grow toward spiritual maturity in the likeness of Christ were ever before them. Far from viewing the Spirit's effects mechanically or magically, they acknowledged the arduous work behind biblical study, preaching, and teaching. For them, personal faith and prayer in no way canceled the careful use of reason. The Cappadocian fathers viewed reason as a gift of God, indeed as "the highest faculty" which marked the very image of God in human beings.[33] But they also recognized that, as Gregory of Nyssa puts it, "subtle dialectic possesses a force that may be turned both ways, as well for the overthrow of truth as for the detection of falsehood."[34] Faith, as well as love of God and love of God's people, could be relied on to guide reason toward constructive ends.

Moreover, moments of "inspiration" could also be caused by self-deception and demonic instigation. The authenticity of one's gift of interpretation must therefore be tested in the life of the Church. A willingness to consider other views and openness to change one's mind are required.[35] Above all, the interpreter must

(margin handwriting: "The Church fathers knew of neither cheap grace nor cheap scholarship")

---

[33] See J. Pelikan, *Christianity and Classical Culture*, p. 128.

[34] From his work *The Soul and the Resurrection*, a dialogue between Gregory and his sister Makrina, quoted by S. J. Dennin-Bolle, "Gregory of Nyssa: The Soul in Mystical Flight," *GOTR* 34 (2, 1989), p. 102.

[35] Perhaps the most famous example of this is St. Basil's initial hesitation to affirm the full divinity of the Holy Spirit, given the unclear biblical evidence, and his subsequent affirmation of this truth in his struggle against the Eunomians and under pressure by the theological reasoning of his friend Gregory the Theologian.

have genuine regard for the integrity of the Church's faith. The struggles of the Church itself, not infrequently caught up in theological and administrative controversies, provided no great comfort. Yet, hope burned invincible that in the end darkness would not overcome light. This assurance was grounded not in human capacities but in God's grace and faithfulness. The Lord himself had promised that he would always be with his people and that the gates of hell would not prevail against his Church, which is both responsible for and accountable to the gospel and its effective proclamation in the world (Mt 16:18; 28:20).

Chapter Five
Modern Biblical Scholarship

The reading of Scripture which is informed and responsible cannot bypass the challenge of scholarship. Scholarship is concentrated and systematic study of a subject, an immensely fruitful and praiseworthy activity as old as civilization. The ancient Egyptians and Babylonians had their teachers of wisdom. Jews, Greeks, and Romans highly valued learning and education.[1] The Bible itself is a product of scholarship and gives evidence of scholarly activities within it. For example, the Book of Sirach explicitly identifies one of the teachers of Israel, who ran a school and composed this book which was later translated into Greek by his nephew.[2] The Gospel of Matthew, written by a Christian teacher who brought "out of his treasure what is new and what is old" (Mt 13:52), gives evidence of careful intellectual labor behind its collections of the teachings of Jesus in long discourses such as the Sermon on the Mount (Mt chaps. 5-7).[3] St. Paul, a former Pharisee and a trained multilingual scholar of the Law, was capable of extensive argumentation on controversial issues among Jews and Christians as evident in his Letters to the Romans, Corinthians, and Galatians. The Church fathers, as well, cultivated scholar-

---

[1] H. I. Marrou, *A History of Education in Antiquity*, trans. G. Lamb (New York: Sheed and Ward, 1964) and William Barclay, *Educational Ideals in the Ancient World* (Grand Rapids: Baker Books, 1974).

[2] See the interesting prologue of Sirach and Sir 39:1-11; 50:27; and 51:23.

[3] The other discourses are in Matthew, chaps. 10, 13, 18, 23, and 24-25.

ship on the basis of both Scripture and the classical heritage. Despite Tertullian's famous skeptical question "What has Athens to do with Jerusalem?" the Church fathers valued the classical tradition and did what scholars most always do: they encouraged and nurtured education according to the tools and needs of their epoch.

Modern biblical studies in universities, colleges, and seminaries continue this broad tradition of education. Contemporary biblical scholars labor under modern circumstances and with current methodologies. Their basic purposes are to cultivate knowledge through their particular fields and to benefit the course of civilization. It is of no surprise that they engage, as the Church fathers did in their own era, the intellectual dynamics, the language and methodologies, as well as the social and political issues of contemporary times.

Yet it must also be acknowledged that, along with brilliant and lasting results, aspects of modern biblical scholarship have caused, directly or indirectly, considerable confusion and no less anxiety among students, pastors, and ordinary believers. Biblical scholars themselves have raised serious questions about the nature and spirit of modern biblical criticism.[4] The crux of the problem is that, on the one hand, biblical criticism proposes to explore and interpret the Scriptures in all their richness and diversity, and presumably to illuminate in the end their positive value as a great literary and religious legacy of civilization. But on the other hand, biblical criticism frequently gives the impression of being negative criticism, dismantling the Scriptures and rejecting essential elements of their witness in radical ways. Instead of a fair and sympathetic appreciation of the Bible, biblical scholarship seems all too often to present a chaotic

---

[4] For example, Walter Wink, *The Bible in Human Transformation*; Peter Stuhlmacher, *Historical Criticism and Theological Interpretation of Scripture;* Martin Hengel, "Historical Methods and the Theological Interpretation of the New Testament," in his *Acts and the History of Earliest Christianity*, pp. 127-136; and Eta Linnemann, *Historical Criticism of the Bible: Methodology or Ideology?* The last carries the subtitle "Reflections of a Bultmannian turned evangelical."

picture of divergent methodologies and conflicting results, heavily influenced by philosophical presuppositions and ideological standpoints alien to Scripture. A balanced perspective on the strengths and weaknesses of the prevailing academic study of Scripture is, therefore, a crucial matter having to do with freedom of scholarly research, the nature of truth, as well as the importance of the Bible for the Church.

The character and spirit of modern biblical criticism are determined, both positively and negatively, by the legacy of its origins as much as its methodologies. The history of biblical criticism is a long and complicated one. There can be no question here of attempting a descriptive account of the history of biblical research.[5] A sketch of the academic study of Scripture among Protestants, Roman Catholics, and Orthodox was provided in Chapter Two. Overall, the field is extremely diverse and marked by objective critical analysis as well as bias, by genuine advances as well as false directions, by solid results as well as seemingly impenetrable problems. While making valuable contributions to our literary and historical understanding of the Bible, biblical studies have been in a continuous state of crisis in terms of hermeneutical approaches and theological consensus. In this chapter, we intend to present a broad assessment of biblical scholarship by highlighting certain basic features in three areas: a) historical origins, b) methodologies, and c) strengths and weaknesses.

Historical Origins

The origins of biblical criticism go back centuries and are rooted in five interacting streams of tradition:

1) *The exegetical heritage of the Church fathers.* The beginnings

---

[5] For such accounts, see the relevant articles on biblical criticism in *The Anchor Bible Dictionary* and *The New Jerome Biblical Commentary*. For the New Testament, see further S. Neill and T. Wright, *The Interpretation of the New Testament 1881-1986*; E. J. Epp and G. W. MacRae, eds., *The New Testament and Its Modern Interpreters*; and W. G. Kümmel, *The New Testament: The History of the Investigation of its Problems*, trans. S. MacLean Gilmour and H. C. Kee (New York: Abingdon, 1970).

of the systematic study of Scripture in terms of study of the original languages, comparison of manuscripts, use of available methodologies, as well reflection on theoretical hermeneutical principles are to be found in Origen, who is himself indebted to earlier Greek and Jewish philologists and interpreters. While the study of Hebrew and the critical comparison of manuscripts waned, the Church fathers on the whole left an impressive exegetical heritage. One of the valuable fruits of this tradition is the concentration on the grammatical-contextual principle of exegesis practiced by Athanasios, Basil, Jerome, Theodore Mopsuestia, Cyril of Alexandria, and others. This principle, applied in a far more systematic and analytic fashion, has been the primary driving force behind the success of modern biblical studies.

2) *The ideals of medieval humanism.* The emergence of universities, the systematic pursuit of knowledge for its own sake, and the Renaissance stimulus to revive classical studies established professional structures and precedents that effected all learning and education. In recent centuries, these factors have inevitably led to specialization and compartmentalization of disciplines. They have also made the classroom and the professional guild the bases of operations. In biblical study, the Scriptures were thus gradually taken away from the life of the Church. From a living source of pastoral nurture, the Bible gradually became instead an object of academic analysis.

3) *The Reformation.* The Reformation, along with effecting tremendous ecclesial, social, and political consequences, focused attention on the sole authority of the Bible and the right of private interpretation over against the Church and tradition. Luther and other Reformers did not develop new methodologies as such. However, the force of these two factors, namely, the sole authority of Scripture and the right of individual interpretation, led on the one hand to an immense intellectual concentration on the Bible and on the other hand to a highly problematic diversity of interpretation. Thus, both the gift of the rediscovery of the Bible as well as the bane of

hermeneutical confusion became hallmarks of modern biblical scholarship cultivated above all in Protestantism.

4) *The Enlightenment.* The Enlightenment's motto "dare to think," attributed to the German philosopher Emmanuel Kant, signified the rejection of all authority in the quest for "objective" truth and enthroned autonomous reason as the primary criterion in all matters. These accents reinforced the individualism of the Reformation. Coupled with the developing scientific method of experimentation, they produced astounding achievements in Western civilization, including an amazing expansion of fields of study in the hard and soft sciences. The underside of this phenomenal success was, of course, the whole complex of enormous economic, social, and environmental problems which beset the modern world. Moreover, the independent, creative spirit of the Enlightenment included an animus against tradition, religion, revelation, the Church, and even God – all forms or expressions of authority. This spirit still vitiates the "objectivity" of many modern intellectuals. In theological and biblical study, the intellectual inheritance of the Enlightenment, which accentuates the supremacy of reason and undercuts the very notion of divine revelation, is most problematic and controversial and the source of much confusion in methodology and research results.

5) *The revolution of historical studies.* The decipherment of hieroglyphics (1827) and cuneiform (1846) opened up the study of Egyptian and Babylonian records and accelerated the accumulation of historical knowledge about ancient civilizations. In nineteenth century historical studies, a presumption surfaced that historians, just as scientists studying nature, could reproduce an objective account of the past exactly as it happened ("historicism"). Significant historical and archaeological discoveries have continued well into the twentieth century, including dramatic findings of Greek papyri in Egypt (nineteenth century), Ugaritic tablets in Ras Shamra, Syria (1929), Gnostic documents at Nag Hammadi, Egypt (1945), and Jewish scrolls at Qumran near the Dead Sea (1947–1956).

This rich harvest of historical knowledge cast new light on the background of the development of Judaism and the origins of Christianity. Moreover, science had long undermined belief concerning the biblical views of the creation of the world, the age of the universe, and the miraculous. Scripture could no longer be viewed as revelation separated from ancient history and culture. A "historical consciousness" emerged about evolution and diversity in the complex historical process involving all human affairs. Scholars came more fully to perceive the contingency of historical events and the relativity of historical truth, both of which remain major issues in biblical hermeneutics.

Methodologies

Biblical scholarship in modern times has developed numerous approaches to Scripture. These involve the comparative study of ancient languages and manuscripts, the critical analysis of the literature and history of the biblical world, as well as interpretive ways by which to derive relevant meaning from the Bible. It is no surprise that, as in any other scientific field, critical biblical studies are defined by technical terminology, complex aspects, and diverse theories. Both the methods and results of biblical studies must be evaluated ultimately on the basis of their presuppositions and of their adequacy to the theological subject matter of Scripture. However, a coherent description of contemporary scholarly methodologies is virtually impossible because of their divergent, even conflicting, nature and purposes. The following overview of methods and approaches employed by the prevailing biblical scholarship today is presented according to three categories, each being less cohesive than the previous one.

The first major category is the *historical-critical* method. This approach has dominated biblical studies in the last two centuries as the "scientific" study of Scripture. It is critical in the sense of carefully searching for and weighing all the available evidence. It is historical in the sense of seeking to illuminate the truth of the evidence in terms of the historical context and background. It is scientific not in the strict manner of the hard sciences but in the sense of operating systematically and by means of defined criteria which are always open to modification.

The historical-critical method does not represent a single and rigid method but rather a broad approach consisting of a fluid cluster of related methods. At ground level is *textual criticism*, sometimes called "lower criticism," which involves the comparative study and classification of thousands of manuscripts of the Bible. Since none of the scriptural books survive in the original manuscripts or *autographs*, the goal of textual criticism is to recover, as closely as possible, the original wording of each book by comparative study of the extant manuscripts, usually relying on the most ancient ones. The result is a "critical scientific text" of the Hebrew and Greek originals, always open to revision, on which are based virtually all the modern translations of the Bible, such as the New Revised Standard Version, the New American Bible, or the Revised English Bible.

More controversial has been "higher criticism" or what has been generally known as *historical criticism*. This entails a broad area of research seeking to ascertain the origins of each biblical writing, its authorship, sources, literary form, cultural background, conceptual content, and relationship to historical reality. For example, why are the four gospels similar in some ways and different in others? Who wrote them, when, and under what circumstances? What sources were used? How are the gospels interrelated? How accurately does each present the actual ministry of Jesus? How can their discrepancies in chronology and striking differences in presenting Jesus and his work be explained? One can easily understand why a free exploration of such questions would cause misunderstanding among believers holding a reverent view of Scripture. For this reason, scholars and teachers have a responsibility to put things in perspective when exercising their functions in order to avoid needless offense.

The philological dimension of historical criticism includes

several refined areas of research. *Literary criticism* first involved the search for possible, usually written, sources behind a given biblical document. This area of research is now more accurately called simply *source criticism* to avoid confusion with "post-modern" literary studies mentioned below. In the twentieth century, source criticism developed into more refined tasks of philological research which are discussed under the section on the gospels in the second volume of this work. Here they may be simply mentioned. *Form criticism* identifies the small forms or units of scriptural books, such as laws, prayers, wisdom sayings, prophetic utterances, parables, etc., which go back to oral tradition and their use in the ongoing life of the religious community. *Redaction criticism*, also called *composition criticism*, examines the final shape of a book to discern how a particular author used available oral and written sources and what the author's specific interests were in so doing. *Tradition criticism* is a more delicate and highly conjectural effort to examine the intermediate stages to see how particular parables, miracle stories, prayers, etc., were possibly shaped by tradition before an author gave them final form. *Genre criticism* has to do with the study of the wholistic form or literary type of entire books such as gospel, acts, letter, treatise, and apocalypse. All of the above are part of the broad historical-critical approach to Scripture which has dominated modern biblical studies and has produced rich results for the understanding of the origins and composition of the gospels and other biblical writings.

A second, fairly recent category of methodologies is known as the *new literary criticism*.[6] These methodologies follow, as in the earlier case of historical criticism, precedents and techniques developed in secular academic studies. As applied to the Bible, they have emerged in part as a result of dissatisfaction with the predominant historical-critical approach and in part as a refinement and enrichment of it. Although these new method-

---

[6] See T. J. Keegan, *Interpreting the Bible: A Popular Introduction to Biblical Hermeneutics*; E. V. McKnight, *Post-Modern Use of the Bible*; and S. L. McKenzie and S. R. Haynes, *To Each Its Own Meaning: An Introduction to Biblical Criticisms and Their Application* (Louisville: Westminster, 1993).

ologies have roots in earlier philological studies, they are referred to as *post-modern criticism* because of their own emphases beyond the historico-critical concern for "objective" truth of the historical-critical method. They include a number of diverse approaches, such as *structuralism* or *semiotic analysis, narrative criticism* or *reader-oriented analysis, rhetorical analysis,* and *chiasmus.*[7] Their broad commonality is, by and large, the setting aside of the question of "historical veracity," which is still mainly left to the historical-critical approach. The goal of the new literary criticism is to enrich the understanding of Scripture by analyzing the biblical documents according to current literary theories and methodologies, including a vital concern for the contextual world and interests of contemporary readers themselves who seek relevant meaning from the Bible. The assumption is that a literary work once committed to writing has a life of its own beyond the intentions and historical context of its author and first readers. Philological scrutiny of a literary work can reveal deep structures of human communication, complex literary patterns, and diverse impacts on later readers which significantly contribute to the understanding of that particular work. The new literary criticism in its various expressions is at the beginning stages. A fuller appreciation, as well as a fairer assessment of these diverse literary approaches will depend on the value and permanency of their future results.

Finally, there is a third category of methodologies of which some are related and others are totally unrelated. What they formally share in common is that they are driven by definitive interests that go beyond historical and literary study. From the perspective of tradition, *canonical criticism* concentrates on the

---

[7] Daniel Patte, *What is Structural Exegesis?* (Philadelphia: Fortress, 1983); M. A. Powell, *What Is Narrative Criticism?* (Minneapolis: Fortress, 1990); J. P. Tompkins, *Reader–Response Criticism: From Formalism to Post-Structuralism* (Baltimore: John Hopkins, 1980); and George A. Kennedy, *New Testament Interpretation through Rhetorical Criticism* (Chapel Hill: University of North Carolina, 1984). The Orthodox biblical scholar John Breck has contributed the major work *The Shape of Biblical Language: Chiasmus in the Scriptures and Beyond* (Crestwood: St. Vladimir's Seminary Press, 1994).

study of the authoritative process of formation of the biblical writings and their final form as appears in the canon.[8] The interest here is to underscore the authority of Scripture in its theological witness by demonstrating the inter-relationship between the biblical writings and the religious community that produced and canonized them as the community sought to express normatively its faith and identity. From a philosophical perspective, *existentialist* interpretation, coupled with a program of "demythologization," was practiced notably by the late brilliant scholar Rudolf Bultmann.[9] A reductionist approach, it endeavored to contemporize Scripture by interpreting its "myths," such as the resurrection of Jesus and the gift of the Spirit, as expressions of the new self-understanding of early Christians, albeit a self-understanding actualized by God's grace.

From a social and political perspective, *liberationist* interpretation opts for a preferential emphasis on the poor and the oppressed, seeking to exploit those elements and themes in Scripture that give comfort to the underprivileged and support their socio-political and economic interests, especially in the third world.[10] In parallel fashion, *feminist* interpretation,

---

[8] The main exponents, with important differences between them, are Brevard S. Childs in his *Introduction to the Old Testament as Scripture*, *The New Testament as Canon: An Introduction*, and *Biblical Theology of the Old and New Testaments: Theological Reflection on the Christian Bible*; and J. A. Sanders, *Torah and Canon* (Philadelphia: Westminster, 1972), *Canon and Community*, and *From Sacred Story to Sacred Text*. Childs prefers to speak of a "canonical approach," not canonical criticism, because historical criticism still remains in force, albeit significantly tempered by attention to the authoritative theological witness of Scripture. In contrast, Sanders insists on the complexity and diversity of the canonical process itself within the ongoing community, rather than on the authoritative witness of the final form of the canon, and thus advocates a pluralistic approach to the contemporary interpretation of Scripture. For more nuanced distinctions and further developments, see Gerald T. Sheppard, "Canonical Criticism," *ABD*, Vol. 1, pp. 861-866.

[9] R. Bultmann, *Jesus Christ and Mythology* (New York: Scribner's, 1958); *Kerygma and Myth*, ed. H. W. Bartsch and trans. R. H. Fuller (New York: Harper, 1961), and Ian Henderson, *Rudolf Bultmann* (Richmond: John Knox, 1966).

[10] For example, R. S. Sugirtharajah, ed., *Voices from the Margins: Interpreting the Bible in the Third World* (Maryknoll: Orbis, 1991).

which appears in various forms from mild to radical, derives from and serves the interests of the women's struggle in modern society.[11] From the perspective of the social sciences, *sociological* and *psychological* approaches to Scripture have also made contributions to biblical studies.[12] These socio-psychological approaches, including feminist interpretation, have to do with the social and personal dynamics of the readers as they interpret and apply the Bible. Such studies should be distinguished from the historical works on the social world of the Bible based on the historical-critical method.[13]

The above overview sums up the various approaches and methods of the prevailing academic study of Scripture in modern times. A reaction to this liberal academic tradition is the *fundamentalist* interpretation, ranging from simplistic to sophisticated expressions.[14] Although fundamentalist interpretation developed in deliberate opposition to liberal biblical studies, especially historical criticism, it was compelled to imitate some of the perceived enemy's tools. Based on its own ideological interests, its definitive feature is the use of rationalism, even if artificially, to defend positions such as creationism and the absolute inerrancy of Scripture. A particularly American phenomenon since the late nineteenth century,

---

[11] Numerous works have been written, including M. Letty, ed., *Feminist Interpretation of the Bible* (Philadelphia: Westminster, 1985); Elizabeth Schüssler Fiorenza, *Bread Not Stone: The Challenge of Feminist Biblical Interpretation* (Boston: Beacon, 1984); and by the same, *Searching the Scriptures, Vol. 1, A Feminist Introduction* (New York: Crossroad, 1993) and *Vol. 2, A Feminist Commentary* (New York: Crossroad, 1994).

[12] For example, W. Wink, *The Bible in Human Transformation* and W. G. Rollins, *Jung and the Bible* (Atlanta: John Knox, 1983).

[13] See Carolyn Osiek, R.S.C.J., *What are they saying about the social setting of the New Testament?* (New York: Paulist, 1984); J. E. Stambaugh and D. L. Balch, *The New Testament in Its Social Environment* (Philadelphia: Westminster, 1986); John H. Elliott, *What Is Social-Scientific Criticism?* (Minneapolis: Fortress, 1993).

[14] For a critique of the fundamentalist approach, see Stanley B. Marrow, *The Words of Jesus in our Gospels: A Catholic Response to Fundamentalism*, and two works by J. Barr, *Fundamentalism* (Philadelphia: Westminster, 1978) and *Beyond Fundamentalism* (Philadelphia: Westminster, 1984).

Fundamentalism

it has spread as well to other areas of the globe in the wake of conservative Protestant missions. The fundamentalist approach is ideological in that it is inclined to defend an absolute position of the plenary inspiration, propositional revelation, and total inerrancy of Scripture regarding all truth – scientific, historical, and theological – beyond the claims and evidence of Scripture itself. While the intent to uphold the authority of Scripture is commendable, the extremes to which it has led, including a kind of intellectual sophistry and fanaticism, are indefensible. Christian fundamentalism, whether among Protestants, Roman Catholics, or Orthodox is on the whole an obscurantist reaction, albeit understandably so, to the bewildering excesses of modernism. It is often based on unconscious fear of losing the objective grounds of one's security of faith in the face of new findings by scientific and historical research. However, as has been noted by many, refusal to face reasonable facts of science and history is not evidence of sound faith but lack of it.

Beyond fundamentalism, in evaluating the various methodologies employed by biblical scholars, it must be affirmed that all of them, given their particular purposes and limitations, have their usefulness and can enrich one another. Methodologies as such, especially those pertaining to the historical-critical approach and the new literary criticism, are ideally neutral heuristic approaches seeking to elucidate the full meaning of the biblical text from various perspectives and at different levels. No historical and literary insight need be ignored, granted some reasonable scholarly self-discipline, but may be brought into full light in the interpretation of Scripture, including its background, exegetical meaning, history of interpretation, as well as its perceived multiple meanings and applications by contemporary readers. Problems arise in the actual use of these methodologies due to exclusive claims or philosophical assumptions held by their practitioners, especially with regard to the question of the final or normative meaning of the biblical text. This is most obvious in the cases of ideological interpretations. The historical-critical and the literary approaches, as well, can become ideological either by reason of hidden philosophical presuppositions or by abandoning altogether the question of the normative meaning of Scripture.

However, the question of normative meaning is one of a different order, having to do in principle more with hermeneutics than with specific exegetical methodologies. What one may consider the normative meaning of Scripture depends on the choice of and commitment to ultimate principles and values on the basis of which the contents of Scripture are inevitably selected and received. Here one moves, consciously or unconsciously, a crucial step beyond specific methodologies and perhaps even beyond hermeneutics as abstract speculation, into the realm of one's personal existence and the community to which one affirms loyalty, whether religious, socio-political, or academic. This personal and social ground of all values forms the primary basis of the human quest for meaning. That the question of the normative or final meaning of Scripture cannot in the end be settled by any methodologies or combination thereof, and probably neither by any hermeneutical theory as such, constitutes an important limitation of biblical studies vis-a-vis the Church, a limitation is problematic to the degree that it is unrecognized. These matters are discussed further in the following chapters on hermeneutics.

Strengths and Weaknesses

A fair assessment of biblical scholarship must take into account the major strengths and weaknesses of the field. The strengths of modern biblical studies are both obvious and numerous. The following list has in view the achievements of biblical studies from the perspective primarily of the historical-critical approach, which has prevailed since the nineteenth century.

1) One of the greatest strengths of biblical scholarship lies in its ideal of honest, critical search for truth by means of objec-

tive, historical, and philological criteria. There is something genuinely creative and refreshing about the historical-critical approach to ancient documents and the layers of accumulated tradition. In principle, the historical-critical method applies equally to all theological disciplines, including biblical study, patristics, Church history, dogmatics, and liturgics. Although absolute objectivity is impossible, significant measures of it are indeed possible as attested by the positive scholarly results in all these fields. While there can be a negative and destructive element in the critical spirit, it has also demonstrated a cleansing effect on religious traditions, illuminating their deepest insights and moderating their rigid and fanatical tendencies. The positive role of the human critical faculty in the discovery of truth must be affirmed. It is also exalted by the great fathers of the Church, such as the Cappadocians.[15] The critical function is an essential aspect of theology as a discerning, not merely repetitive, discipline which seeks to distinguish between truth and falsehood. While biblical critics have made foolish claims and grave errors, the critical approach has also demonstrated distinct capacity for self-criticism and self-correction, which are intrinsic and permanent elements of sound scholarship.

2) The success of biblical criticism in linguistic and textual studies is indisputable. Scholars have devoted exhaustive attention to the original languages of Scripture and to comparative analysis of the thousands of biblical manuscripts.[16] They have produced a scientific "critical text" of Scripture in the original, which serves as the basis of virtually all modern

---

[15] "The speculative, critical, and world-surveying faculty of the soul is its peculiar property by virtue of its very nature, and thereby the soul preserves within itself the image of divine grace." So states Gregory of Nyssa reporting a dialogue with his sister Macrina and cited by J. Pelikan, *Christianity and Classical Culture*, p. 128. Pelikan, *ibid.*, pp. 215-230, provides an excellent account of the relationship between faith and reason according to the Cappadocian fathers.

[16] For a fascinating account of the comparative study of New Testament manuscripts, see Bruce M. Metzger, *The Text of the New Testament* (New York: Oxford University Press, 1992).

translations of the Bible by biblical experts.[17] The fruits of scholarly linguistic work also include an amazing array of grammars,
lexica, concordances, and other aids for the systematic study of
Scripture.

3) Biblical scholarship in general has yielded an astonishing
body of knowledge about the Bible and its contents, the origins
and development of Judaism and Christianity, as well as their
surrounding cultures and religions. The sheer number of
dictionaries, encyclopedias, commentaries, books, and
periodicals dealing with the study of Scripture is staggering. A
magnitude of reasonably accurate information about the Bible
and its world is at our fingertips thanks to the meticulous labors
of scholars.[18]

4) Critical biblical studies have also elucidated countless
biblical institutions, concepts, and themes such as election,
covenant, prophecy, kingdom of God, and eschatology. We know
more about these subjects now than at any time before. Further,
biblical studies have shed unexpected light on major issues that
have traditionally divided Christians, for example, Scripture and
tradition, law and gospel, word and sacrament, and faith and
works. Thanks to historical critical scholarship, those who delve
into these matters in an open and honest way can achieve a

---

[17] In the case of the New Testament, the scientific critical text, which has had a
long history, is currently edited by Kurt Aland and others, *The Greek New Testament* (United Bible Societies, 1993, 4th revised edition) and the same text is also
published under the title *Novum Testamentum Graece* (Stuttgart, 1993, Nestle-
Aland 27th edition). This text is based primarily on two fourth-century manuscripts, Vaticanus and Sinaiticus. A number of conservative Protestant scholars
support an alternative critical text based on the majority of extant, later manuscripts of the New Testament, which derive from the Byzantine tradition. See
Maurice A. Robinson and William G. Pierpont, *The New Testament in the Original Greek According to the Byzantine/Majority Textform* (Atlanta: The Original Word
Publishers, 1991) and Zane C. Hodges and Arthur L. Farstad, *The Greek New
Testament According to the Majority Text* (Nashville: Thomas Nelson, 1982). A
critical text based on a limited number of Byzantine manuscripts had been previously prepared by the Orthodox biblical scholar Vasilios Antoniadis and published by the Ecumenical Patriarchate of Constantinople in 1912.

[18] Two recent monumental achievements of biblical scholarship are *The Anchor
Bible Dictionary* in six volumes and *The New Interpreter's Bible*, which will appear

consensus about what? (handwritten, left margin)

surprising level of consensus today.[19] This ecumenical aspect of biblical scholarship has facilitated dialogue not only among the Christian churches, but also between Christianity, Judaism, and other religions. *Well, yee ha, cowboy!* (handwritten)

5) By uncovering the historical complexities behind Holy Scripture, biblical scholarship has disclosed in dramatic ways the diversity and development of institutions and ideas within the revealed traditions of Judaism and Christianity. The undeniable reality of growth and diversity in the Bible has heightened our awareness of the incarnational and human aspects of Scripture, corroborating and refining the dynamic view of inspiration and revelation. A healthy by-product has been a kind of epistemological humility about claims based on Scripture, recognizing that Scripture can be used or misused in its application. For example, using different texts from Scripture, one could make a case for the freedom and liberation of oppressed people, just as another might make a case for the conquest and domination of others, indeed even a case for holy war, based on religious claims. But the latter would certainly illustrate an evil use of the holy book. A similar scholarly temperance about the complexity of history and the profundity of Scripture's ultimate subject, which is the mystery of the living God, seems to be leading many scholars to the realization that biblical experts themselves may not have all the answers about the Bible either.

Modern biblical scholarship must be measured, as well, by its weaknesses, which are just as obvious as its strengths. Again, at a grave risk of generalization, a number of shortcomings may be pointed out. Amidst the diversity of scholars and approaches, not all display these shortcomings in the same way or in equal measure, and many perhaps not at all. Yet, as one surveys the field, three major areas of weakness stand out, which seem to mark negative aspects of modern biblical studies in the

complete in more than a dozen volumes.

[19] For bibliography on several topics of ecumenical discussion, see Chapter Three, note 12.

prevailing liberal tradition. These areas of weakness involve the important elements of the theology, spirituality, and truth of Scripture.

1) Historical-critical analysis, a great strength of scholarship, has also turned out to be a heavy liability. Critical analysis has tended to so concentrate on the historical and literary details of texts and their background that, without appropriate synthesis, or rather, with a seeming inability to provide a synthesis adequate to Scripture, biblical scholarship has lost sight of the saving witness of Scripture, the substance of theology. One can rightly accuse biblical scholarship of promoting not salvation by grace, but salvation by the works of critical analysis, although it seems not to have found salvation at all. A theological discipline has paradoxically been reduced to an historical discipline. It has changed the Bible from a source of pastoral nurture into a complex, if impressive, museum of literary, historical, and religious data.

To object that biblical scholars must do the analysis while others pick up the pieces and engage the theology of the Bible is an indefensible position as viewed by other professionals, clergy, students, and ordinary lay people. Georges Florovsky more than a generation ago wrote about "the lost Scriptural mind" and how, in contrast to the Church fathers, modern scholars seem to deal with "maps" rather than "real things" in biblical study – the great saving events and central theological themes of Scripture.[20] He urged concentration on the full truth of the gospel, Christ, the classic creeds, and the Church. Whatever the strengths of biblical scholarship, the field is marked by disarray when it comes to the religious and theological value of the Bible. Where the Church fathers were strongest, namely, the christocentric theology of Scripture, biblical scholarship is weakest. Modern biblical studies urgently need to correct the impression that they have become theologically irrelevant, even bankrupt, seemingly drowning in a sea of historical and literary waves largely of the

---

[20] G. Florovsky, "The Lost Scriptural Mind," in his *Bible, Church, Tradition: An Eastern Orthodox View*, pp. 9-16, originally published under the title "As the Truth Is in Jesus" in *The Christian Century*, December 19, 1951.

field's own making.

2) A second serious shortcoming of biblical scholarship is a kind of professionalism that fails to do justice to the spirituality of the Bible. There is a healthy professionalism based on institutional procedures and instrumental criteria by which experts carry out their work and actualize the value of their field. An unhealthy professionalism sets in when the experts become too self-enclosed, too engrossed in their own skills and methodologies, too blind or uncaring about the final adequacy and value of their work as compared to the subject matter of their study. The Bible is a fruit of and bears testimony to the experience of God, the source of the confident joy and hopeful promise of life, amidst the suffering and corruption of this world. Where is Scripture's song to be heard in the works of biblical experts? Is it not right to expect that musicologists play the masterpieces, as well as analyze them? Should not the same be required of biblical scholars if justice is to be done Scripture's spiritual dimensions?

St. Basil called some interpreters of his time, who strained the letter but missed the spirit of Scripture, "technologists" (τεχνολογοῦσι, οὐ θεολογοῦσι) rather than theologians.[21] For him and other Church fathers, the study of Scripture was accompanied by prayer and Christian living in the context of the life of the Church. Those committed to such engagement had a vocational calling to ministry and consequently emerged as leaders of the Church. Indeed, most of the great interpreters of Christian antiquity were also bishops of the Church. Theologizing was a matter of deep personal faith dedicated to the nurture of the Church's life. In contrast, contemporary theological studies find their home in the classroom and in institutions of higher learning. The focus is less on prayer and Christian living and more on completion of academic programs and granting higher degrees. Both as teachers and students we seem to be caught up

---

[21] St. Basil, *Letter 90*, Loeb Classical Library: *St. Basil, Letters*, Vol. 2, trans. R. J. Deferrari (Cambridge: Harvard University Press, 1962), p. 124. So also St. Gregory of Nyssa in his *Second Book Against Eunomius*.

in an inescapable professionalism, despite frequent complaints by many. A hunger for expressions of personal faith and spirituality goes unsatisfied even in seminaries. During graduation festivities, academic achievements are applauded but hardly anyone asks if the theological school graduate has yet learned to pray.

Again, to object that in institutions of a pluralistic society, especially secular colleges and state universities, personal faith and spirituality cannot or should not shine through one's work, is a poor excuse for bad professionalism. Is not a Marxist political theorist allowed to present the case of Marxism and to disclose his own convictions directly or indirectly in these institutions? Should not a philosopher sing the praises of Plato's vision of the good life in the college classroom? Surely it is intellectually far more challenging and personally far more engaging to take a course on Judaism from a knowledgeable and committed Jew or, likewise, a course on Islam from an informed and devout Moslem, than from a neutral or unsympathetic expert. Is it not a plus for our civilization to expose university students to the spirituality of the Bible and other sacred documents together with the scholarly study of them?

Good point

Moreover, there are professional and institutional standards which can, given reasonable flexibility, safeguard the classroom from unqualified, proselytistic, or fanatical exponents. The academic context of higher educational institutions provides an excellent forum for the free exchange of ideas and convictions reasonably argued. In such academic contexts, the intrinsic truth of any subject has a chance to win a place in the hearts of thinking people as they exercise the right of their personal freedom in a pluralistic society. From this perspective, the Bible has been devalued even in theological schools by biblical experts who have often not risen to the task of grappling with the Bible's spiritual treasures.

In fact, professionalism in biblical studies is at times marked by a kind of negativism and cynicism that subtly vitiate scholarly work and the classroom, a spirit students easily detect but the experts seem mindlessly to ignore. This negativism goes beyond the occasional aloofness that a professional might sometimes display in claiming more for one's field or one's own positions than seems appropriate. It goes beyond even professional indifference, jargon, excessive conjectures, empty speculations, the unrelieved "problem-centered approach," and provocative phrases such as "the Christ–myth," "New Testament disunity," and the "anatomy" of this and that in the Bible. All these, too, no doubt startle, perplex, and disappoint students who enroll in biblical courses thinking to find some personal satisfaction and life value in them as taught by experts, but to no avail.

However, beyond all such professional drawbacks, one sometimes detects among some scholars an animosity toward the subject matter itself, the Bible, and its claims. It can be seen in the negative spirit with which the expert may critique biblical events and ideas. It can be observed in the sinister, whether hidden or overt, pleasure of shaking up the weak or uninformed faith of students.[22] Behind such attitudes lie a scholar's own unresolved issues of religious faith, various forms of an inferiority complex in the face of the prevailing intellectualism, even a kind of self-hatred for being in a field the expert neither loves nor truly believes is of any value to anyone. In a scholarly milieu of this kind, a student who may eagerly enter the field as a vocational goal can in the process lose his or her own faith and eventually become "twice as much the child of Gehenna" (Mt 23:15). This indeed is a pernicious and destructive professionalism that does great disservice to the Bible and to those engaged in its academic study.

3) The third area of weakness in modern biblical studies, in some respects closely related to the second, is the source of the

_____

[22] For example, C. Jack Eichhorst, a Lutheran pastor, bitterly laments "all the efforts in Lutheran colleges and seminaries to knock the stuffings of pietistic or fundamentalistic views of the Scripture out of students ... [a] critical overkill that has produced ... skepticism, cynicism and rank unbelief about the Bible ... I now find myself to be part of a church where ultimately the Bible is trashed more than trusted, pious rhetoric notwithstanding, and belittled more than believed," in "There Is a Deep Spiritual Sickness," *LF* 28 (3, 1994), pp. 25-26.

gravest problems. Here we are dealing with the philosophical presuppositions of the Enlightenment, which have had an enslaving grasp on the majority of the practitioners of liberal biblical criticism from Hermann Samuel Reimarus (1694–1768) to the contemporary participants in the Jesus Seminar. At the heart of the matter is nothing less than the essential question of truth about Christ, the gospel, the Church, and Christianity as a whole. By setting up autonomous reason as the arbiter of all truth, the Enlightenment worldview has been heavily biased toward empiricism and logical positivism. These philosophies not only question the reality of biblical events and miracles, but also axiomatically preclude the truth of a living God intervening in history and in particular human lives. In this fashion, with one arbitrary sweep of the philosophical hand, they render the Bible irrelevant as a source of saving truth and strike at the heart of the faith of religious communities based on revelatory traditions such as Judaism and Christianity.

To be sure, within modern theological scholarship the Enlightenment legacy often hides in subtle ways behind appeals to reasonableness, relevance, and the objectivity of scholarly research. It is also easily combined with the use of traditional language understood in metaphorical and humanistic ways. A favorite expression of some biblical scholars has been to talk about the "stories" or "narratives" of Scripture. While this is an appropriate and useful way to interpret the Bible for the modern reader, the whole enterprise becomes hollow unless there is revelatory basis behind the scriptural stories and narratives. It is a crucial matter whether the whole biblical story is grounded on events of revelation or is merely a summary of the primitive religious configurations of ancient peoples. In similar fashion, scholars talk about a "methodological bracketing," that is, scholarly analysis of texts and interpretation of narratives without raising the question of truth. Again, while such a methodological device may lead to more nuanced understanding of ancient documents, the whole effort becomes superficial without reference to saving theological truth and the momentous question of encounter with the living God.

Whatever the case, the Enlightenment rationalistic stance deserves to be exposed for what it is in its most sinister depth: a kind of diabolical impulse, both arbitrary and nihilistic, which is bent on effacing faith in God from the earth and on destroying any semblance of revealed truth claimed by humanity. This corruptive element of the so-called "modern mind," namely, the humanistic reliance on autonomous reason as the key to reality conceived as a closed system, has long been discredited by philosophy and physics. It has also failed to achieve its pretentious goals as evidenced by the crises of modern civilization as well as the "post-modern" resurgence of the suppressed religious spirit, often finding expression in bizarre forms. Yet, Enlightenment presuppositions still dominate the mindset of many intellectuals in the academies, continuing to spread confusion and darkness both in the classroom and contemporary culture. Regrettably, the same is true of liberal biblical scholarship which, despite its positive contributions, has caused a deep crisis in Protestantism by undermining the role of faith and the authority of Scripture.

The above criticisms should not be construed as a call to dispense with modern critical study of Scripture as useless and dangerous. Biblical scholarship is marked by indisputable strengths as well as glaring weaknesses. Its strengths are grounded on objectively verifiable observations and standards that sharpen our insight into and enrich our knowledge of the biblical world. Its weaknesses are exaggerations that can be corrected or wrong directions that can be retraced and rerouted. As is the case in all other fields, there can be no question of abandoning critical biblical studies for an uncritical reading of Scripture either for the informed believer or, much less, for the Church. The true challenge is the challenge of positive and sound scholarship which, without precluding honest disagreements, seeks an appropriate balance between the tasks of critical analysis, the theological witness of the biblical texts, as well as the authentic claims of the religious communities for which these texts constitute

Holy Scripture. That balance can only be worked out with due regard to the hermeneutical question, which is addressed at length in the remaining chapters.

Chapter Six

The Hermeneutical Question I: A Critical Overview

Problem or Problems?

The hermeneutical question is a rather paradoxical matter. On the one hand, biblical hermeneutics has to do with epistemology, namely, the nature of the study of Scripture and its interpretation. Described as the "art of understanding,"[1] hermeneutics seeks to clarify how and why we do what we do with the Bible. Through systematic reflection on the methods, principles, and dynamic factors of biblical study it attempts to construct a coherent theory of communication — how meaning and value are derived from Scripture and how they are applied in life.[2] On the other hand, hermeneutics is

---

[1] Bernard C. Lategan, "Hermeneutics," *ABD*, Vol. 3, p. 149.

[2] Gordon D. Fee, *Gospel and Spirit*, correctly stresses and provides numerous illustrations of the connection between hermeneutics and the actual use of Scripture, which is very often selective on all sides. According to Fee, hermeneutics significantly involves both "the meaning and application of Scripture," a matter of daily challenge, since all Christian life and ministry necessarily presuppose hermeneutics, or as Fee puts it, "thinking about and reflecting on Scripture in such a way that one brings it to bear on all aspects of human life," p. 24. Hermeneutics, whether implicit or explicit, is inescapable and must be articulated with utmost care, responsibility, and consistency. Unfortunately, many hermeneutical thinkers seem to deal with the subject in terms of abstractions, as if building castles in the sky, with no tangible connections to the biblical texts and the reality of everyday life.

seemingly beset by intractable questions and conflicting proposals. Reading in the relevant literature discloses such diverse presentations and approaches that even defining the hermeneutical problem becomes an elusive task. Impressive theories developed by brilliant thinkers ranging from Schleiermacher to Gadamer have come and gone. In our generation, proposals by Paul Ricoeur, David Tracy, and many theorists of the so-called new literary criticism have been put forward with no consensus in sight. W. Randolph Tate concludes that "the task of hermeneutics ... is never complete ... [but] ever-changing, never-ending," and accompanied by inevitable frustration.[3] In his overview of the contemporary situation, Raymond Brown likens the quest for "*the* way to interpret Scripture" to the quest for the Holy Grail, as undying as it seems futile.[4] It is indeed paradoxical that a discipline aiming at clarification should generate so much confusion.

Yet, the perplexity in hermeneutics can be explained in terms of the complex and fluid factors involving the Bible, its readers, and the life context in which Scripture is read and applied. Regarding Scripture, there are numerous queries about its historical and literary origins, its diversity of teachings and institutions, its human and divine aspects, its role and authority in church and culture throughout the ages. How is God's will to be discerned within the variety of Scripture's witness as well as in its multiple ways of interpretation in history? Regarding the readers, there are equally numerous queries about their personal interests and biases, their ecclesial and cultural backgrounds, their views of inspiration and revelation, as well as their implicit or explicit principles of interpretation. By what motivations and criteria does a reader seek to understand, interpret, and apply Scripture? Regarding life context, it is obvious that different burning issues arise in various times. For St. Paul and the early Church, such issues included the role of the Mosaic Law and the relations between Jews, Jewish Christians, and Gentile

---

[3] W. Randolph Tate, *Biblical Interpretation*, p. 212.
[4] R. Brown, "Hermeneutics," *NJBC*, p. 1158.

Christians. In the fourth century, the trinitarian debates preoccupied all. At the end of the twentieth, socio-political questions about government and religion, gender and sexuality, medical ethics and human rights are discussed. How does the reading of Scripture influence critical issues of the day and how do such issues in turn qualify or refine the role and interpretation of Scripture?

These considerations indicate that the hermeneutical "problem" is in reality not one but many simultaneously. Complex factors and diverse dynamics play into defining the elusive nature of the hermeneutical quest. What may be an immense problem for a particular reader, religious community, or generation may be no problem at all for another. One reader rejoices in Scripture's claim that God personally made himself known to specific persons such as Abraham and St. Paul, while another is highly skeptical about it. One interpreter anchors a hermeneutical model on the authority of Scripture and Church, while another constructs a different model, rejecting both authorities. Various ecclesial and academic uses of Scripture rely on different hermeneutics whether implicit or explicit. As concrete issues arise and debates develop in a given epoch, the hermeneutical task may be specified and refined. Theorists can sort out elements of agreement and disagreement. But hermeneutical discussion can also become extremely narrow, technical, and abstract to an extent that it becomes far removed from the biblical text as well as from the interest of most readers. The challenge is thus to identify the structure of the hermeneutical quest, that is, to define basic dimensions and crucial points of convergence and divergence, in order to establish some coherence and clarity in the hermeneutical inquiry.[5]

The Hermeneutical Question in the Ancient Church

The biblical authors themselves were unavoidably involved in hermeneutical dynamics but rarely raised the hermeneutical

---

[5] See also the preliminary discussion of hermeneutics in Chapter Three.

question in a conscious way, and then only indirectly when dealing with disagreements. For example, St. Paul's distinction between letter and spirit (2 Cor 3:6) in reading the Old Testament is a rudimentary hermeneutical reflection. Although he inherits this distinction from the Jewish background, he applies it in his own way. He implicitly acknowledges that Jews and Christians read the same Bible differently but he does not engage theoretical considerations about theological principles and exegetical methods. He simply declares that a blinding "veil" impedes unbelieving Jews from true understanding of the Pentateuch, an impediment which can be removed only through faith in Christ and by the power of the Spirit (2 Cor 3:14-18). When advocating the cessation of the Mosaic Law and that "there is no longer Jew nor Greek" (Gal 3:23-28), Paul knows as well that a number of Jewish and Christian contemporaries vehemently disagreed (Gal 2:4-5; 11-14; cf. Acts 15:1-2). He seeks to demonstrate his claim through reasoning and biblical interpretation (Gal 3:6-29). But his unreflected hermeneutics relies far more on his own faith experience of Christ (Gal 1:11-17) as the hermeneutical key, and the reality of his Gentile congregations as the hermeneutical ground, for that claim. The decisive hermeneutical significance of the larger ecclesial reality, although unreflected, is shown more clearly in the case of the Apostolic Council (Acts 15:1-29). To maintain unity between Jewish and Gentile Christians, the Jerusalem Assembly took what amounts to be a momentous hermeneutical position on the Mosaic Law – removing the burden of its observance from Gentile Christians – and justified its decision chiefly with the declaration "it has seemed good to us and to the Holy Spirit" (Acts 15:28).[6]

[6] According to the sketchy account in Acts, which no doubt omits a full exchange of views for and against the obligation of Law observance by Gentile Christians. The hermeneutical question is indirectly raised again and again in the Fourth Gospel where the correct understanding of Christ and his ministry is frequently at the forefront, (e.g., Jn 6:44-45; 7:16-17; 12:37-40; 16:12-15). Interestingly, the declarative mode of divine revelation in the Fourth Gospel is accompanied by references to the role of the Holy Spirit as hermeneutical agent (Jn 6:63; 7:39; 14:16-17, 26; 16:13), both of which are expressions of the hermeneutical stance of the Johannine community.

In the patristic tradition, the question of hermeneutics gradually gained the level of conscious reflection. Because of ongoing doctrinal disputes, most of which involved biblical interpretation, the Church fathers developed sophisticated hermeneutical distinctions regarding the nature of Scripture, its role and interpretation in the Church, as well as appropriate exegetical methods and principles.[7] Numerous examples can be given. In the debates with Jews and Marcionites over the Old Testament as witness to Christ, St. Justin Martyr forged the first systematic qualification of the unity of Scripture, that is, his tripartite classification of the Old Testament into prophecy, moral law, and temporary historical legislation for Jews.[8] The last of the three elements constitutes the first explicit relativization of the massive authority of Scripture inherited from Judaism.[9] A generation later, St. Irenaios, who bears clear testimony to a universal Christian Church and a Christian Bible composed of Old and New Testaments, established important theological principles for the unity and interpretation of Scripture.[10] For Irenaios, Christ is the central hermeneutical principle for the entire Bible, a principle that undergirds the unity of Scripture as well as the viability of typological interpretation of the Old Testament. Equally important is his appeal to the "rule of faith" as an interpretive perspective, which is essentially an appeal to the doctrinal sense of the Church as a hermeneutical principle so crucial

---

[7] See Chapter Four for the patristic views on Scripture, exegetical methodology, and bibliography.

[8] *Dial.* 44.2.

[9] Justin's concern was to maintain the authority of the Old Testament as a Christian book, while allowing for partial relativization of its authority through acknowledgment that the ritual Law was temporary and no longer binding on Christians. What was implicit in St. Paul's thought (Gal 3) becomes explicit in Justin's. See further Hans von Campenhausen, *The Formation of the Christian Bible*, trans. by J. A. Baker (Philadelphia: Fortress, 1972), pp. 88-102, and Theodore Stylianopoulos, *Justin Martyr and the Mosaic Law*, (Missoula: Society of Biblical Literature, 1975), pp. 51-68 and 153-163.

[10] See J. L. Kugel and R. A. Greer, *Early Biblical Interpretation*, pp. 109-113; F. Sadowski, *The Church Fathers on the Bible*, pp. 27-44, and B. de Margerie, *The Greek Fathers*, pp. 51-77.

in Christian history. His lasting hermeneutical achievement is the conscious binding together of Scripture and Church, the latter being the proper context of interpretation of Scripture as Scripture.

In the third century, hermeneutical reflection reached an apex in the work of the great Origen who was a philologist, exegete, catechist, homilist, theologian, and philosopher.[11] As a man of the Bible and the Church, Origen was greatly impressed by both the scriptural treasures and the missionary success of Christianity. Working with the intellectual tools of his time and addressing all thinking persons, Origen constructed a systematic vision of Christian education (παιδεία) centered on Christ, whom Origen rightly perceived to be the central focus of as well as *the* hermeneutical key to Scripture. Ancient and modern interpreters, many in grossly unfair and anachronistic ways, have vilified him for his allegorical excesses and some fantastic speculations, yet all owe something to him. No one has equaled his total exegetical achievement from textual studies to interpretive actualization of the biblical witness. His value for hermeneutics lies not simply in his formulation of a distinct hermeneutical theory based on body, soul, and spirit, as many scholars seem to think, and which he himself did not follow consistently, but precisely in the cohesion of his interpretive and theological vision integrating contemporary methods of study, the authority of Scripture, the authority of the Church, and the challenges of his day. It was within this vision that "spiritual exegesis," including use of allegory without losing sight of the historical grounding of revelation, proved an effective tool in promoting the biblical witness among believers and pagans. John Panagopoulos, who sees Origen as a faithful and brilliant thinker dealing with the interactive hermeneutical currents of Judaism, Christianity, and hellenism, writes these bold words about the great Alexandrian:

---

[11] A recent brief evaluation of this great but controversial figure is provided by B. de Margerie, *The Greek Fathers*, pp. 95-116. For Origen's texts in English translation see K. Froehlich, *Biblical Interpretation in the Early Church*, pp. 48-78; J. W. Trigg, *Biblical Interpretation*, pp. 71-115; and F. Sadowski, *The Church Fathers on the Bible*, pp. 89-125.

"Origen was and remains the founder and pioneer of biblical hermeneutics, the inexhaustible fountain of sound ecclesial biblical interpretation."[12]

After Origen, in both East and West, hermeneutical sophistication continued to develop as Church fathers countenanced not only heretics but one another over the question of correct biblical interpretation adequate to its subject matter. Patristic interpreters such as Diodore of Tarsus and Theodore of Mopsuestia in the Eastern tradition, as well Augustine and Jerome in the Western tradition, engaged specific issues of exegetical methodology, technical terms, translation, and rules of interpretation.[13] One of the hermeneutical fruits was the formulation of the standardized fourfold sense of Scripture – literal, allegorical, tropological (moral), and anagogical (eschatological) – which first appeared in John Cassian,[14] happily as much an Easterner as a Westerner. In the case of the Cappadocian fathers, we find a philosophically conscious hermeneutic seeking to maintain a critical balance between faith and reason, between the experiential and discursive dimensions of theology, including "an effort to reconcile theological data and scientific thought" of their times.[15] Rich diversity in methodology and interpretation marked the patristic heritage, but a diversity within the broad unity of the doctrine and life of the Church.

Hermeneutically, the crucial issue was, and is, not methodology or plurality of interpretations, but the relationship between the authority of the Bible and the authority of the Church, that

---

[12] John Panagopoulos, Ἡ Ἑρμηνεία τῆς Ἁγίας Γραφῆς στὴν Ἐκκλησία τῶν Πατέρων Vol. 1, p. 280.

[13] K. Froehlich, *Biblical Interpretation in the Early Church*, pp. 82-132; J. W. Trigg, *Biblical Interpretation*, pp. 163-295; and F. Sadowski, *The Church Fathers on the Bible*, 143-243.

[14] K. Froehlich, *Biblical Interpretation in the Early Church*, p. 28. The standard example was Jerusalem which literally is the Jewish city, allegorically the Church, tropologically the soul, and anagogically the heavenly Jerusalem of the kingdom, according to Cassian's *Conferences* 14.8. See *John Cassian: Conferences*, trans. Colm Luibheid (Mahwah: Paulist, 1985), p. 160.

[15] The quoted statement is by J. Daniélou, cited by B. de Margerie, *The Greek*

is, the Church's doctrinal sense regarding potentially divisive matters of interpretation. As noted above, in the classic Christian era, Scripture and tradition were interdependent and mutually supportive.[16] The Christian Bible, according to R. Greer, had authority only when read in the light of the Church's rule of faith.[17] But the rule of faith and the central message of the Bible were seen as intimately connected, even identified. In the early Christian centuries, there were no exact canonical delineations of either the Bible or the rule of faith. The apostolic tradition, whether oral or written, loomed large. As Greer points out, in one sense the rule of faith was authoritative because it cohered with Scripture's central message; in another sense it was the developing rule of faith that essentially determined the acceptability of the biblical writings and thus created the Christian Bible.

One should note perhaps more clearly than Greer does that, functionally, the critical hermeneutical factor in both cases was the ongoing and open-ended living tradition of the great Church and its doctrinal discernment. This was a matter of historical and theological inevitability insofar as the apostolic tradition, granted its decisive importance, could not of itself be transmitted and defined apart from the self-identity and interpretive decisions of the living community of faith. In this light, one can fully agree with Greer's two general and abiding points of hermeneutical discussion arising from the patristic exegetical legacy. In Greer's words:

Fathers, p. 219. See further the extensive discussion by J. Pelikan, *Christianity and Classical Culture*, pp. 215-230, entitled "Faith as the Fulfillment of Reason," and more recently J. A. McGuckin, "'Perceiving Light from Light in Light' (*Oration* 31.3): The Trinitarian Theology of Saint Gregory the Theologian," *GOTR* 39 (1-2, 1994), pp. 32. Philip Rousseau, *Basil of Caesarea*, pp. 106-111 and 322-323, underscores Basil's sensitivity toward clever dialectics against which the Cappadocian guarded by relying on a literal interpretation of authoritative Scripture and then accommodating all other knowledge.

[16] See the discussion under "Scripture and Tradition" in Chapter Two.

[17] Rowan A. Greer, "Biblical Authority in the Early Church," *ABD*, Vol. 5, p. 1027.

First, the early Church [i.e., up to the fifth century] did not think of the authority of Scripture apart from its relation to the theological tradition expressed in the rule of faith or apart from the use of Scripture in Christian worship. The authority of Scripture was bound to the life of the Church. Scripture, the theological tradition, and the worship of the Church were not treated as alternative points of departure for articulating the meaning of the faith, nor were they regarded as alternative authorities to be played off against one another. Second, the authoritative meaning of these norms of belief and practice was intended to establish unity for the Church, but not a unity involving uniformity.[18]

The Hermeneutical Crisis in Western Christianity

In modern times, the patristic hermeneutical vision was broken in two ways, through the Reformation and through the Enlightenment. The Reformation, as a protest movement against perceived abuses and distortions in the Western Christian tradition, established the foundational principle of "Scripture alone" (*sola Scriptura*) and thereby rejected in principle the interdependence between Bible and tradition. We now recognize, of course, that the Protestant "scriptural principle" is a polemical one, a corrective to the excesses of tradition, and does not stand of itself. Neither the Bible, nor faith, nor grace, nor Christ, ever "stand alone." Primacy yes; singularity no. The simple reason is the necessity of the receiving human subject, the necessity of interpretation, which inevitably cause the interpreter to carve

who are we?

---

[18] *Ibid.*, pp. 1026-1027. Historical scholarship has gradually compelled many Protestants, conservatives as well as liberals, to acknowledge the role of tradition in the canonization of Scripture, a rather significant issue in hermeneutics and ecclesiology. For example, Gordon D. Fee, *Gospel and Spirit*, p. 17, writes: "What most evangelicals tend conveniently to ignore is that it was tradition in this sense that was responsible, under the guidance of the Spirit, for the canonization of the [scriptural] tradition."

out, consciously or unconsciously, his or her own tradition of interpretation.

The Reformers, on the one hand, by their rejection of the authority of the Church and, on the other hand, by their double, related emphasis on *sola Scriptura* and the right of individual interpretation, created a new tradition, in fact, eventually many interpretive traditions as the fragmentation of the Protestant movement proceeded. One can, of course, argue that the Western medieval Church had already distorted the interdependence of Scripture and tradition by heavily tilting the balance toward tradition, which stifled the voice of Scripture. If and when the beliefs or practices of the Church, whether Western or Eastern, become perceptibly removed from or inconsistent with Scripture's witness, then the principle of interdependence becomes unconvincing and meaningless in practice.

Eastern Orthodox theologians have mused whether the Reformation could have occurred in Eastern Christianity. From an Orthodox perspective, the hermeneutical position of the Reformation is attractive but imbalanced. On the one side, it is clear that Luther and Calvin marked a return to classic patristic hermeneutics.[19] They recovered the authority and centrality of Scripture in the life of the Church. They stressed the central aim (σκοπὸς) and the unity of Scripture, which they located in Christ. They insisted on the primacy of reading Scripture contextually in the light of Scripture. They discerned an interplay between letter and spirit, between abstract theory and spiritual wisdom, given that the mystery of God must be approached with faith and prayer and cannot be resolved into a rational system. They acknowledged and developed the principle of accommodation, that is, that along with its inspired character, the Bible also reflects human limitations.

---

[19] D. H. Kelsey, "Protestant Attitudes Regarding Methods of Biblical Interpretation," in *Scripture*, ed. by F. E. Greenspahn, pp. 134-141; D. G. Bloesh, *Holy Scripture*, pp. 192-195, and Donald K. McKim, "Biblical Authority and the Protestant Reformation," *ABD*, Vol. 5, pp. 1032-1035.

On the other side, the rejection of the final hermeneutical authority of the Church in matters of faith, expressed not through the papal magisterium but through representative councils voicing the doctrinal discernment of the whole Church, amounts to a hermeneutical crisis. The principle of *sola Scriptura* and the concomitant right of individual interpretation drive a wedge between the authority of Scripture and the unitive theological tradition of the Church, thus creating a hermeneutical impasse. The hermeneutical question in its peculiarly Protestant expression emerged as an intractable theological and ecclesial problem. The history of Protestantism amply shows that the various Protestant traditions established their own hermeneutical perspectives within which they read the Bible, but found no hermeneutical way to maintain unity in diversity. The Reformation's rediscovery of Scripture is welcome but the "dogmatic" position on *sola Scriptura* is highly problematic. The "scriptural principle," without the balance of an "ecclesial principle," recoils upon itself and becomes self-defeating. It destroys any possibility of an integrative hermeneutic because, in the absence of a final hermeneutical authority, individual interpretation reigns supreme. The historical developments in Protestantism, including Protestant Orthodoxy, Puritanism, Spiritualism, Millenarianism, Pietism, as well as modern mainline confessions and fringe groupings give evidence of the hermeneutical diversity and confusion in Protestantism.

The patristic hermeneutical vision was broken in a second and even more radical way by the Enlightenment, through its impact on Protestant theological and biblical studies.[20] Specifically, the convergence of developing Enlightenment rationalism and historical criticism, both based on the scientific principle of analogy, raised the hermeneutical question in a different and most radical form. Previously, the hermeneutical problem centered on the question of ecclesial or individual discernment as final hermeneutical arbiter. Now the hermeneutical problem

---

[20] See the relevant remarks and bibliography on the academic use of Scripture and biblical scholarship in Chapters Two and Five.

shifted to the question of revelation or reason as the final hermeneutical criterion. In the Enlightenment heritage, the presumptuousness of unbridled reason, against which Luther had emphatically warned, eventually led to a wholescale rejection of the revelatory authority of Scripture. Lessing debunked the central truths of Scripture because he was an enlightened "man of the eighteenth century" and perceived an ugly chasm or ditch between the revelatory claims of Scripture and the new thinking of intellectuals like himself. With the rise of science, the emergence of historical criticism imitating the scientific method, and the secularization of Western culture, gradual accommodation to Enlightenment thinking systematically undermined the authority of the Bible and caused among Protestants "the crisis of the Scripture principle."[21]

The hermeneutical impact of the Enlightenment on Protestantism had shattering repercussions. Deep fissures appeared among conservative and liberal Protestants and shades thereof, dependent on the degree of acceptance of or resistance to the new thinking. On the one hand, the Western religious heritage, through its rigid views of Scripture and its authoritarian control of society, fueled the new questioning of authority and the desire for emancipation. On the other hand, the biblical debate between conservatives and liberals was cast, according to Walter Brueggemann,[22] in the Enlightenment categories of scientific accuracy or historical precision, which were alien to the Scriptures and, one might add, alien as well to the classic patristic tradition. Sharing implicitly the same presuppositions, one side excessively relativized while the other side excessively absolutized the authority of Scripture. As Protestantism traumatically

[handwritten margin note: TWINS BORN OF THE SAME MOTHER THE ENLIGHTENMENT]

---

[21] The expression is W. Pannenberg's, a chapter title in his *Basic Questions in Theology*, Vol. 1, trans. G. H. Kehm (Philadelphia: Westminster, 1970), p. 1. For a sketch of the complex story of how Scripture's authority was both overemphasized and then undermined by developments chiefly among Protestants, see H. G. Reventlow, "Biblical Authority in the Wake of the Enlightenment," *ABD*, Vol. 5, pp. 1035-1049.

[22] Walter Brueggemann, "Biblical Authority in the Post-Critical Period," *ABD*, Vol. 5, p. 1050.

The Enlightenment's battle cry: "Reason alone!"

reformed into fundamentalist, conservative or evangelical, and liberal camps, with differentiations among them, the implicit or explicit diversity of hermeneutics was accentuated.[23] The consequences can hardly be overestimated. They concern heavy charges of heresy against liberal Protestantism by Karl Barth and others.[24] They involve questions about the very vitality and future of Protestant Christianity in the modern and post-modern world.[25]

One might have thought that liberal Protestants on the common basis of critical reason as a standard of truth could have worked out an integrative hermeneutic but, to no avail. On the contrary, it is within the liberal tradition of Protestantism, where the individualism of the Reformation was transformed into a wilder form of individualism through the Enlightenment stand on autonomous reason ("reason alone!") that one finds virtual hermeneutical disintegration.[26] Earlier, if the medieval Church had distorted the patristic interdependence of tradition and Scripture one way, the Reformation did so in the opposite way. Later, the Enlightenment proceeded to destroy the patristic

Liberal hermeneutic disintegration

---

[23] For a typology of current Protestant approaches to Scripture, see D. H. Kelsey, "Protestant Attitudes Regarding Methods of Biblical Interpretation," in *Scripture*, ed. F. E. Greenspahn, pp. 151-161. For the commonalities, diversity, and dynamics among Evangelicals, see Mark A. Noll, *Between Faith and Criticism*, pp. 142-185.

[24] Cited with approval by Carl E. Braaten, a mainline Lutheran, in his "Response to Manfred K. Bahmann," *LF* 28 (3, 1994), p. 11. Of course, Fundamentalists and Evangelicals consistently view liberal Protestantism as heresy. Gordon D. Fee, *Gospel and Spirit*, takes into view heresies by conservatives as well and writes the following: "To put it baldly, where there is no appreciation for tradition … [that is, "historic orthodoxy," p. 25], Protestantism has spawned a mass of individual heresies, all vying for center stage as the single truth of God," p. 80.

[25] For a recent discussion from an Evangelical perspective, see Alister McGrath's, *Evangelicalism & the Future of Christianity* (Downers Grove: InterVarsity Press, 1995), who perceives that the future belongs to Evangelicalism by its stand on enduring scriptural values, whereas liberal Protestantism has enfeebled itself by its very accommodation to rapidly changing culture.

[26] As reflected in the accounts of Hans W. Frei, *The Eclipse of Biblical Narrative: A Study in Eighteenth and Nineteenth Century Hermeneutics* (New Haven: Yale University Press, 1974) and David H. Kelsey, *The Uses of Scripture in Recent The-*

The Hermeneutical Crisis in Western Christianity 159

interdependence of faith and reason. Thus, curiously, the "'tyranny of the church' ... [evolved] into the 'tyranny of the academy' over the voice of the Bible."[27] It is clear that once Lessing's ugly ditch between biblical and modern thought is posited in substantive terms, applied even to the very notion of revelation of a personal God, there is no rational way to bridge the chasm. There is an *a priori* denial of what is to be demonstrated. The Reformation rendered the hermeneutical problem intractable by its rejection of the ecclesial principle in favor of the scriptural one. The Enlightenment rendered it intractable by its rejection of the scriptural principle itself, that is to say, the very categories of revelation and faith as authoritative ways of knowing, in favor of autonomous reason as the criterion of all truth. In its hermeneutical impact, the Enlightenment, it should be noted, drives not only Protestant but also Roman Catholic scholars insofar as they consciously or unconsciously come under the sway of Enlightenment presuppositions.

Great hermeneutical thinkers in the liberal tradition such as F. Schleiermacher, W. Dilthey, and R. Bultmann have labored mightily to bridge the alleged chasm between Scripture and modern thought, not content with the extreme rationalists to cast the Bible to the heap of ancient mythology. These herculean efforts, intellectually impressive and stimulating in themselves, have not yielded compelling and lasting results because they give away too much philosophical ground to the Enlightenment. Having surrendered the classic Christian view that the Bible provides sufficient and true knowledge about God and his purposes, they could not make up the difference by brilliant hermeneutical theories. Critiques of these theories and new

---

ology (Philadelphia: Fortress, 1975). Dennis Nineham, *The Use and Abuse of the Bible* (New York: Harper & Row, 1977) seems to debunk all hermeneutical attempts by conservative and liberal Protestants alike as futile and useless in demonstrating any authoritative relevance of the Bible for the present. He opts for a view of the Bible as a document of the ancient past whose world view cannot be genuinely recovered in modern society.

[27] W. Brueggemann, "Scriptural Authority in the Post-Critical Period," *ABD*, Vol. 5, p. 1053.

proposals by H. Gadamer, P. Ricoeur, and D. Tracy redress the balance by underscoring the importance of a hermeneutical dialogue with the theological subject matter of Scripture.[28] However, following in the liberal tradition, these corrective proposals too seem to grant excessive weight to the so-called "distance," not only cultural but also theological, between the Bible and modern thought, which is presupposed as the primary hermeneutical problem. Unacceptable ambiguity is left about the truth of Scripture and normative hermeneutical access to it. These refined hermeneutical proposals are cogent as epistemological theories, that is, they explain the dynamics of the transference of meaning in human rational terms. However, they give insufficient attention to the revelatory authority of Scripture in its relationship to the Church, as well as the role of faith and the Holy Spirit as critical elements in receiving and actualizing the saving message of Scripture. Liberal scholars themselves have continued to question the whole enterprise of biblical criticism and its implicit or explicit hermeneutics.[29]

In recent years, various related and unrelated hermeneutical perspectives have been pursued. One set of variant efforts is represented by the "new literary criticism," such as structural,

---

[28] For a concise presentation of these new proposals, see David Tracy's contribution in Part 2 of the revised and enlarged edition of *A Short History of the Interpretation of the Bible* by R. M. Grant and D. Tracy, pp. 153-187.

[29] For example, P. Stuhlmacher in his *Historical Criticism and Theological Interpretation of Scripture*, M. Hengel in his reflection on the same topic in *Acts and the History of Early Christianity*, pp. 127-136, and B. S. Childs in his several books. See also the manifesto by P. C. McGlasson, *Another Gospel* with a supportive foreword by B. S. Childs. Of course, the critiques from conservative Protestants continue unabated as reflected in the works of C. H. Pinnock, D. G. Bloesch, D. A. Carson, J. D. Woodbridge, J. I. Packer, and others. From the Roman Catholic side, Raymond Brown in his many works has strongly supported historical biblical criticism as the primary tool for biblical study; however, he has also on the one hand rejected its Enlightenment rationalistic freight and on the other hand supported, while qualifying, the interpretive authority of the magisterium. See especially R. Brown, *Biblical Exegesis and Church Doctrine*, where he both answers traditionalists and critiques radicals, as he carves out a "centrist position" in line with and officially supported by the Church.

narrative, and reader-oriented, following precedents in the study of literature.[30] Their purpose is to grant a kind of independence to the text of Scripture and to recover the meaning of Scripture as religious literature in the context of contemporary readers. Another set of efforts, represented by feminist and liberationist thinking, has been called "advocacy hermeneutics" because of its ideological grounding in contemporary political and socio-economic struggles.[31] All these approaches endeavor in their own ways to bridge the presupposed distance between the Bible and modern readers, but apart from the Enlightenment concern for "scientific" verification of truth. However, they still operate on the basis of either the primacy of reason or contemporary ideological interests in order to glean whatever relevant meaning from the Bible may be found, given its enduring cultural authority as a literary classic or historical source of diverse values. For now, these new directions have added to the hermeneutical pluralism. Their merit has been more of a corrective rather than of a programmatic nature. While their lasting impact remains to be seen, they have not presented a compelling integrative perspective in hermeneutics. Like previous liberal Sisyphian efforts, they seem to be pushing up the mountain another version of Enlightenment epistemology, only to have the hermeneutical rock roll back down again.

The Hermeneutical Question in Eastern Orthodoxy

Orthodox scholars have long recognized the importance of the hermeneutical question in its various dimensions – exegetical, theological, and ecumenical.[32] Their literary output has pri-

---

[30] See T. J. Keegan, *Interpreting the Bible* and E. V. McKnight, *Post-Modern Use of the Bible.*

[31] A strong challenge is presented by Elisabeth Schüssler Fiorenza, "Toward a Feminist Biblical Hermeneutics: Biblical Interpretation and Liberation Theology," in *A Guide to Contemporary Hermeneutics*, ed. D. K. McKim (Grand Rapids: Eerdmans, 1986), pp. 358-381. See also her books *Bread Not Stone* and *Searching the Scriptures: A Feminist Introduction.*

[32] See the diverse bibliography in Chapter Two, notes 51 through 54. From an

marily dealt with general aspects of the question as Orthodox thinkers have worked toward an explication of Orthodox hermeneutics. Virtually all have written from within the security of the tradition. For the Orthodox, the hermeneutical problem does not have the burning urgency it does for Western Christians because the Orthodox presuppose the problematics of neither the Reformation nor the Enlightenment. Of course, the influence of the Enlightenment heritage through science, education, technology, and secularism strongly affects all Christians, including the Orthodox everywhere. But Orthodox thinkers sense that they have theoretical and practical tools to countenance contemporary culture as long as they do not capitulate to the presuppositions and false dichotomies of Western problematics. They perceive that for them, the burning hermeneutical problem is not at the level of theoretical principles, which nevertheless need clarification, but at the level of life. Their catchword is ὀρθοπραξία, right practice, which embraces a wide vision of renewal according to authentic Orthodox ecclesial and theological principles (ὀρθοδοξία), including giving full voice to the witness of Scripture through sound scholarship.

Nevertheless, a vital Orthodox witness cannot occur apart from efforts to formulate an explicit hermeneutic in both general and specific terms. For the Orthodox, Georges Florovsky has established the broad framework of discussion by defining the ethos of the Orthodox Church in terms of "a neopatristic synthesis ...

---

ecumenical perspective, largely centered on the work of the World Council of Churches, sample contributions include Metropolitan Chrysostomos Konstantinidis, "The Significance of the Eastern and Western Traditions within Christendom," *Orthodoxy: A Faith and Order Dialogue*, (Geneva: WCC, 1960), pp. 62-72; Nikos A. Nissiotis, "The Unity of Scripture and Tradition: An Eastern Orthodox Contribution to the Prolegomena of Hermeneutics," *GOTR* 11 (2, 1965-1966), pp. 183-208; and Ion Bria, *The Sense of Ecumenical Tradition* (Geneva: WCC Publications, 1991). A standard for the ecumenical discussion is *The Bible: Its Authority and Interpretation in the Ecumenical Movement*, ed. Ellen Flesseman-van Leer (Geneva: World Council of Churches, 1980).

the task and aim of Orthodoxy theology today."[33] According to Florovsky, the "neopatristic synthesis" embraces inseparable theological and spiritual dimensions. One dimension is doctrinal which is anchored on the christological and trinitarian mysteries apprehended and celebrated as saving truth. The other dimension is spiritual, which is anchored on a recovery of "the mind of the Fathers," a discerning, creative vision rooted in faith and the new creation within the life of the Church, the body of Christ. The two dimensions are inseparable because the ultimate truth is not an abstract principle but a person, Christ. Theologizing must be done, in the words of St. Gregory the Theologian, "in the manner of the Apostles, and not in that of Aristotle (ἁλιευτικῶς οὐκ ἀριστοτελικῶς)."[34] Florovsky wrote: "Apart from the life in Christ theology carries no conviction, and, if separated from the life of faith, theology may easily degenerate into empty dialectics, a vain πολυλογία (verbiage)."[35] Florovsky himself embodied this neopatristic vision in both his fidelity to the tradition and his scholarly pursuit of truth.

On biblical topics, Florovsky expounded dynamic views of Scripture, revelation, inspiration, tradition, and Church in a patristic key.[36] On the grand scale of theology, his contributions are classic. He underscores the authority of Scripture as revelation while he points out the authority of tradition as "hermeneutical principle." For him, tradition does not "add" something to Scripture but discerns and actualizes its true meaning. Tradition as living tradition functions as a hermeneutical principle not only through the normative rule of faith, that is, the transmission of inherited doctrines, but also through the actualization of the saving message of Scripture in catechesis, preaching, and the entire life of the worshiping

---

[33] G. Florovsky, "The Ethos of the Orthodox Church," in *Orthodoxy: A Faith and Order Dialogue*, pp. 45ff.

[34] Cited by Florovsky, *ibid.* p. 41.

[35] *Ibid.*

[36] The relevant articles on these subjects have been conveniently collected in his book *Bible, Church, Tradition: An Eastern Orthodox View.*

Church, "a continuous life of truth." He quotes with approval Ellen Flesseman-van-Leer:

> Scripture without interpretation is not Scripture at all; the moment it is used and becomes alive it is always interpreted Scripture.... Real interpretation of Scripture is Church preaching, is tradition.[37]

However, Florovsky does not engage the hermeneutical question in its modern discussion and does not himself show how theologizing according to the mind of the Church fathers can creatively address new questions and arrive at renewed answers. He does not critically discuss questions such as the Enlightenment influence on modern theology or the nature of historical studies.[38] Much less does he take up specific questions such as the comparative role and validity of literal-grammatical, typological, and allegorical approaches to Scripture. What exactly is the authoritative role of Scripture on tradition and by what means is it applied? What is the relationship between the homiletical and critical interpretations of the Bible? What of the misinterpretations and misapplications of Scripture in the popular tradition of preaching? And how can we deal with contemporary issues, let us say, about gender and sexuality, in an authentic Orthodox way? Florovsky has left such challenges to others who are also grounded in the patristic principle of the positive relationship between Scripture and tradition, and who have tried to advance the hermeneutical discussion in greater detail. It is appropriate to review, under the light of these considerations, the hermeneutical efforts of several contemporary Orthodox scholars in Greece and the United States. Our purpose is positive, that is, to develop a structured position of

[37] G. Florovsky, "The Function of Tradition in the Ancient Church," *GOTR* 9 (Winter, 1963-1964), pp. 187-188, and reprinted in *Bible, Church, Tradition.*

[38] Even Florovky's articles "The Predicament of the Church Historian," in *Religion and Culture*, ed. W. Leibrecht (New York: Harper & Row, 1959), pp. 140-166, and "The Patterns of Historical Interpretation," *ATR* 50 (2, 1968), pp. 144-155, are written in a grand theological perspective rather than a truly critical one, as for example by Van A. Harvey, *The Historian & the Believer* (New York: MacMillan, 1966).

Orthodox hermeneutics through constructive critique and interactive discussion, both of which are evidence of maturing scholarship.[39]

Panagiotis *Andriopoulos* Some twenty years ago, Panagiotis Andriopoulos, an instructor at the University of Athens, took a bold leap into modern hermeneutical thought with his voluminous and perceptive work entitled *Τὸ Πρόβλημα τοῦ«Ἱστορικοῦ Ἰησοῦ» ἐν τῇ Συγχρόνῳ Ἑρμηνευτικῇ τῆς Καινῆς Διαθήκης ὑπὸ τὸ Φῶς τῆς Θεολογίας Κυρίλλου τοῦ Ἀλεξανδρείας* [*The Problem of the "Historical Jesus" in Contemporary New Testament Hermeneutical Thought in the Light of the Theology of Cyril of Alexandria*].[40] Given the traditional character of Greek theological studies, this was a rare and rather striking intellectual incursion into Bultmannian problematics. After a review of the hermeneutical thought of Schleiermacher, Dilthey, Heidegger, and Gadamer, Andriopoulos took on the hermeneutics of Bultmann and his students in relationship to their discussion of the "new quest" of the historical Jesus. In parallel, he presented the christological thought of Cyril of Alexandria. Although incisive in his descriptive accounts of both, his comparative work was inadequate because he did not sufficiently engage the question of their disparate contexts and differing epistemological presuppositions. He ended perplexed about how the Bultmannians, given the Protestant principle of *sola Scriptura*, could have come up with such unacceptable christological conclusions.[41] He did not seem to perceive that Bultmannian problematics were crucially determined by the Enlightenment heritage and the consequent "crisis" of the authority of Scripture in Protestantism. By assuming that "mod-

---

[39] Orthodox theological scholars have tacitly shown extreme sensitivity about constructive mutual criticism. Although they quote one another in oblique or supportive ways, each usually presents his or her own ideas apart from direct engagement of the ideas of other Orthodox authors. But advancement in Orthodox scholarship cannot occur without honest, interactive discussion on the basis of mutual respect and the putting aside of personal attacks and recriminations.

[40] (Athens: Maurogeorges, 1975). A fervent believer and inspiring teacher, Andriopoulos died at a young age, a great loss to Orthodox biblical studies.

[41] *Ibid.*, pp. 405-408.

ern man" needed something like Bultmannian hermeneutics to countenance "genuine questions" of modernity, Andriopoulos did not discern the particular philosophical grounding, nor the passing value of Bultmannian thought as Western scholars had already done. Despite his impressive and laudable efforts to grapple with modern hermeneutical thinkers, his is an example of the difficulties of Orthodox attempts to engage highly de-fined issues in pluralistic Western theology without due atten-tion to larger epistemological issues.

Savas Agouridis, a professor of biblical studies in Thessalonike and then Athens for many years, and a stimulating thinker among contemporary Greek intellectuals, has tackled the hermeneutical question from various angles in his numerous works.[42] The centerpiece of his hermeneutical thought is a lengthy work entitled Ἑρμηνευτικὴ τῶν Ἱερῶν Κειμένων [*Hermeneutics of the Sacred Texts*].[43] His achievement has been to raise the hermeneutical question in the light of contemporary life. He offers challenging and often eloquent explorations of the themes of Church and society, Scripture and tradition, revelation and history, patristic and modern biblical studies, theology and spiri-tuality, liturgy and biblical scholarship, all with a passionate, prophetic tone.

Nevertheless, Professor Agouridis' hermeneutical achievement is ambiguous. Despite his many insightful observations, his work suggests an overall need for greater clarity and integration of thought. He accepts that the "agonizing" hermeneutical prob-lem is caused by the "distance" between biblical and modern thought, but does not seem to recognize the extent to which this conceptualization of the question is due to negative aspects of the Enlightenment, which he rejects elsewhere in passing.[44] Because he is committed to historical scholarship, he rightly dis-

---

[42] For bibliographical entry into his works, see Chapter Two, notes 52 through 54.

[43] Ἑρμηνευτικὴ τῶν Ἱερῶν Κειμένων (Athens, 1979). See also his forthright and stimulating article on biblical studies in modern Greece mentioned and com-mented on in Chapter Two, note 53.

[44] *Ibid.*, pp. 8-9, 16, 57-58, 328.

tinguishes between exegesis and interpretation, and highly values freedom of research; yet, he finds that the realm of worship expresses the essence of Scripture without indicating the epistemological relationship between liturgy and critical study.[45] He affirms that tradition is the bearer and guarantor of revealed truth, but neglects to discuss the interdependence of tradition and Scripture in view of Scripture's authority in and for tradition.[46] He holds that essential theological truth is disclosed at the experiential and communal rather than rational levels, but takes no account of the hermeneutical function of the rule of faith, the doctrinal sense of the Church, and does not seem to perceive that his own perception of the hermeneutical question is partly fed by a rationalistic perspective.[47] In substance, he contends that the decisive Orthodox answer to the hermeneutical problem lies in an ambiguous combination of the eschatological vision of the liturgy and the concept of universal history held by Pannenberg, but without attempting to bridge the epistemological gap between their respective hymnic and philosophical modalities of thought.[48] A haunting combination of grandness and frustration seem to mark Professor Agouridis' efforts. While he engages relevant broad themes, he does not specify the critical aspects and the crucial points of the hermeneutical problem. Clearer formulation of Orthodox hermeneutics must be sought through a more nuanced discussion of the various hermeneutical levels as well as the hermeneutical factors of faith and reason, Scripture and tradition, Church and modern culture in specific terms.

Father John Breck, an American Orthodox biblical scholar, has devoted several pieces to the hermeneutical discussion. The

---

[45] *Ibid.*, pp. 45, 61ff., 71-72, 339, 342, 349, 360.

[46] *Ibid.*, pp. 318ff. and 326ff.

[47] *Ibid.*, pp. 8-9, 57-58, 67, 323-327. In his passionate concern for the hermeneutical question and pastoral care, he expects that scholars, students, and lay people alike must bear the same hermeneutical burden without qualification, pp. 14-15, 315-316, as if all must experience the gap or distance between Bible and modern thought before they can derive any value from Scripture.

[48] *Ibid.*, pp. 16, 71-72, 302, 310-315.

primary contributions are two articles published in 1976 and 1983 and his book *The Power of the Word in the Worshiping Church,* which appeared in 1986.[49] A subsequent lecture to a mixed Christian audience summarized his thought.[50] Father Breck's main purpose is to find an Orthodox way between fundamentalist and historicist approaches to Scripture. He, too, rightly distinguishes between exegetical and interpretive levels and perceives that the main hermeneutical problem lies at the interpretive level. For him, historical-critical methodology is in itself neutral. He thus grants full weight to rigorous scientific study for both discovering and contemporizing the message of Scripture, "the very ground of Orthodox faith and life."[51] However, neither historical critical studies nor Western hermeneutical approaches have proven adequate to the task of conveying the power of God's word. The decisive hermeneutical answer, according to Professor Breck, is to be found in the patristic teaching of θεωρία, the act of receptivity or spiritual vision of God's saving presence and action testified by the biblical word and supremely actualized in the Church's worship.[52]

Certain similar questions can be raised about Father Breck's hermeneutical thought as in the case of Agouridis. Father Breck, too, assumes an unqualified notion of the chasm between biblical and modern thought, and thus speaks of the need to render Scripture's message meaningfully to the "modern mind" and "a

---

[49] The two articles are "Theoria and Orthodox Hermeneutics," *SVTQ* 20 (4, 1976), pp. 95-219 and "Exegesis and Interpretation: Orthodox Reflections on the 'Hermeneutic Problem,'" *SVTQ* 27 (2, 1983), pp. 75-92. These are essentially reproduced in his book, published by St. Vladimir's Seminary Press in Crestwood, New York, which includes substantive additions on patristic exegesis and rich sections on Scripture as "living Word" in liturgical celebration, creedal confessions, and iconography.

[50] John Breck, "Orthodoxy and the Bible Today," in *The Legacy of St. Vladimir,* ed. John Breck and others, pp. 141-157.

[51] John Breck, "Theoria and Orthodox Hermeneutics," pp. 195-196; "Exegesis and Interpretation," pp. 75-76; *The Power of the Word,* pp. 25-28.

[52] John Breck, "Theoria and Orthodox Hermeneutics," pp. 196, 211, 217-219; "Exegesis and Interpretation," pp. 78-84; 90-92; *The Power of the Word,* pp. 9-10, 28-36, 44-47, 109-113.

world of instinctive skepticism."[53] But it is not at all clear that "scientific study" as such can accomplish this task of contemporization, that is, to convey effectively the meaning and power of Scripture to modern readers. On the basis of what criteria and in what forms are we to seek relevance with modernity? Father Breck takes into account neither liberal Christianity's failure on account of its accommodation to modern culture nor the epistemological problems raised by the Enlightenment as widely discussed, for example, by Evangelical scholars.[54] His comparative paradigm of the hermeneutical bridge between Scripture and modern man – the sermon for Protestants, the papal magisterium for Roman Catholics, and the Holy Spirit for the Orthodox is far too general.[55] It passes over not only the hermeneutical pluralism among Protestants and Roman Catholics alike, but also the fact that all Christians value the Holy Spirit, the sermon, and forms of authoritative interpretation.[56]

Professor Breck's main focus is on the patristic θεωρία, which is indeed a valuable but one-sided hermeneutical anchor. In his understanding of θεωρία while rejecting allegory, Professor Breck wholly justifies typology without critical reference to superficial typological interpretations in the tradition. He also rightly connects θεωρία with the liturgical dimension, which he discusses at length in his book. The difficulty is that θεωρία is essentially a spiritual vision, as Professor Breck himself ends up affirming, and not an exegetical method. As an all-embracing spiritual receptivity, θεωρία qualitatively effects one's approach to Scripture and everything else, but it cannot swallow up the discursive

[53] John Breck, "Exegesis and Interpretation," p. 76; *The Power of the Word*, p. 28.

[54] For example C. H. Pinnock, *The Scripture Principle*; D. G. Bloesch, *Holy Scripture: Revelation;, Inspiration & Interpretation*; M. A. Noll, *Between Faith and Criticism*; and many others in *Scripture and Truth*, ed. D. A. Carson and J. D. Woodbridge.

[55] John Breck, "Exegesis and Interpretation," pp. 80-84; *The Power of the Word*, pp. 31-36.

[56] For example, M. A. Noll, *Between Faith and Criticism*, pp. 151 and 205, finds forms of a Protestant magisterium among Evangelicals based on the priesthood of all believers and in the pronouncements of exalted Evangelical leaders.

task of dealing with the "intellectual contours" of Christian truth in the phraseology of Florovsky. In his reading of the Church fathers, Professor Breck does not grant sufficient critical difference between θεωρία as an exegetical method and θεωρία as inspired perception, a distinction comparable to discursive and mystical theology or between theological reasoning and doxological expression. Certainly, Athanasios, Basil, and his brother Gregory, however much they worked within an all-embracing spiritual vision, also interpreted Scripture in reasoned contextual and grammatical terms, especially in their discursive debates with heretics. Although the two dimensions cannot be separated, they do involve distinguishable hermeneutical operations; one cannot cancel out the other.

Consequently, the technical term should not obscure the fact that, as spiritual vision, θεωρία is nothing other than the horizon of living faith – the faith commitment and spiritual openness – that apprehends the transforming saving power of the biblical word released by the Holy Spirit, whether through sermon, individual reading, or corporate celebration in worship.[57] All Christians, Orthodox, Roman Catholic, and Protestants affirm this truth. Despite the lack of liturgical richness among many Protestants, it is not true that the emphasis on the sermon, that is, the Bible and its exposition, renders "the Word" a "purely verbal phenomenon."[58] All traditional Christians hold to the teaching concerning the inner illumination by the Spirit. All nurture verbal and contemplative dimensions and should seek a right balance between the two. On the Orthodox side, "eucharistic fulfillment" without verbal explication of biblical truth can become distorted in ritualistic ways. Faith, prayer, attentiveness to the biblical word, whether read, heard or

---

[57] In a different chapter of his book, pp. 117-122, Father Breck himself includes an inspiring section on faith but apparently does not see its affinity to the patristic θεωρία.

[58] John Breck, *The Power of the Word*, pp. 32 and 35. Father Breck himself, p. 31, defines the classic Protestant position as "charismatic," that is, anchored on the principle of the personal illumination by the Holy Spirit, which is to be applied to the congregation as well as the preacher during the sermon.

preached, as well as corporate worship and committed Christian living, all these make up the spiritually receptive realm in which the Holy Spirit transforms the biblical word into a living word for all Christians.

Let us fully grant that the Church fathers, following the biblical authors, elaborated diverse typological and allegorical interpretations from the perspective of an inspired "theoretic" vision. But from the same perspective, they also provided a mass of straightforward interpretations applied to faith and practice. The bulk of these, as in Chrysostom's homiletical commentaries, are given without one-sided reference either to θεωρία or the eucharistic vision, which may well be presupposed, but are not explicitly invoked or necessary for the understanding and application of biblical instruction. Moreover, in the milieu of hellenistic higher philological and philosophical education, the Cappadocian fathers inclined toward careful contextual and grammatical exegesis, especially in connection with the doctrinal controversies that put the question of syllogistic precision and coherence into the forefront.[59] Therefore, the perspective of θεωρία, whether explicit or implicit, yielded an abundance of literal-grammatical, typological, as well as allegorical interpretations among the Church fathers.

If both allegory and typology issue from a "theoretic" perspective, why then dismiss the former and take pains to justify the latter? Are they really so different as methods to validate the one and reject the other? Also, why neglect the numerous straightforward instructional and ethical interpretations, which are neither allegorical nor typological? Why not, for clarity's sake, distinguish the literal, allegorical, and typological interpretations and call them by their right names as rep-

---

[59] For example, Gregory of Nyssa, prior to the controversy with Eunomios and his followers, practiced mostly allegorical exegesis. But the controversy led him to a much more precise and contextual approach to the biblical text on the basis of a more sophisticated understanding of epistemology and the philosophy of language. So Mariette Canévet, *Grégore de Nysse et l'herméneutique biblique: Étude des rapports entre le langage et la conaissance de Dieu* (Paris: Études Augustiniennnes, 1983). I owe this reference to my colleague Nicholas Constas.

resenting various methodological approaches, and leave θεωρία in its proper spiritual and mystical function of appropriating the transcendent, saving power of God's word, which is in itself weighty? If Antiochene θεωρία inclined to take the biblical text and history more seriously than did Alexandrian θεωρία, this fact alone neither transforms typological interpretation into historical-critical exegesis nor renders allegorical interpretation useless. Both allegory and typology go beyond the level of contextual-grammatical exegesis and must be appreciated at the hermeneutical level of their purpose and function. While both can lead to exaggerations, both also have their respective merits, but neither as historical-critical exegesis.

The hermeneutical conundrum in Father Breck's thesis may be clarified by distinguishing two epistemological dimensions at the interpretive level, one primarily discursive and critical, the other primarily contemplative and intuitive. In support of θεωρία as perception of divine truth inspired by the Holy Spirit, and in advocating "theoretic" exegesis as the ideal for interpreters today, Father Breck looks to the purpose and function of liturgy. He writes: "Just as the Jew *participates* in the Exodus at every Passover festival, so the Christian *participates* in the crucial moments of Christ's life and ministry,"[60] that is, in the Church's worship. However, worship is a realm of spiritual appropriation, not intellectual evaluation of the truth of a community's sacred traditions. By its very nature, worship is a contemplative interpretive level on which any religious community celebrates and perpetuates its sacred texts and the experience of God enshrined in them. It can yield Orthodox, Roman Catholic, Protestant, and Jewish "theoretic" interpretations. Crucial as worship is for its own purpose and function, it cannot substitute for critical theology, that is, for the discursive approach to truth as abundantly evidenced by the doctrinal debates, which at the forefront were syllogistic rather than "theoretic" appeals in the interpretation of biblical texts by fathers and heretics. Nor can one, as a way out of the conundrum, refer

---

[60] The emphasis is Father Breck's in *The Power of the Word*, p. 104. Cf. pp. 110-113.

to patristic appeals to the authority of the liturgical tradition for the explication of doctrine because such explication occurred at the level of discursive theology.

Following the Church fathers, then, one can hardly endorse critical biblical study and anchor one's hermeneutic one-sidedly on spiritual perception, which anyone can claim. Of course, neither should one underestimate spiritual perception as a decisive mode of personal and corporate appropriation of the saving truth and power of God's word. But such appropriation, if it is not to lapse into unacceptable subjectivism, must be closely related to and anchored on the "intellectual contours" of the biblical witness by some methodology involving concentrated syllogistic activity based on the patristic interdependence between faith and reason. Since all methods in principle seek to provide functional access to the conceptual meaning of biblical texts, no method as such can be either absolutized or eliminated, whether literal, allegorical, typological, or any of the contemporary scholarly methods, but each assessed on its own purpose and merits. The crucial question is not only one of spiritual receptivity but also of theological truth.

From this perspective, if one is not to yield to uncontrolled diversity and ecclesial disunity, the critical hermeneutical factors are what the Church fathers long ago discerned: the truth claims of Scripture which, when disputed, must be authoritatively interpreted according to the doctrinal consensus of the Church. Strangely, neither Professor Agouridis nor Professor Breck take up for critical discussion the doctrinal connection in hermeneutics.[61] Yet, the Archimedian hermeneutical reference

---

[61] In Part II of his *Power of the Word,* Father Breck includes lengthy chapters on creedal formulations in the New Testament and the liturgical tradition but oddly does not raise the question of the hermeneutical role of doctrine, that is, the quest for normative truth. Thus, Part I on "Interpreting the Word" and Part II "Living the Word" seem essentially unconnected. Father Breck's connection of course is θεωρία as the only hermeneutical key. The erroneous impression remains that the "living word" occurs only in worship and not other areas of ministry, for example, biblical teaching, which is part of theology's burden for the world. In his later article "Orthodoxy and the Bible Today," pp. 149-150, Father Breck does include

is precisely the quest for truth, normative theological truth, which functions both as the unitive framework and the ultimate measure of the various methods and diverse interpretations of Scripture. It is in this same quest for normative truth that the contemplative and the discursive, the mystical and the rational, faith and reason are critically inseparable when engaging the sharpest hermeneutical question of all. On what terms can tradition as living and creative tradition authentically encounter new circumstances and new knowledge? That is to say, by what criteria can we discern and define what is normative for faith and practice not merely in the distant past but also in the challenging and open-ended present as new issues arise?

The hermeneutical position of Father John Romanides, the final one to be reviewed here, in part answers the last questions. Such questions could be addressed if one could point to a living authority which would combine in itself the mystical and the discursive, the transcendent and the practical, and thus act as normative criterion and unfailing discernment of Christian truth in the ever changing present and unknown future. This is exactly the hermeneutical position of Father Romanides, who constructs an entire theological and biblical hermeneutic based on the model of the charismatic saint.[62] The following paragraphs summarize his position.

For Professor Romanides, the saints *par excellence* were the prophets and the apostles, those who had direct experiences of God in a continuous and dynamic state of glorification, which

---

an incipient discussion of how doctrinal formulations should "determine hermeneutic presuppositions," an issue that needs far greater attention.

[62] A comprehensive statement of his position may be found in his lengthy article "Critical Examination of the Applications of Theology," in *Procès-Verbaux du deuxième Congrès de Théologie Orthodoxe*, ed. Savas Agouridis (Athens, 1978), pp. 413-441. Father Romanides many years ago was my first theology professor at Holy Cross Greek Orthodox School of Theology, and he opened my eyes to exciting theological insights and to the necessity of paying close attention to "presuppositions." To him I owe my foundational theological thinking, albeit qualified by critical historical scholarship of the Bible and the Church fathers. Father Romanides is now retired but still active in Greece and abroad.

is called by the Church fathers θεωρία or θέωσις by grace. According to Professor Romanides, the sublime revelatory experiences of the prophets and the apostles were beyond speculative concepts and images, granting to the beholders immediate knowledge of God and enabling them to guide others toward God infallibly through concept-bearing words and images appropriate to the level of understanding of their hearers. This tradition of the vision of God and participation in the divine glory is a living tradition in Eastern Christianity, continuing in a presumably limited number of known and unknown saints today – an ongoing Pentecost that constitutes the highest revelation and knowledge of God. An intriguing point by Father Romanides is that the true meaning of *sola Scriptura* is none other than θέωσις, deification by grace, summing up the unity and identity of the direct experience and knowledge of God among prophets, apostles, and saints. The same unitive experience is the "key to opening the Bible's secrets ... [without which] the Bible remains a hidden mystery even to biblical scholars,"[63] whether Orthodox or not. For Romanides, only the true saint ("saint alone?") – the one who has moved beyond the stage of purification and has reached the stages of illumination and perfection – can unerringly interpret biblical revelation at the level of words and concepts by virtue of enjoying the "same species of knowledge" as did the prophets and the apostles themselves.

Professor Romanides' hermeneutical proposal vigorously claims interdependent theoretical aspects and practical applications,[64] that is, it advocates a unity of the mystical and the practical. On the practical side, one can find today unnamed saints who have attained θεωρία, are wholly liberated from the enslavement of sin, the devil, and selfish love; and who, in God's

---

[63] *Ibid.*, p. 423 and more broadly pp. 421-426.

[64] Father Romanides time and again confidently parallels his theological and hermeneutical approach to the experimental method of the hard and soft sciences, involving both interdependent theorizing and actual testing by observable and measurable standards, pp. 413, 423, 432, and 436-437.

glory and selfless love are infallible witnesses and instructors of the ways of God. They are theologians in the classic sense of the word – authoritative knowers and spokespersons of God not by speculative reason but by direct experience of God in the manner of the prophets and the apostles. Such persons and only such persons, who have been cleansed of their evil passions and have reached at least illumination and the discernment of spirits, if not actual θέωσις, can be true guides in biblical interpretation. All others are only "so-called theologians," presumably impostors and perverters of truth in varying degrees. According to this "θεωρία – based theology," learning and application go together. The student must attach himself to a teacher who has experienced illumination. The teacher, as spiritual father, can guide the student but cannot actualize in him θεωρία, which is a gift of the Holy Spirit alone. Nevertheless, all this means that

> an Orthodox theologian and spiritual father is the same thing. One cannot be a theologian without being a spiritual father and one cannot be a spiritual father without being a theologian.[65]

On the theoretical side, Father Romanides offers equally important observations. He raises the question of the critical presuppositions of theologizing as such. According to Father John, the Augustinian approach to Scripture and theology departed from the biblical and patristic experiential model and lost sight, as well, of the decisive distinction between Creator and creature. It assumed in platonic fashion the existence of eternal archetypes or uncreated universals, and thus presupposed a real similarity or analogy between the uncreated and created orders of being, as if both belonged to a single system of truth, which could be penetrated by the human intellect. In specific moments of inspiration, so Augustine taught, according to Professor Romanides, God infallibly conveyed what he wanted to the biblical authors in concept-bearing words and images that

---

[65] *Ibid.*, p. 434. See also pp. 432-433.

the authors themselves did not necessarily fully understand. In this Augustinian perspective, the Bible was identified with created forms of divine revelation. Revelation itself was erroneously identified with the very words of Scripture. Consequently, the human intellect, ever probing the world of immutable divine truths, could gradually gain higher knowledge of the eternal archetypes, including the mystery of the Holy Trinity – a knowledge that could be even superior to that of the prophets and the apostles themselves. This Augustinian epistemology, according to Professor Romanides, is the fatal substructure of all Western speculative thought, which necessarily cracked in modern centuries as philosophical nominalism and scientific study of the flux of all things "weakened the idea of unchanging and immutable truths so dear to western philosophical and theological systems." In these terms, one could also quite likely explain the general collapse in Western culture of belief in the existence of absolute truth, law, and moral norms as criteria of thought and conduct.[66]

Here is how Professor Romanides sums up his hermeneutical position:

> Dialectical speculation can never become the source of authoritative teaching as though the Church, whether by means of a Pope, or Councils or Protestant Biblical scholars, could transform research into dogma....

> The authority for Christian truth is not the written words of the Bible themselves, which cannot *in themselves* either express God or convey an adequate concept concerning God, but rather the individual Apostle, Prophet and Saint who is glorified in Christ and united in this experience of glory to all the friends of God of all ages.

> Thus the Bible, the writings of the Fathers and the decisions of the Councils are not revelation, but about revelation. Revelation itself transcends words and concepts although it inspires those participating in divine glory to

---

[66] *Ibid.*, pp. 413, 416, 418-421.

express accurately and unerringly what is inexpressible in words and concepts....

For the Fathers authority is not only the Bible, but the Bible plus those glorified.... The Bible as a book is not in itself either inspired or infallible. It becomes inspired and infallible within the communion of Saints who have the experience of divine glory described in, but not conveyed by, the Bible. To those outside of the living tradition of θεωρία the Bible is a Book which does not unlock its mysteries.[67]

Professor Romanides' hermeneutical thought is incisive in both its biblical focus on the direct experience of God, which is the heart of biblical revelation, as well as in its philosophical sophistication, a radical liberation of thought from platonist epistemology. As regards the latter, to affirm that truth must be sought in personal and relational terms rather than abstract and eternal archetypes, is simultaneously relief from the anguish of a philosophical deadend and, as well, the opening of new horizons in the search for lived truth. As regards the former, to lift up the significance of the immediate and direct experience of God is to engage the substance of Scripture's witness and, as well, the essence of the common human odyssey. For nothing is more profound and urgent than for each human being to gain personal intimations of the living God.

Indeed, the personal-experiential and the nominalist-philosophical perspectives are integrated in a most intriguing way by Professor Romanides, a way that simply rings true and gives his thought a powerful and attractive unity. It is certainly a worthy witness of the great Church fathers who, as philosophical sophisticates in their age, increasingly turned their back to Plato and deliberately followed the biblical way of knowing God. Not the least of Professor Romanides' merits is to remind modern scholars of the essential continuity and coherence of biblical and patristic theology. In his own efforts to exorcise the platonist ghost that always drives persons to relate more to ab-

---

[67] *Ibid.*, pp. 427 and 432.

stract truths and absolutes values rather than the living God himself, he has clearly discerned what is the core of patristic thought, namely, the scriptural content and vision. The way of the fathers is the way of Scripture. One could add that faithfulness to Scripture was precisely the driving force that pushed back the horizons of platonism in the thought of ancient Christian thinkers, an interesting way of thinking about how "Moses overcame Plato," that is, how platonist ontology gave way to biblical personalism.[68]

However, the hermeneutical proposal by Professor Romanides is burdened by one-sidedness in its own way because of certain unnecessarily extreme claims that detract from the value and persuasiveness of Father John's thought. On the philosophical level, leaving aside the question of the interpretation of Augustine to experts in this area, a radical kind of nominalism must be tempered with the consideration that "concept-bearing words and images" carry a certain stability of meaning. While rejecting the idea of eternal universals and archetypes, one must still take account of the biblical and patristic view that there are in Scripture clear and abiding teachings about God and his ways accessible to all. One does not necessarily have to adopt platonist metaphysics about immutable truth to affirm that the Bible, at the communication level of words and images, contains abiding insights, principles, and truths concerning such things as God and idols, grace and free will, love and hate, honesty and lying,

---

[68] J. Pelikan, *The Christian Tradition 2: The Spirit of Eastern Christendom (600-1700)* (Chicago: University of Chicago Press, 1974), p. 33, writes that, according to the Eastern fathers, "theology was not a science of divine ontology but of divine revelation." The patristic emphasis on faith and Scripture, rather than on reason and philosophical speculation – while viewing the two perspectives as complementary and mutually supportive, not antithetical – is more fully laid out by Pelikan in his *Christianity and Classical Culture*. In contemporary Orthodox theology, biblical and patristic personalism as contrasted to Greek philosophical ontology is the touchstone of the work of John D. Zizioulas, *Being as Communion* (Crestwood: St. Vladimir's Seminary Press, 1985) and Christos Yannaras, *The Freedom of Morality*, trans. Elizabeth Briere (Crestwood: St. Vladimir's Seminary Press, 1984).

forgiveness and retaliation, justice and exploitation, giving and selfishness, hope and despair.

One does not have to read very far in the theological and practical writings of the Church fathers, such as Basil and Chrysostom, to see the massive authority they attached to the letter and plain meaning of Scripture as secure instruction about God and his will for all. These fathers relied heavily on the clarity and stability of meaning resident in the biblical text they derived by grammatical exegesis and assumed that any reader could follow without esoteric techniques. To claim that "the Bible is not inspired" as it stands is to fly into the face of the whole patristic tradition and undercut Scripture's plain witness to God's dealings with all people. To seem to claim that stable and secure meaning at the level of words and images cannot at all be gained by ordinary human understanding is to undercut at once human communication, scholarship, as well as the hope of meaningful dialogue and possible reconciliation between disputants, whether orthodox or heretical. We are not saying that the plain meaning of words and images available to all is everything but that it is an integral part of that same truth about God and of God, which all are invited to seek.

The central difficulty of Professor Romanides' proposal is the extreme convergence on the charismatic saint who seems to be raised above the Bible, above the Councils, and even above the Church. We do not question the rich and valued tradition of spiritual fathers in Eastern Christianity.[69] Nor do we question the foundational role of the key biblical figures and of the great saints in the total life of the people of God. What we do ques-

---

[69] See Kallistos Ware, "The Spiritual Father in Orthodox Christianity," *CC* (Summer/Fall, 1974), pp. 296-312, and Irénée Hausherr, S.J., *Spiritual Direction in the Early Christian East* (Kalamazoo: Cistercian Publications, 1990), with a foreword by Kallistos Ware. Douglas Burton-Christie, *The Word in the Desert*, ends his study on the ancient monastic use of Scripture by underscoring the significance of persons who lived Scripture and were "Christ-bearers" and "mediators of God to humanity." His ending sentence reads: "The ultimate expression of the desert hermeneutic was a *person* [his emphasis], one who embodied the sacred texts and who drew others out of themselves into a world of infinite possibilities," p. 300.

tion is the exclusivity of the charismatic model, which seems to raise the saint to a theological super figure. One is tempted to compare the vagueness of the ideal saint of whom so much is required to the vagueness of the Protestant emphasis on the word of God to which similar superiority is attributed.

But who are these supreme saints who enjoy an exactly identical experience of God and can communicate unerringly between them and with others who are not blessed with θεωρία? After the experience of the transfiguration of Jesus, John and James were not above looking for special honors in the coming kingdom they apparently still awaited in earthly form (Mk 10:35ff.). Despite their unarguable stature, the apostles Peter and Paul could have a striking difference on an important matter of ecclesial life, which compelled Paul to face up to Peter publicly (Gal 2:11-14).[70] The Book of Acts also reports "a sharp contention" between Paul and Barnabas over John Mark's instability which caused their separation in missionary work (Acts 15:36-41). If such disputes occurred among the apostles, one would not be hard pressed to provide numerous examples from among the Church fathers themselves. In fact, most heretics could be described as charismatic figures.

What evidence does Professor Romanides provide for the above hermeneutical model? Three references from St. Gregory the Theologian about the impossibility of conceiving God and the necessity of spiritual cleansing when seeking knowledge of the sublime mystery of God.[71] He also refers to the verb θεωρέω ("observe," "perceive," "behold," etc.) used in the Gospel of John in connection with seeing and knowing Christ. Father Romanides takes the liberty of translating this verb as a noun ("may have θεωρία," Jn 17:24) and thereby injecting in it the

---

[70] One can understand but not accept the interpretation of some Church fathers, going back to Origen, that Peter and Paul simulated the conflict in order to teach a lesson to Jewish and Gentiles Christians. But, on the premise of the dignity and unfailing agreement between apostles, would not these Christians also be offended even by a simulated conflict, just as later Christians were apparently offended who took the disagreement as real?

[71] *Theological Orations*, 1.3; 2.3, and 2.14.

technical patristic meaning. But the noun is never used in the Gospel of John and only once in the entire New Testament and there with a different nuance (Lk 23:48), hardly sufficient scriptural evidence for a technical, heightened understanding of θεωρία. In fact, the Fourth Gospel offers an abundance of gnosiological terms (εἰδέναι, γιγνώσκειν, πιστεύειν, βλέπειν, ὁρᾶν, θεωρεῖν, etc.), all of them applied indiscriminately to Christ's relations to all, believers and unbelievers.

With regard to Gregory, the intent of the first two cited orations is that, duly cleansed, "let us philosophize within our proper bounds"[72] because "the divine nature cannot be apprehended by human reason."[73] Gregory is talking about proper use of reason fulfilled by faith.[74] His appeal to mystical knowledge is over against Arian and Eunomian rationalism, not the ordinary use of reason in gaining biblical knowledge about God, which is available to all. Gregory himself makes ample use of both reason and rhetoric gained from his classical Greek education, not least in his use of the Greek notion of θέωσις which, to be sure, he fills with biblical meaning. All this is by no means to deny that the experiential and mystical dimension is unimportant in either the Fourth Gospel or Gregory. On the contrary, we affirm its importance in both. However, it is to point out that neither the Fourth Gospel, nor Gregory, in their overall witness raise the charismatic believer or saint as *the* infallible criterion of the knowledge of God and about God above Scripture and above the Church. The total testimony of the Bible

---

[72] *Theological Oration*, 1.5.

[73] *Ibid.*, 211.

[74] See *Faith Gives Fullness to Reasoning: The Five Theological Orations of Gregory of Nazianzen* by Frederick W. Norris who lifts up the following Gregorian citation, p. v: "When we abandon faith to take the power of reason as our shield, when we use philosophical enquiry to destroy the credibility of the Spirit, then reason gives way in the face of the vastness of realities.... Give way it must ...[being] the frail organ of human understanding. What happens then? The frailty of our reasoning looks like a frailty in our creed. Thus it is that as Paul too judges, smartness of argument is revealed as a nullifying of the Cross. Faith, in fact, is what gives fullness to our reasoning" (*Oration* 29.21).

and the fathers does not support such an exclusive model as a hermeneutical criterion.

In biblical and theological hermeneutics, we cannot be satisfied with a proposal that seems to suggest that the authoritative charismatic figure is beyond critique, a position open to the charge of arbitrariness and subjectivism. The charismatic figure is important in the Judaeo-Christian tradition but cannot be separated from the people of God, the realm of the faith community whose corporate character is the prevailing point of reference. The apostolic advice is: "Do not believe every spirit, but test the spirits to see whether they are of God; for many false prophets have gone out into the world (Jn 4:1)." Among the Church fathers, St. Symeon the New Theologian advocated, as perhaps no other Orthodox saint, the unerring wisdom and even sinlessness of the beholder of Christ's glory, and himself claimed to be such. Nevertheless, despite his strong statements about the spiritual blindness of all others, he invites his hearers, who had not yet beheld the glory of the risen Christ, to judge for themselves the truthfulness of his own words. For example, he writes: "This, in my opinion, is the truth of the matter, and such is God's counsel toward us ... You, on your part, must see and test that which we say."[75]

Charismatic claims must be tested out by the communal tradition and the life of the Church as the final criterion. Experience of God belongs to the whole Church and not only to an elite group, which would smack of gnosticism. Personal mystical cognition has significance, especially for the beholders of the glory of God, but cannot exclusively either dominate or absorb access to knowledge of God available to all. For otherwise, not only would the faithful be deprived of their role of guardians of the faith but also the Church would be cut off from communication with the world to which it is charged to preach the gospel meaningfully. Rather, a hermeneutical model is needed that takes into account a greater balance between faith and reason, mystical cognition and scholarship, individual and faith community,

---

[75] C. J. deCatanzaro, trans., *Symeon the New Theologian: Discourses*, p. 354.

Church and culture, according to the testimony of the Church fathers.

Chapter Seven

The Hermeneutical Question II: An Ecumenical Proposal

A Multilevel Hermeneutic

After critiquing the views of others, one has the obligation in turn, to lay out his own for criticism. What follows is a hermeneutical proposal based on the concept of "neo-patristic synthesis,"[1] which intends to integrate "what is new and what is old" (Mt 13:52). It is grounded in the patristic ideal of the mutual interdependence of Scripture and tradition, as well as of faith and reason, factors that should be viewed as essentially synergistic rather than conflicting according to the Church fathers. The value of critical scholarship and openness to culture are taken for granted on the premise that the Holy Spirit, the Scriptures, authentic tradition, as well as the gifts of faith and reason, of themselves prompt critical discernment of truth which, as truth, is both addressed and relevant to all and in all cultures. The following paradigm invites critical thinking on the permanent structure, as well as the fluid aspects of hermeneutical inquiry. As a heuristic model, it applies to all readers of the Bible and ecclesial bodies, and thus presumes ecumenical significance. It calls for irenic disclosure of confessional and scholarly commitments in order to achieve honest, critical

---

[1] The expression coined by Georges Florovsky. See above, Chapter Six, at the beginning of the section "The Hermeneutical Question in Eastern Orthodoxy."

discussion of points of convergence and divergence and, in the end, if necessary, to agree to disagree amicably.

The keystone of the proposal is the position that there is not one hermeneutical problem, nor one hermeneutical key, but many, according to several interrelated hermeneutical levels at which several interrelated sets of hermeneutical factors play varying interactive functions. As a formal discipline, hermeneutics deals with epistemology, the theory of knowledge. It seeks to elucidate the principles and elements of communication, that is, the transference of meaning with ultimate reference to truth. But knowing or understanding something and, certainly, knowing the meaning and claims of biblical texts has several levels or dimensions.[2]

In biblical hermeneutics, three fundamental levels can be differentiated which are nevertheless closely interrelated. One level pertains to understanding or knowing what the biblical document conveys according to its contextual sequence of words and overall conceptuality in its own historical world, a level that is called "exegetical." This level is often regarded as the "historical" or even the "academic" study of Scripture. Another level is evaluative, involving the reader's assent or dissent to Scripture's ideas and claims, presumably on the basis of some authority or evaluative criterion, explicit or implicit. This second level may be called "interpretive" or "evaluative," and mainly concerns what is perceived as the "theological interpretation" of Scripture. Still another even more profound level is that of personal appropriation of biblical truth, which may be called "transformative" or "transformational." This is the level of existential engagement, whether individual or corporate, with the truth claim of what is understood by the reading or hearing

---

[2] Pertaining to biblical study, M. Hengel, *Acts and the History of Earliest Christianity*, p. 131, touches on a crucial hermeneutical point when he writes, "one could speak of three possible 'stages of knowledge': knowing, understanding and assenting or dissenting. The possibility of controlling communication diminishes with each stage." I agree and I hope in a different and more analytic fashion to offer a structured and more detailed hermeneutical model that may be helpful in the ongoing hermeneutical discussion.

of the text, and then assented to or dissented from, a level often referred to as the "spiritual reading" or "devotional use" of Scripture. Thus we have three hermeneutical levels or dimensions – exegetical, interpretive, and transformative – which are ultimately inseparable and yet can be differentiated by their distinct hermeneutical "problems" and operations.[3]

There are additional decisive hermeneutical factors that operate at these three hermeneutical levels and make the hermeneutical inquiry even more complex. At least five sets of factors may be formally identified. One set is faith and reason as epistemological ways of knowing truth, that is, as "hermeneutical modes" of approaching Scripture and its claims. A second is Scripture and tradition as "hermeneutical testimonies" to truth.[4] A third is the community of faith and individual members as "hermeneutical agents" and arbiters of truth. A fourth is church life and ongoing culture as "hermeneutical contexts" of discussing and settling truth. And a fifth set is human capacity and divine grace as "hermeneutical initiatives" in the discernment and actualization of truth. All these factors are interrelated according to each set and all sets between them as they become dynamically operative at the three hermeneutical levels.

---

[3] Most biblical scholars distinguish between historical exegesis and evaluative interpretation, and associate hermeneutics mainly with the second task. See, for example, Gordon D. Fee, *Gospel and Spirit*, pp. 200-227, whose hermeneutical thinking I value highly. However, bearing in mind R. Bultmann's caveat about the impossibility of presuppositionless exegesis of Scripture as a whole, the question of what is exegesis and what is eisegesis, as well as critical assessment of critical methodologies claiming to get at the true exegetical meaning of Scripture, all require careful hermeneutical reflection. Hermeneutics has to do not only with what we do with the meaning of Scripture, but how we arrive at that meaning in the first place. Hermeneutical reflection must consider the whole process from a) exegesis of specific texts, to b) evaluation of their truth content, and to their c) impact on actual life when applied.

[4] Not only tradition but also Scripture itself constitutes "hermeneutical testimony" to transcendent truth insofar as it is a record of revelation and as such involves interpretation of the understanding of God, his activities, purpose, and will for humanity and creation, including essential focus on what is true and false about all these matters.

Formally speaking, the above fundamental hermeneutical levels and basic sets of hermeneutical factors are constants in hermeneutical theory. They constitute the permanent theoretical structure of biblical hermeneutics. However, in practice their interaction is almost incalculably dynamic and elusive, rendering the hermeneutical quest extremely difficult. Clarity in hermeneutical discussion can be achieved to the degree that the proposed structure of biblical hermeneutics is maintained and the various levels and factors are comparatively taken up for critical examination. The preeminent challenge is to maintain the balance of the paradigm, both by distinguishing as well as by relating the interactive levels and factors, whether they are viewed as synergistic or conflicting in varying degrees. The following attempt to do just that may indicate, as well, that general biblical hermeneutics could be conceived of as a formal, neutral discipline, a kind of hermeneutics of hermeneutics, on which particular confessional or ideological hermeneutics could be mapped out.

The Exegetical Level

We begin with the exegetical level. By exegetical is meant the level of understanding of the biblical text in its historical context of literary form and conceptuality according to the etymological meaning of exegesis as opposed to eisegesis. Although some would dispute it,[5] the level of the text is fundamentally the level of the author because no other controlled access to the author's thought is available other than the text itself. Even if the author meant something more than what the author actually wrote (a kind of *sensus plenior*, that is, "fuller meaning"), that something can be critically gleaned at the exegetical level only by close study of the author's entire work, that is, the text itself. The ideal at the exegetical level is to comprehend and describe – not to evaluate, assent to or dissent from, or render relevant to contemporaries – the author's own understanding of

---

[5] I have in mind the new literary critics who view the text as independent of the author and the author's historical context.

God, the world, humanity, salvation, historical events, predilections, concerns, and specific points of discussion, as accurately as possible.[6] This level may be formally designated "exegetical" rather than "historical" to avoid the usual contrast between "historical" and "theological." Such a contrast is fundamentally ambiguous because historical records register theological claims, and theological claims are made by concrete persons and communities in historical contexts. In a certain sense, everything is theological and everything is historical. One must be clear that the exegetical approach deals with all matters in the texts whether specifically grammatical, literary, historical, sociological, theological, cosmological, or eschatological.

Critical analysis and synthesis at the exegetical level can move freely in all directions, but must strive to explicate the biblical author's own realm of understanding, convictions, and truth claims within the author's total religious and social world. For example, the exegete can explicate Paul's views of the Mosaic Law, the people of God, the Messiah and so on, and even critique to what degree these may or may not be consistent with other Jewish and early Christian views, explore why, and set down the definitive features of Paul's own positions. The exegetical level necessarily involves "evaluation" and "interpretation" but always in terms of the thought patterns of the author and his historical circumstances, not in terms of the values and perceptions of later generations up to contemporary times. This exegetical level is the foundation of biblical study as a scientific discipline which should, ideally, be not Orthodox, Roman Catholic, or Protestant, but simply biblical, just as the field of patristics should have its own context and integrity and not be

---

[6] Of course I have in view Krister Stendahl and his classic article "Biblical Theology, Contemporary," *IDB*, pp.418-432, as well as other works, who first opened my eyes to the methodological distinction between descriptive exegesis and normative interpretation, and thus made it possible for me in good conscience to study in Protestant graduate schools many years ago. To him and to those schools I am deeply grateful for the challenges and the opportunities that expanded my horizons.

Orthodox, Roman Catholic, or Protestant.[7] Examples of scholarly work at the historical, exegetical level are the writings of such contemporary biblical scholars as Raymond Brown, Martin Hengel, E. P. Sanders and N. T. Wright, to name a few. It is at this historical, descriptive level that cooperative study of the Bible is fruitful among various scholars, whether committed believers or not, and forms the scholarly basis for serious ecumenical and inter-religious dialogue.[8] The hermeneutical "problem" at the exegetical level is none other than how to do accurate historical, critical work, and the solution is a sound theory of historical biblical criticism in its analytic and synthetic functions. At the exegetical level, faith plays virtually no role apart from the sympathetic affirmation that something decisively important is at stake because of Scripture's sacred status and the value of encountering its own authentic witness. The scholar and critical reason – the hermeneutics of historical scholarship – must be given primacy and complete freedom of research. Descriptive exegetical truth

[7] This was the basic argument of my articles "Historical Studies and Orthodox Theology or the Problem of History for Orthodoxy," *GOTR* 12 (3, 1967), pp. 394-419 and "Biblical Studies in Orthodox Theology: A Response," *GOTR* 17 (1, 1972), pp. 69-85. Although I would now qualify a number of points, I still stand by the fundamental thesis. Today I would argue more precisely about the integrity, not autonomy, of biblical scholarship. I see more clearly that historical criticism is an essential but preparatory or ancillary approach to the theological interpretation of Scripture. On the other hand, theological interpretation without sound exegetical basis builds on weak foundations. From a broader philosophical and theological perspective, I am no longer impressed by the so-called "distance" between Scripture and modern culture, nor expectant that historical criticism, however objectively conducted, has the decisive answer. Rather, I perceive that the ultimate Christian answers to life lie in one's experiential understanding of God within a vibrant and praying community of faith that holds to the authority of Scripture and classic Christian doctrine in matters of faith and morals, yet always remains self-critical and open to ongoing culture.

[8] I agree with many scholars, including Gordon D. Fee, *Gospel and Spirit*, p. 26, that "frankly it [i.e., the exegetical task] is one that believer or unbeliever alike can engage in with a relative degree of objectivity." The caution should be added that an unbeliever must have professional sympathy for the subject matter and that a believer should take care that too much sympathy may well impede exegetical understanding.

must be derived on the basis of scholarly standards, open to all methods and sources, including exegetical insights from the tradition, without special pleading.

However, historical critical reason must be thoroughly cleansed from the philosophical presuppositions of logical positivism, the heaviest liability of modern biblical criticism. To yield to the positivistic "principle of analogy" means to vitiate historical research and to preclude *a priori* the possibility of encounter with the most essential elements of Scripture's claims. This does not mean that the scholar should not critically assess, to the degree that evidence allows, the reported accounts of the ministry of Jesus, including the infancy narratives, baptism, transfiguration, and resurrection.[9] Nor does it mean that a critical sifting of the evidence of the Gospels in order to reach the level of the "historical Jesus," extremely difficult as this task is, should be declared theologically inappropriate. But it does mean that the scholar at the exegetical level has no right to foreclose the transcendent dimensions of Scripture's truth claims. To do so smacks of philosophical arbitrariness, which stifles the voice of Scripture, deprives non-professionals of their right of free response to that voice, and undermines scholarship as prejudicial. It goes without saying that critical reason must do its work in a sensitive manner recognizing that the Bible, as in the case of the sacred texts of all people, deserves respectful treatment whether or not one agrees with its message.

Exegetical hermeneutics, first of all, requires integrity in the discursive, exegetical discourse through heightened awareness of the nature and limits of historical reason. Exegetical study of biblical texts quickly confronts profound theological claims that cannot be dismissed on account of philosophical bias and historicist prejudice, which are two grave shortcomings of modern biblical scholarship. On the contrary, the exegetical approach itself demands focused attention to the text and its central aim or σκοπός, to use the terminology of the Church

---

[9] An example is R. E. Brown's, *The Birth of the Messiah* (Garden City: Doubleday, 1977).

fathers. On this basis, the theology and spirituality of Scripture require significant attention because the original deserves to be fully presented in its own thrust of originality. Hermeneutical thought at this level must seek to clarify how the various aspects of exegetical analysis and synthesis bear on the original meaning of the text, what is exegesis and what is eisegesis, and to what degree various methods, old and new, uncover or distort that meaning. Stripped of their philosophical and ideological biases, critical historical and literary methodologies, which are modern refinements of the patristic literal and grammatical approach to Scripture, seem most adequate to the exegetical task. However, even distinctly ideological hermeneutics such as the liberationist and feminist approaches to Scripture can provide insightful and challenging contributions at the historical, exegetical level. *yeah, right.*

To be sure, the scientific exegetical task is a narrow and professional one, requiring scholarly training and critical standards. Just as in all literary and historical study, there are strengths[10] and weaknesses.[11] No critical study as such can preclude occasional arbitrariness, especially in breaking new

---

[10] Historical critical reason has brilliantly analyzed the literary forms and complex traditions within Scripture, the interrelationship of biblical books such as the Pentateuch and the Synoptics, the historical developments of Judaism and Christianity, and has offered plausible and useful reconstructions, although often hypothetical and conflicting. However, in this overall perspective, historical reason has discovered the crucial reality of the faith community and tradition behind the Bible and the undeniable fact that the biblical books are largely faith documents, expressing the historical struggles and the religious values of the Jewish and Christian communities. It has also uncovered the immense variety and diversity of the biblical material, a welcome perspective on the human character of the Bible, tempering absolutist and pernicious uses of the sacred book. Its greatest success has been in the descriptive exegetical results, detailed and thematic, pertaining to specific books. One must freely grant that the positive results of exegetical studies have surpassed the patristic exegetical heritage to such an extent that one is hard pressed to find fruitful contact between the two at the historical exegetical level, except in isolated instances.

[11] Aside from the ambiguities and differences of critical opinions due to lack of sufficient evidence, there are other greater shortcomings due to "historicism," that is, the misuse of historical reason when: a) critical inquiry becomes so absorbed in historical and literary analysis as to neglect the religious and theological content of

ground. The exegetical approach, paradoxically by forgetting the σκοπός of Scripture, which is preeminently religious, can also become antiquarian and pedantic. Such tendencies or excesses should be addressed by the community of scholars exercising balanced judgment in a continuous process of self-correction.[12] Apart from such self-criticism and sound judgment, biblical scholarship loses credibility on its own grounds as well as in the eyes of the community of faith, which itself has a tremendous investment in Scripture. However, when pursuing its exegetical ideal, biblical scholarship can and progressively has laid out accurate and panoramic accounts of the diverse world of the Bible in all its historical, literary, and religious dimensions. The descriptive task embraces not only inspiring biblical teachings, such as to love one another and to practice social justice, but also morally disturbing aspects, such as the idea of holy war and prayers for the destruction of enemies. Of course, if the exegete is to pronounce value judgments from a modern perspective or the exegete's own life stance – and the exegete would have a philosophical right to do so – he or she must disclose and define these value judgments for what they are, hers or his, not the

---

Scripture, and b) inquiry is overtaken by programmatic skepticism about biblical events either for lack of desired evidence or by philosophical predilection. In the first case, instead of partaking of the banquet of Scripture in its literary, theological and spiritual richness, where the Church fathers are strongest, historical reason exhausts itself trying to figure out what exactly happened in the kitchen, that is, the "background"– an unfulfilling effort that renders the banquet tacitly irrelevant. In the second case, prevailing skepticism about biblical events casts a cloud of doubt over the whole Bible and its overall veracity. But the essential problem is not whether all the tribes of Israel left Egypt together or whether Jesus cleansed the Temple once or twice, since a degree of relativity is intrinsic to reporting and reconstructing historical events. Rather, the problem is radical skepticism about any reliable knowledge about Moses and Israel's exodus experience, Jesus and his ministry, Peter and the pentecostal experience of the Church. Many critics speak and write with such a skeptical tone that virtually all biblical events seem to vanish from sight and one is left wondering what then explains the undisputed emergence and endurance of Judaism and Christianity.

[12] This is recently demonstrated by the impressive efforts of N. T. Wright in his *The New Testament and the People of God*, a breathtaking project aimed at a fresh reconstruction of the world of the New Testmament and early Christianity.

Bible's. Such value judgments involve another hermeneutical level, which must critically be considered in its own right. Without this clear distinction and appropriate notice to unwary readers, the "exegete" subtly takes on the role of "interpreter," a most confusing and pernicious habit of many scholars.

The important hermeneutical point is that the exegetical approach, which in principle is functional and instrumental, and thus neutral, can provide a veritable banquet of biblical knowledge and do so with an exciting sense of discovering the dynamic and diverse world of the Bible. Its unarguable advantage is that it gives direct and refreshing, if also at times disturbing, access to Scripture's original voice in all its richness and variety. To object to the ideal of uncovering the witness of Scripture at its own level is hardly tenable, unless one either despairs about or is afraid of historical truth, though such truth is inevitably relative. On the contrary, granted human limitations, the outcome of sound exegetical work is not only good historical scholarship which can be pursued properly and with great benefit at higher educational institutions in a pluralistic society. Exegesis is also the first level of solid theological scholarship, to be encouraged above all by the Church, because Scripture in its canonical authority is the primary text bearing witness to divine revelation through human words and images.

What has been said thus far about the historical, critical study of Scripture applies equally to other theological fields, such as liturgics, patristics, church history, and the history of doctrine. As historical disciplines, these do not have to retain their polemical vestiges, nor continue to harbor hidden epistemological agendas. We are fully aware of the so-called "hermeneutical circle." Since no study is free of "pre-understanding," there is no absolute point of neutrality and objectivity. Yet, this epistemological view by no means gives free license to prejudicial historical scholarship. On the contrary, part of being "critical" calls for the ongoing exposure of "pre-understanding" to critical scrutiny in order that interpretation and evaluation of data at the historical level may achieve the highest degrees of relative

objectivity and accuracy.[13] "Pre-understanding" at this epistemological level should be limited to the minimal extent
necessary for widely-based scholarly study of historical records.
If the inexorable nature of the "hermeneutical circle" can at all
be minimized or neutralized, it is precisely at the historical level,
apart from the question of the relevance and normative value of
texts. Integrity in the pursuit of truth invites deep self-criticism
and mutual scholarly correction of hidden agendas in order to
work toward areas of consensus in all these fields. The fresh yields
of historical critical results themselves help us to see that the
question of their normative evaluation and contemporary
relevance involves epistemologically other and far more complex hermeneutical levels.

The Interpretive Level

The second hermeneutical level is the interpretive or evaluative in the normative and/or contemporary sense. At this level,
the world of the reader is fully engaged. Here the reader's assenting or dissenting response to Scripture's witness is decisive, determined by the reader's questions, motivations, needs, values,
philosophical presuppositions, purposes, and goals, whether explicit or implicit. The determinative element is the value that is
sought or found in Scripture according to the diverse interests
of the users of Scripture, experts or not. For the Christian

---

[13] Interesting parallels of corrective revisions of secular history gained popular
attention in the United States during the summer of 1995 as Americans com-
memorated the fiftieth anniversary of the dropping of the atomic bomb on
Hiroshima. See *The Boston Globe*, July 25, 1995. The standard view held that the
dropping of the bomb was justified to save American lives in view of an impend-
ing invasion of Japan and the desire to secure its unconditional surrender. The
revised view advocated different reasons for the nuclear holocaust: while Japan
was poised to surrender anyway, and a mere demonstration of the frightful dimensions of the bomb would have sufficed, nuclear-driven officials carried out this act
of unprecedented destruction for domestic political reasons and to intimidate the
next enemy, the Soviet Union. Similar debates among Americans have occurred
over the prolonged conflict in Vietnam, the winning of the Cold War, and the
conquest of the lands of the American Indians, standard and revised views vying
for public acceptance.

*The Christian Churches [?]
would be a [?] of the break [?] the
The Russian Orthodox Church and not [?] to its heretical
Orthodox [?]
patriarchies/
assemblies?
sects*

churches throughout the centuries, the chief interest is the saving message of Scripture for pastoral nurture transmitted through worship, proclamation, catechetics, and guidance in faith and practice. For theologians, it is exposition of the mystery of God, his being, ways, purposes, and will. For poets and hymnologists, it is exaltation of God's glory. For the average Christian reader, it is practical, finding inspiration and wisdom to live out the day. For modern historians and scholars of ancient cultures and languages, the contemporary interest, the driving force of their professions and livelihood, may be primarily antiquarian. For scholars of religion and theological academicians, it may be exploration of the human experience in terms of symbolic constructs and religious patterns of meaning. For socio-political scientists and critics it may be ideological, according to burning issues of the day. For literary authors and film makers, it may be a combination of aesthetic, ideological, and general human interests. Because of the plurality and divergence of interests, the second hermeneutical level may be formally designated "interpretive" or "evaluative," rather than "theological" because the latter represents one specific among many interpretive interests.

The hermeneutical problem at this epistemological level is obviously as elusive as it is immense. If the Bible is a most controverted book, it is not because basic sense cannot be made of it historically, but because it is a valued book and various people take diverse things from it in different ways. The very formulation of the hermeneutical "problem" and its "solution" at the interpretive level are crucially determined by the question "for whom?" since readers can and do come to the Bible from diametrically opposed perspectives. What is true or false, normative or optional, relevant or irrelevant, varies widely according to diverse readers and various communities, whether religious or secular. All inevitably have their implicit or explicit "pre-understandings" or "hermeneutical agendas" determined by the interplay of many factors. We have specified above five sets of key hermeneutical factors. The most crucial of these, to which the others are related, are what the Church fathers long ago identified: on the one hand faith and reason as ways of knowing, that is, "hermeneutical modes," and on the other hand Scripture and tradition as vehicles of truth, that is, "hermeneutical testimonies." These two sets of hermeneutical factors need extensive comparative attention.

Faith is the positive response to revealed truth. It is the gift and capacity of assenting to the authoritative witness of Scripture in its overall message of salvation, an authority intrinsic to Scripture's truth claims as God's word and received canonically by the Church in its apostolic and patristic tradition. This faith, which is not only individual but above all the corporate faith of the Church, has decisive epistemological value insofar as it affirms, reflects upon, celebrates, and applies the knowledge derived from Scripture as true knowledge that ultimately comes from God. For centuries faithful Christians and their communities have derived decisive religious value from Scripture apprehending its broad themes and specific instructions by common sense and various methods from the contextual grammatical to the allegorical.[14] This faith perspective, which includes the cooperative use of reason, is the perspective of the biblical authors themselves who affirm true knowledge of God not only in terms of their personal experience of faith but also through their communal tradition of faith and their sacred texts.

The biblical notion of revelation, which precludes human manipulation of God either by religious consciousness or philosophical reason, necessitates faith as the fundamental response

[14] Only foolish and presumptuous people would dare think that past Christian generations missed the essential message of Scripture because they lacked the benefit of modern biblical criticism and contemporary hermeneutical theories. Pertinent in this regard are David Well's polemical words quoted by Mark Noll, *Between Faith and Criticism*, pp. 152-153, which in part run: "Why is it that only now, two thousand years after the event, we are at last beginning to understand what Christianity is all about?... Are we to suppose that the real interpretation of Jesus is alone accessible to a tiny minority in the church – its learned scholars – and that the remainder of Christian believers is excluded from such knowledge?" The implication is that those who presume that only modern scholars have true knowledge of the Scriptures presuppose views of Scripture and truth that need thorough criticism.

to the mystery of God's self-disclosure to which Scripture is the recorded witness. The uniqueness of Scripture lies exactly in its transcendent claims about God and his saving activity in history. If the σκοπὸς of Scripture, its main subject matter, is theological, that is, the knowledge of God anchored on God's personal revelation, then the faith perspective is the primary perspective for understanding and appropriating the transcendent reality to which Scripture uniquely bears testimony. From a hermeneutical standpoint, faith has decisive epistemological value insofar as, according to the essential witness of Scripture, God has communicated knowledge not only of his numinous power but also of his attributes and moral demands. Otherwise, if faith is not granted cognitive value, then an unbridgeable gap is created between God's self-disclosure and human understanding.

Having cognitive value, faith is inseparable from reason, the attribute that gives intelligible structure to faith. Faith and reason work together in appropriating true knowledge of God, although faith clearly has primacy. Reason itself is a gift of God, a capacity to be used to its fullest extent provided it recognizes its proper functions and limits in various areas, such as the hard sciences, historical study, philosophical analysis, and the revelation of God. In its capacity to study the biblical writings, although often caught up in historicist interests, critical reason has demonstrated brilliant results. It has also provided welcome and far-reaching cleansing effects on obscurantist, fanatical, and immoral uses of the Bible and religious traditions. However, on its philosophical side, seeking to penetrate the transcendent claims of Scripture, critical reason has been marked by precipitous failures. It has questioned the very core of the truths of the apostolic faith and tradition, for example, the deity of Christ, the pentecostal gift the Spirit, indeed the very truth of a living God concretely active in his reign and righteousness among his people.

In a kind of epistemological hubris, philosophical reason has not only undercut the biblical category of revelation but has also misused rational inquiry into the historical records, resulting in radical reconstructions of the normative patterns of the ancient Church.[15] When hermeneutical approaches lead to such developments and still claim the designation biblical study, something has gone terribly askew with the mixture of biblical interpretation and Enlightenment philosophy. According to Martin Hengel, critical reason has replaced naive understandings of history with naive philosophical views of the transcendent mystery of the living God. The sane and succinct answer is Hengel's:

> Lessing's criticism that "accidental truths of history can never become proofs of the necessary truths of reason" reminds the theologian that he is not primarily concerned with "necessary truths of reason" but with God's free self-disclosure of himself in Jesus Christ.[16]

Hermeneutics at the interpretive level, whether implicit or explicit, shifts from one end of the spectrum to the other according to the beholder's "pre-understanding" of the relationship of faith and reason. To put it in extreme terms, on the one hand, for the rationalist Lessing and his intellectual heirs, the hermeneutical problem is virtually insoluble because the perceived "chasm" between faith and reason, biblical and modern thought, is unbridgeable and traditional theology is useless. The core saving truths of Scripture are not only rejected as irrelevant but also viewed with contempt as harmful to

---

[15] According to the assessment of some critics, gnostic Christianity represents an option equal to, perhaps in some respects better than, second-century catholic Christianity as an interpretation of the apostolic tradition. This amounts to saying in parallel that the Judaism of the false prophets and Jewish practicioners of Canaanite idolatry are on a footing equal to, perhaps in some respects better than, that of the canonical prophets as interpreters of the Sinaitic tradition. For many of us, it is both a happy fact and a matter of divine providence, that the Great Church, rather than the Gnostic sects, won out in antiquity. Although we would attribute an absolute inerrancy neither to Scripture nor tradition, we find no need whatever to be either apologetic or defensive about the magnificent achievement of the ancient universal Church amidst its hard struggles within and without. The saving message of Scripture, the truth of Christ, as well as the identity of the Church were at stake.

[16] M. Hengel, *Acts and the History of Earliest Christianity*, p. 133.

human progress. On the other hand, for a fanatical believer who unquestionably accepts the authority of "inerrant" Scripture, the hermeneutical "problem" is virtually non-existent and the entire text of Scripture is revealed truth relevant for all times. Any verse from any book of Scripture at any time may be lifted out as normative for contemporary life.[17] For the former, autonomous reason is the evaluative criterion that inescapably leads to skepticism about even the very notion of a personal God revealed in history. For the latter, blind faith is the evaluative criterion that invariably inclines toward fideist, literal acceptance of a six-day creation, biblical history at face value, and a final consummation through divine acts of unprecedented cosmic violence.

Accordingly, at the interpretive epistemological level, the hermeneutical problem as discussed by contemporary scholars and theologians goes beyond an understandable gap between professionals and ordinary people that can somehow be bridged by increased publication of popular works on hermeneutics.[18] It goes beyond an inevitable degree of relativism in critical research, differences of opinions among scholars, and semantic disputes about what is relevant or irrelevant. It has to do with deeper philosophical attitudes and choices that involve a total life perspective about what is true and right.

In modern times, the interplay of faith and reason, and therefore the discussion of the hermeneutical problem, are inescapably qualified – but not necessarily determined – by the Enlightenment accent on reason, the scientific experimental method, and the rise of the historical consciousness since the nineteenth century. The poisonous element in the mixture is not reason or the use or reason, which are welcome, but autonomous reason as the criterion of all truth, the keystone of the

---

[17] This is the hermeneutical implication of the fundamentalist dictum: "The Bible means what it says and says what it means."

[18] Welcome as these are, they are often written from a narrow hermeneutical standpoint across the spectrum of the interplay of faith and reason, and thus confuse the reader by not presenting the wider landscape of the hermeneutical problem.

philosophies of logical positivism, empiricism, and modernism. These philosophies have tried to marginalize religion and replace it with the myth of progress. However, events of the twentieth century, including apocalyptic intimations of nuclear and ecological disaster, have deflated the myth of progress and have shaken secular faith in autonomous, scientifically objective reason. As Western culture moves beyond modernity to what is variously called postmodernity or ultra-modernity, the myth of autonomous universal reason is being dethroned by a sense of the radical contingency of all knowledge. Yet the myth of human autonomy remains and falsely validates all sorts of current subjectivist constructions of reality. In our hypermodern age, we have what J. Richard Middleton and Brian Walsh have described as an unstable hybrid of epistemological realism and autonomous subjectivism seeking to get the world right but in accordance with human aims. As ultra-modern people "even if we don't believe we can get the world right, we do believe we can make the world anything we want."[19] In this cultural context, the Christian faith perspective gains a new hearing, while Christian epistemology remains challenged to affirm that truth is ultimate truth and not merely a human construct.

Against this broad cultural and philosophical background, it is possible to sketch a rough map of contemporary hermeneutical positions at the evaluative or interpretive level, granted a colossal risk of oversimplification. The hypothetical center is the patristic ideal of a balanced interdependence between faith and reason in the contemporary study of Scripture. Scholars from different ecclesial backgrounds such as Peter Stuhlmacher, Raymond Brown, J. I. Packer, and Brevard Childs try to hold to the center through equal concern for critical exegesis and theological interpretation, with primacy falling to faith. Although differentiated by confessional interests, their position may be

---

[19] From an interview of J. R. Middleton and B. Walsh, "How Pomo Can You Get?" in *Academic Alert* 4 (2, 1995), p. 1, to whom I owe this critique of postmodern culture. The interview announces their forthcoming book, *Truth Is Stranger Than It Used to Be*, published by InterVarsity Press.

Enlightened conservativism

It seems to me and Basil right that sts Athan should be to the for the Trad and ws the

broadly described as enlightened conservatism, a position that was arguably exemplified by the great Church fathers such as Athanasios, Basil, and Augustine. To the right of center are numerous shades of positions on the conservative and tradition-alist spectrum, whether Protestant, Roman Catholic, or Orthodox. The common mark of all these diverse positions is a distinct theological orientation in hermeneutics.

Conservative liberalism

To the left of center one perhaps could place numerous shades of positions from that of Wolfhart Pannenberg and many others going back to Schleiermacher, the father of so-called "modern hermeneutical theory," who take on the Enlightenment's challenge frontally. But doing so meant conceding in various degrees that normative access to truth is by means of "scientific" reason.[20] This position, which is highly differentiated by corrective qualifications from Hans Gadamer to Paul Ricoeur, as well as Pannenberg himself, may be broadly described as conservative liberalism. The common strand is a distinct philosophical orientation that yields stimulating hermeneutical theories of knowledge but leaves much ambiguity about the specific truth claims of Scripture and normative reception of them.[21] Further on the left side of center ought to be placed, as well, liberationist and feminist approaches which, while yielding important exegetical results, are vitiated by their sociopolitical ideology and tendency to exclusivism. On the far side of the left also belong the Bultmanns, the Tillichs, the Cobbs, the Ninehams, and many others who either are dependent on a contemporary philosophy

---

[20] A substantive critique of this tradition is by Andrew Louth, *Discerning the Mystery: An Essay on the Nature of Theology* (Oxford: Oxford University Press, 1993).

[21] C. H. Pinnock, *The Scripture Principle*, p. 199, is right to suggest that Gadamer's hermeneutic of the fusion of two horizons, the Bible's and the reader's, can mean very different things for the believer and non-believer. The non-believer may still draw out of the Bible according to his dominant "pre-understanding" and remake the biblical message according to his or her own image. The believer will more readily allow oneself to be drawn into the biblical message by the Spirit and be transformed. In both cases, apart from the relevance of Scripture, the question of normative truth and normative interpretation remains.

or even despair about the hermeneutical quest altogether. It is a question of where to place the diverse hermeneutics of the new literary critics who, in reaction to the antiquarian nature and results of historical criticism, seek to make scriptural studies meaningful and relevant to modern readers by refined literary methods. Most literary critics seem to set aside altogether the question of abiding or normative truth, and even reject its relevance for pluralist modern culture. Such interpreters can be classified on the far left either by explicit position or by default.[22]

The right balance between faith and reason, especially in the actual interpretation of specific biblical texts, is of course, a hypothetical ideal perceived by the eyes of the beholder. Nevertheless, in broad strokes it becomes clear what the orientation of a particular evaluative hermeneutic is, whether it inclines toward a faith and ecclesial perspective accepting the authority of Scripture as a book of the faith community or whether it inclines toward a rationalist and humanist perspective questioning that authority and viewing Scripture as any other book. The difference is a veritable crossing of the hermeneutical Rubicon.[23] Those who lean toward the faith perspective view critical analysis as "positive criticism" when operating within that perspective; otherwise it becomes "negative criticism." Those who

---

[22] Overall, the new literary criticism seems to cap a sequential process of hermeneutical orientation in modern biblical studies in four stages: 1) viewing biblical history as reality; 2) seeking to get to the reality behind the biblical narrative; 3) dealing unsuccessfully with interpreted reality; and 4) interpreting Scripture as religious literature quite apart from the question of reality altogether.

[23] Clark H. Pinnock in *The Scripture Principle*, pp. xiv-xv, and 223, observes that the main confrontation in Protestantism is between classical Christianity and liberal neo-Christianity, a confrontation centered around the "Scripture principle," which makes Protestant traditional differences with Roman Catholicism trivial by comparison. He states, pp. 133-144, that apart from the faith perspective the entire Bible becomes implausible and irrelevant; and critical analysis, driven by the serpent's question (Gen. 3:1), turns negative, rendering Scripture into a strange and antique object to be dissected rather than God's word to be heard and obeyed. Pinnock's views of Scripture, including his qualification of *sola Scriptura* (pp. 216-217) and his statement that "Christology, not Bibliology, occupies the center stage

lean toward a rationalist perspective tend to coopt the term
"critical" for themselves, viewing their counterparts as
"uncritical" in various degrees. But the latter critics do so
"uncritically," failing to realize that they themselves speak from
a philosophical faith perspective, that is, faith in reason. Their
faith in reason leads them to suppose that they can ultimately
squeeze compelling meaning from Scripture – on the strength
of reason, but what strength pertaining to ultimates? – to satisfy
"modern" or "ultra-modern" man, a risky enterprise, which has
proven largely a failure as witnessed in the titanic tensions between Christianity and modern culture. For clearly, if there is a
vitality and promise in Christianity at the turn of the second
millennium, instead of a defensive and defeatist spirit, and there
is much vitality and promise, it is found among those
Christians and biblical interpreters who nurture a vibrant faith
perspective in the biblical and traditional sense.

One must draw the conclusion that, at the interpretive and
evaluative level of seeking the abiding or contemporary value of
Scripture, the hermeneutical problem yields to neither stable
formulation nor possible solution. It is a firefly in the dark, an
intellectual quark, its position determined by the eyes of the
beholder. Even if, hypothetically, exegetical scholarship can lay
out before us fairly accurate exegetical results from the New
Testament all could accept, let alone the Old Testament, nevertheless the question of choosing from these results comes to the
forefront.[24] To the degree that interpreters affirm or do not affirm by faith the revelatory authority of Scripture, they will look
upon those exegetical results as bearing true knowledge of God
or as expressing merely human constructs. For the latter, the

in Christianity" (p. 16), are substantive bases on which new and promising ecumenical alliances are currently emerging between Evangelical and Eastern Orthodox Christians around a common affirmation of classic Christian doctrine based
on the primacy of Scripture in patristic perspective.

[24] This is exactly where James Barr's proposal in his *Holy Scripture: Canon, Authority, Criticism* breaks down. While emphasizing the complex pre-history of the
canon (pp. 1-18) and rejecting the notion that either the final canon or church
tradition could serve as adequate hermeneutical criteria (pp. 29-31, 67-72), Barr

Bible is "like any other book" and it is up to the arbitrary value judgments of the readers to take from Scripture desired elements in the process of making the world "anything they want."

For the former, those who in various degrees accepted Scripture's canonical authority, crucial evaluative questions and choices remain and are inescapable. How does one distinguish between the cultural and the abiding, the temporal and the universal, the peripheral and the central elements among the results of exegetical research? Which view of Christian salvation and life should be chosen as the organizing center – the "charismatic" of Paul, the "ethical" of James, or the "apocalyptic" of the Book of Revelation? What of christology, ecclesiology, and the sacred rites of baptism and the Lord's supper? Those inclined by their "pre-understanding" to select a particular "canon within a canon" tend to underscore the "variety" and "diversity" of the New Testament. Those who tend to accept the authority of the whole canon of the New Testament either rationalize their selectivity of biblical teachings[25] or seek to find an integrated "catholic vision" of an interpreted unity between the "charismatic," the "ethical," the "apocalyptic," and all other major perspectives and teachings of the New Testament, precisely on the basis of its canonical unity. Herein lie the deepest contradictions of Protestantism in its many

---

advocates "freedom of research" and a hermeneutical approach based on "the actual datum" of the text and on an ambiguous appeal to whatever is "true" according to all fields of knowledge (pp. 32-37, 110-126). However, the data of the texts present numerous truth claims and philosophical reason can provide no ultimate criterion of "truth." There is an inherent inconsistency in Barr between his emphasis on the community behind the canonical process and his neglect of the decisive hermeneutical role of the ongoing community in the use and interpretation of the biblical tradition. For a more balanced position, see Harry Y. Gamble, "Canon" and Gerald T. Sheppard, "Canonical Criticism," *ABD*, Vol. 1, pp. 852-866.

[25] Gordon D. Fee, *Gospel and Spirit*, time and again exposes such selective readings of Scripture, whether consciously or unconsciously, by Protestants according to their particular confessional biases. For example, "one whole wing of evangelicalism...argues vehemently for the eternal validity of 1 Cor 14:34-35 on the silence of women, while rejecting every other imperative in the chapter, including the final one, not to forbid speaking in tongues," p. 45. Fee's most scathing critique, pp. 73-74, is reserved for Robert Schuller's *Self-Esteem: The New Ref-*

manifestations: on the one hand taking its stand on the canon of Scripture and on the other hand being selective about its use of Scripture; on the one hand anchoring itself on the "scriptural principle" according to the witness of the canon and on the other hand rejecting or resisting the broader "ecclesial principle" according to the witness of the ancient Church which, in the first place, formulated the canon.[26]

From the standpoint of general hermeneutics, the hermeneutical problem at the interpretive level is defined and solved in various ways by the particular hermeneutics of the beholders of Scripture and their communities. The Basils, the Aquinases, the Luthers, the Schleiermachers, the Gadamers, the Ricoeurs, the Florovskys have written from their particular evaluative "pre-understandings" or perspectives, according to their personal intellectual and communal commitments. The hermeneutical problem, which cannot be separated from the hermeneutics of life itself, can be formulated and resolved in some stable and coherent fashion only in reference to community, religious or secular. Accordingly, Christian epistemology and Christian biblical hermeneutics at the interpretive level are necessarily tied to various churches and their respective ongoing traditions. Acknowledgment of this fact, and that the factors of Scripture and

---

ormation (Waco: Word Books, 1982) which, though cloaked with evangelical slogans, is rejected as a modern cultural reversal of the Reformation, blunting God's discomforting word. According to Fee, these selective readings of the Bible, whether in narrow or wholescale terms, may be presented as persuasive and cogent in their apparent logic but the bias is in the fact that "the logic *precedes* the exegesis," p. 77 (the emphasis is Fee's).

[26] Semantic qualifications by various Protestants, such as that the biblical canon "imposed" itself upon or gradually "developed" within the life of the ancient Church by some inner authoritative impulse in the proclamation of the Gospel and guided by divine grace, sound hollow in view of the diverse options available in the second and third centuries, and the necessity of choice at every step of the way by local churches seeking to express and consolidate a catholic identity. Presumably divine grace guided the whole life of these churches as well, and not merely the preaching of the gospel which in the particular form it was defined and preached was inseparable from those churches. For example, the heretic Marcion had his own gospel and his own churches, the two wedded together.

tradition as "hermeneutical testimonies" are operative for all Christians, including Protestants, facilitates ecumenical discussion.[27]

While diversity abounds everywhere, each tradition broadly determines what is negative and what is positive diversity. An allegorical sermon on a biblical text by an Orthodox with a "θέωσις theology" is no more, nor less, appropriate or tasteful than an anecdotal sermon on the same text by a Protestant with a "justification theology." Both preachers exercise a pastoral ministry, seeking to convey a message consistent with what they think is essentially true and relevant according to the deeper, normative truths of their traditions, whether or not their sermons are exegetically on target. Within their normative patterns of faith and practice, all Christian traditions understandably exercise a kind of *sensus plenior,* producing numerous interpretations and applications of biblical texts. The community of faith, whether in Scripture or after Scripture, was always dependent more on established communal norms of faith and practice than on historical exactitude and precise exegesis. The burning hermeneutical point is to submit the norms themselves to critical evaluation in the light of the total witness of Scripture. The "justification theology" focusing on the issue of faith and works is not less traditional simply because a Protestant declares it "biblical." Nor is the "θέωσις theology" focusing on union with Christ in the Spirit unbiblical simply because an Orthodox declares it "traditional." An exegetical approach may well find that both the "participatory" and "forensic" views of salvation are part of the larger biblical witness, and that deeper appreciation of both may be achieved

---

[27] For example, the Evangelical C. Pinnock writes in his *The Scripture Principle,* p. 217, "slogans aside, the Bible is not 'sola' among the factors that influence us. No one can leap over twenty centuries.... Radical biblicism is a delusion." He goes on to affirm both the value of the exegetical wisdom of Christian tradition as well as the safeguard of the living community of believers who collectively have the right and responsibility to assess interpretation. The Orthodox hold exactly to the same position, but in different forms, in that the interpretive decisions of representative ecclesial councils must be accepted by the faithful at large in order to gain permanent legitimacy.

precisely by seeing them in positive comparative light. But the hermeneutical point is that, functionally, whether by selection or omission, Scripture and tradition play equally important roles in every faith community. The difference is that, because of their respective biases, Protestants tend to ignore the role of tradition,[28] whereas the Orthodox tend to boast about it.

In the end, all traditional Christians accept the primacy of Scripture as the hermeneutical ground of truth, but they tend to emphasize different things in Scripture. The element of evaluative choice is inescapable and choices are made according to a respective tradition. Therefore, all Christians as well, including Protestants, explicitly or implicitly, hold to the primacy of tradition as the hermeneutical principle of evaluative interpretation. This is especially true about the ongoing community of faith, which must, in view of changing culture, redefine its positions on vital matters in the light of Scripture and traditional norms. In this case, it is a logical fallacy to speak about either Scripture over the Church or the Church over Scripture because the two factors are of a different order. Scripture is and always remains a "hermeneutical testimony," that is, a record of revelation in need of interpretation. The ongoing community of faith is and always remains a "hermeneutical agent" providing the interpretation. In the functional sense, because Scripture is not a living agent but a written record, and therefore cannot interpret itself, the community of faith has precedence. Christians of all churches are engaged in this kind of dynamic, but they differ significantly regarding the authoritative norms of their respective traditions. In Roman Catholicism, the final authority is the papal magisterium, though not apart from the wisdom of Catholic thinkers, clergy and lay alike. In Orthodoxy, the final authority is conciliar, expressed

---

[28] From the Evangelical side, Gordon D. Fee, *Gospel and Spirit*, pp. 66-82, provides a suggestive analysis of five levels of tradition, including Scripture itself as the first tradition. According to Fee, p. 69, no one escapes the influence of their own confessional traditions which, "wittingly or unwittingly,...shapes both our approach to and our understanding of the biblical texts"; moreover, the unofficial, unwritten traditions may be "sometimes more powerful."

through representative councils, which have authority only as received by the faithful. In Protestantism, the final authority is an elusive combination of individual conscience, popular preachers or authors, and the community of believers as the ultimate reference.[29] Where the authorities are well defined, greater unity is achieved. Where the authorities are not well defined, pluralism reigns.

Where does all this leave us hermeneutically? The answer may be surprisingly simple: with the Bible and the importance of theological scholarship in its exegetical and interpretive tasks. Here is where the two hermeneutical levels, the exegetical and the interpretive, can connect in challenging and fruitful ways. Scripture, as the historical record of revelation, remains the same yesterday, today, and forever. Its witness, in all its historical contingency and religious depth, deserves full exposure on its own terms in every generation. That is the task of historical exegetical scholarship, which should "distance" itself not from the world of the Bible but from the world of contemporary interests. In a second methodological step, speaking formally, all the traditional differences as well as contemporary interests may be fully injected into the discussion at the interpretive level but critically pertaining to what they are and on what assumptions they rely. Exegetes and theologians must work together, being well versed in each other's fields. It becomes fairly clear then, at least for those who strive for a balance between faith and reason, as well as Scripture and tradition, that the interpretive problems are not about a three-storied universe, demons with horns, and ancient forms of slavery,[30] but about current

---

[29] For the Protestant side, see M. A. Noll, *Between Faith and Criticism*, pp.150ff. and 186ff. and C. H. Pinnock, *The Scripture Principle*, pp. 216ff.

[30] Such issues fall on the wayside by the accumulated knowledge and moral sensitivity of ongoing culture. In the case of demonology and angelology, the real issues are not whether demons have horns to frighten people or whether angels have wings to fly, but whether both good and evil have personal dimensions. If one believes that men and women endure beyond the confines of the visible, material world, it is but a small step to believe the demonic and angelic personal beings inhabit a spiritual dimension.

burning issues such as the modern forms of slavery of women and minorities, personal and institutional evil, and the responsible use of and care for creation. These issues cannot, of course, be discussed apart from the broader views of our faith communities about God, Scripture, salvation, the Church, and normative principles of faith and practice. Regrettably, most readers of Scripture, whether expert or not, are so eager to find their own "pre-understandings" confirmed by Scripture or to use data from Scripture polemically in the present, that they mix the exegetical and interpretive dimensions in biblical study. To the extent that sufficient clarity and epistemological humility about all these matters are absent, confusion and presumption prevail.

It seems fairly clear, also, that those who affirm the authority of Scripture and seek to live and work with some balance between faith and reason, will continue to gravitate toward a consensus that is called either "evangelical catholicity" or "catholic evangelicalism" as the enduring Christian option of the third millenium. Semantics apart, historical scholarship has taught us that the nature of Scripture as a book of the Church inexorably drives unbiased Christian thinkers to consider the importance of the "ecclesial principle" and therefore of the normative value of the witness of the historic Church and its classical tradition regarding faith and practice. But the nature of Scripture in its canonical authority also inexorably drives unbiased Christian thinkers to consider the importance of the "scriptural principle" and therefore the normative value of the witness of Scripture for the actual life of the Church. Herein lie the deepest contradictions in catholic Christianity in its Roman Catholic and Orthodox manifestations: on the one hand they tend institutionally to coopt Scripture for themselves in the name of the universal Church, while on the other hand they shirk from measuring their institutional forms and daily habits according to its revelatory authority; on the one hand they pay official respect at the altar of sacred Scripture, yet on the other hand they resist deep renewal in accordance with its evangelical witness.

As Christians countenance each other individually and ecclesially, they have the double burden of being faithful to the witness of Scripture and to the Christian churches that have nurtured them. Hermeneutically, this means that we must be open to the voice of Scripture and its interplay with the voice of tradition, whether weak or deafening within our communities. This is so especially in matters that divide us, including our theologies of θέωσις and "justification." The cutting edge of mutual persuasion at the interpretive level, along with the need of terminological clarifications, is the cogency with which we can explain our particular theological accents in the light of the total witness of Scripture.[31] When our respective biases are unconscious, we can claim some excuse for them. When biases are mutually exposed and retained, they become inexcusable hypocrisies, all the more serious because they involve presumptions about God and his plan of salvation for all people.

In this context, the Church fathers have something important to teach us, not so much on the exegetical level but on the interpretive one, where the patristic hermeneutical interdependence between faith and reason, as well as between Scripture and tradition, is decisive. These hermeneutical factors must not be played off one another. Neither traditionalism nor biblicism, neither fideism nor rationalism, are desirable. We welcome the critical impulse of the Enlightenment, but reject its negative accents. Massive among the Church fathers, the authority of Scripture as the record of revelation is supreme, but Scripture is profoundly a creation of tradition and requires an ongoing ecclesial context of interpretation. Just as tradition must not develop in ways discordant with Scripture, and must be corrected when it does, so also Scripture cannot stifle the creativity of living tradition as it meets new issues in new circumstances.

---

[31] These traditional accents may well be corrected and softened when brought into honest and comparative exegetical and interpretive study, as for example in the cases of texts pertaining to predestination (Rom 9:20-26) and freedom of will (Rom 10:6-13), justification by faith (Gal 2:16-17) and salvation by works (Gal 5:19-21), the saving power of the gospel (Rom 1:16) and the saving efficacy of sacrament (Rom 6:1-11).

Moreover, the Church fathers in their integrative spiritual vision significantly teach us that the pursuit of what is true or false, normative or optional, relevant or irrelevant,[32] has also something essential to do with the hermeneutics of Christian life, the new creation in Christ and the Spirit. The challenge of dealing with our differences and bearing common Christian witness in the third millenium is a call to prayer, repentance, and discernment at the level of a transformed personal and corporate life in which truth itself, the living Lord, is the decisive, persuasive guide.

The Transformative Level

We have come to the third hermeneutical level, the existential or transformative one. This third level is inseparable from the two others and yet distinguishable by its own hermeneutical operations. The following examples may illustrate the interrelationships of the three levels. According to the Gospel of John Christ states: "I give you a new commandment, that you love one another. Just as I have loved you, you also should love one another" (Jn 13:34-35). At the exegetical level, the task is to explore all the nuances of Jesus' teaching about love in the light of his ministry, why the Gospel of John refers to it as a "new commandment," and the comparative importance of love of God and love of neighbor in the Old and New Testaments. At the interpretive level, one faces the evaluative decision whether and how far to assent to Jesus' teaching about love as a relevant or normative truth and resolve to practice it. At the transformative level, one has the possibility of being grasped and changed by the power of Christ's love itself as one fervently embraces the Lord and his words of love in faithful obedience and practice.

---

[32] There is relevance of substance and relevance of function. What is substantively true is always relevant except for those who are unwilling to accept the truth. Yet, a truth needs to be presented also with skill and contextual intelligibility in functional terms. However, a relevance not based on truth but merely on artful sophistry, which can make falsehood seem both relevant and true, is utterly rejectable.

To take another example, St. Paul declares: "No one speaking by the Spirit of God ever says 'Jesus be cursed!' and no one can say 'Jesus is Lord' except by the Holy Spirit" (1 Cor 12:3). At the exegetical level, the task is to ascertain contextually what blasphemers Paul might have had in view, pagans, Jews, gnosticizing Christians and why; what is the background and meaning of the christological title "Lord"; what is the relationship between Lord and Spirit in Paul's thought, and the like. At the interpretive level, one faces the faith decision whether and how far to assent to or dissent from this christological truth on the basis of Paul's testimony. At the transformative level, the personal confession of Jesus as Lord and a new life under his transforming lordship is at hand.

Similar hermeneutical dynamics apply to countless biblical teachings about the person of Christ, the Spirit, the gospel and the kingdom, sin and forgiveness, new creation and the fruit of the Spirit, the Church and its mission in the world. The exegete freely explores the biblical world and can illuminate the background and meaning of biblical concepts and truth claims. When and if the exegete gets out of the historical inquiry – and the danger of historicism is very real in scholarship – he or she is faced with an evaluative decision about the ultimacy of these religious claims. In the latter case, the exegete becomes an interpreter in the deeper sense, which inescapably involves some faith perspective, religious or philosophical. The non-expert reader may be greatly helped by the exegetical details as well as communal interpretive norms, but is not necessarily dependent on them because such a reader encounters the biblical claim ("love one another" or "Jesus is Lord") as it stands. For any reader, transformation hinges more on inner receptivity and the action of the Spirit rather than on the accuracy of exegetical and interpretive knowledge as such. At the transformative level, a simple believer embraces the biblical truth, and is transformed by it through grace without any need whatever to know anything about the various hermeneutical levels and sets of hermeneutical factors. It goes without saying that, for those who do not accept the revelatory character and claims of the biblical witness, talk about a transformative level is meaningless.

Therefore, the role of exegetical hermeneutics is not to make the biblical truth claims "relevant" but to explore the full extent of their meaning for the biblical authors and their communities. The role of interpretive hermeneutics is to take seriously the exegetical results and clarify for the modern readers the range of possible evaluative choices according to faith and reason, Scripture and tradition, Church and culture – and not to make those choices for the readers. While any reader or faith community will unavoidably adopt or assume a particular interpretive hermeneutic, they may not pretend that different options do not exist for others according to their particular presuppositions and community norms. Of course, the common burden of all is to justify the cogency of their particular hermeneutic in view of the exegetical results, especially for those who affirm the authority of the Scriptures.[33] Finally the role of transformative hermeneutics is to reflect on the dynamics of how biblical teachings are actualized in personal and corporate life, that is, how they become the living word of the living God in the present.[34]

The transformative hermeneutical level, which is the level of the direct experience of God and his blessings, is most profound and least open to discursive reason. The decisive interpreter here is the Holy Spirit through his personal initiative and gracious

---

[33] Essentially this implies holding in dialogical, critical comparison on the one hand the exegetical results and on the other the normative principles of life and thought on which a hermeneutic is usually based. Acting in good faith would mean being open to appropriate revision of one's hermeneutic or hermeneutical accents.

[34] What is discussed here as the transformative level is in accordance with traditional biblical and patristic spirituality. An excellent example of this spiritual hermeneutic is Douglas Burton-Christie's *The Word in the Desert*, dealing with the application and actualization of Scripture in the ancient monastic tradition. This perspective is very different from, but not necessarily opposed to, Walter Wink's proposal in *The Bible in Human Transformation* and *Transforming Bible Study* (Nashville: Abingdon, 1980). Wink's view of human transformation relies on the human side of the ledger, that is, on psychoanalytic and neurological considerations

presence. "The Spirit blows wherever it chooses" (Jn 3:8). Conceptual knowledge about God is not crucial, nor is syllogistic analysis of theological and exegetical insights, but the immediate action of divine grace, which is equally available to the simplest believer. "Anyone who claims to know something does not yet have the necessary knowledge; but anyone who loves God is known by him" (1 Cor 8:2-3). The witness of Scripture has to do not only with the intellectual contours of truth, but more deeply with the mystery of God in his personal presence and mercy. While God's gifts and blessings, his kingdom and righteousness, love and forgiveness, healing and renewal, may be provisionally described and interpreted with human words and concepts, they can never be deeply known in the biblical sense except by grace through faith. To quote the psalmist, "For with you is the fountain of life; in your light we see light" (Ps 36:9).

The actualization of this deepest value of Scripture cannot occur apart from the present action of the risen Christ and the Spirit in the context of obedient, humble, and prayerful Christian living. Only God can reveal God, and God does so to receptive minds and repentant hearts as they encounter the good news. Habakkuk declared that "the righteous live by their faith" (Hab 2:4). St. Paul, quoting Habakkuk applies this declaration to the preaching of the gospel through which "the righteousness of God is revealed through faith for faith" (Rom 1:17). He asks

---

of left-brain and right-brain operations and on engaging biblical readers in wholistic, interactive encounters based on existential questions (for example, when meditating on the healing of the paralytic, what are the forms of my and your own paralysis, etc.?). Although help from the medical and social sciences in Christian nurture is welcome, one sorely misses in Wink the focus on Christ, the Spirit, faith, repentance, prayer, and Christian daily conduct. Thus one remains with the impression that Wink's proposal for transformation is equally achievable with any significant texts or stories drawn from any literature, religious or secular. While this is not a bad thing in itself – people are renewed and transformed in their own way by vital connections with their literature – Wink's proposal lacks the theological foundation and vision proper to the biblical witness. In liberal fashion, it seems to use Scripture in a functional way for "human" transformation but does not take from Scripture the core of its own message and witness.

the Galatians, "Did you receive the Spirit by doing the works of the law or by believing what you heard" (Gal 3:2)? The biblical and patristic hermeneutical circle is thus complete: the same Spirit that inspired the sacred text is also its chief interpreter. At this level, the reading and appropriation of Scripture constitute charismatic activity. It is at this level that the issue of the *sensus plenior* in its proper sense arises. It is here that interpretation, spirituality, theology, and practice are integrated aspects of the one reality of the new life in Christ.

From the patristic tradition, a striking example of transformative hermeneutics at work is provided by the Orthodox saint and mystic, Symeon the New Theologian (949-1022). In his discourse *On Spiritual Knowledge* (see Appendix 2), St. Symeon writes about the theologians of his time who – Symeon does not essentially dispute the fact – know and teach theological knowledge but "lean on the mere study of the Scriptures." As in the case of the biblical authors whom he has constantly in view, Symeon does not take up the "hermeneutical problem" for theoretical discussion, but what he does have to say carries immense hermeneutical implications. According to Symeon, scholars may have expert knowledge of Scripture, but no experiential inkling of the transformed life to which Scripture testifies. He expresses amazement that theological scholars of his time would claim true knowledge and assume the role of leaders and teachers, yet concede that they have never consciously experienced the Spirit's presence and radiance. For Symeon, true knowledge is experiential knowledge of the transcendent realities attested by Scripture, and not mere conceptual knowledge of biblical teachings gained by erudition, even though this too may be derivatively called knowledge. The spiritual treasures of the Bible are so sealed to ordinary discursive thinking that it is not "by the Scripture that the contents of Scripture become clear." At this deep level of knowledge, it is not the Bible that makes the Bible clear! According to Symeon, only the risen Christ and the Spirit can disclose the spiritual treasures of Scripture to those who in the process, provided their life of faithful obedience to Christ and the Spirit, are inwardly renewed and "born from above."[35]

Faith and reason, experiential and conceptual knowledge, are not opposed by Symeon, himself a man of notable discursive and literary talents. But "the hidden power of faith," illuminated and energized by the Spirit, moves beyond human skill and erudition to apprehend existentially the essence of Scripture's testimony, a dynamic state of θεωρία or mystical cognition,[36] which makes a great deal of difference how one ultimately views Scripture and what one does with it. Correct conceptual knowledge is necessary but experiential knowledge is fullness of life given to those who believe in word and deed. The key to true knowledge is the Holy Spirit in whom the Father and the Son are known in the biblical sense. Mystical cognition has to do not with abstract theological truths, that is, conceptual maps, but rather with the reality of new creation, that is, personal knowledge of the living God in his presence and power, who shines light and life in the hearts and lives of believers. Hence St. Symeon's remarkable statement: "Knowledge is not the light! Rather, it is the light that is knowledge, since 'in it [him] and through it [him] and from it [him] are all things.'"[37]

Although charismatic and mystical, Symeon's appeal is decidedly not esoteric because he is talking about the experience of God and his blessings, an experience open to every reader of the Bible. It is most interesting that Symeon is dependent on straight reading of the Bible with no reliance on allegorical or

---

[35] St. Symeon in his writings clearly teaches an adult baptism of the Holy Spirit, not in opposition to but in renewal of sacramental baptism. In a remarkable passage he writes the following: "We shamelessly presume to teach the multitude about the light of knowledge, and even to show them the light of knowledge itself! Knowledge is not the light! Rather, it is the light that is knowledge.... We refuse the vision of light, and so make it plain that we have not been born again, and have not attained to the light that comes from above ... we who rush to the sacred places and take possession of apostolic thrones!" See C. J. deCatanzaro, *Symeon the New Theologian: The Discourses*, p. 301.

[36] See James R. Price, "Mystical Transformation of Consciousness in St. Symeon the New Theologian," *Diakonia* 19 (1-3, 1984-1985), pp. 6-16.

[37] C. J. deCatanzaro, *Symeon the New Theologian: Discourses*, p. 301, who renders the pronoun for light as "it." However, Romans 11:36, which Symeon is

typological interpretations. For transformative reading of Scripture, what is required is neither great learning nor some esoteric technique, but rather a living faith and prayerful obedience demanded by Scripture's own plain witness. Given such faith, according to Symeon, God's gracious action in the reader is unfailing because of God's love and faithfulness beyond all syllogistic analysis and proofs.[38]

Accordingly, the hermeneutical problem at the transformative level is essentially not an intellectual but a spiritual one. The crux of the problem is lack of faith, unwillingness to hear and obey God's word, unbelief in all its spiritual, practical, and psychological dimensions. The resolution lies in the personal act of faith and all that is implied by the life of faith, including genuine repentance, struggle against sin, and maturation in

---

quoting, and certainly the discourses of Symeon himself, indisputably point not to abstract but personal light, the Lord himself.

[38] In Discourses 28-36, St. Symeon, with flaming zeal, expounds on the reality and accessibility of the new life in Christ for every person, presenting "the truth from divine Scripture and from experience," C. J. deCatanzaro, p. 352. "We restore the teachings of the Master and the apostles that some have perverted. From the very divine Scriptures themselves we collect that which strengthens and corrects their thinking and that of their followers," p. 354. He tells of leaving every other occupation in life to labor day and night excavating the Scriptures (p. 355) until, by Christ's luminous intervention, they yielded their spiritual treasure, the reborn and risen life in Christ, which requires crucifixion of the old nature in Pauline terms. Though accused of being boastful, he boldly parallels his witness to that of the apostles and the Church fathers who had the mind of Christ, a "ministry to the Spirit" (p. 350), against which resisters and opponents commit the unpardonable sin of blasphemy. Nothing can hinder, nor is more critical than, this apostolic witness to the renewed life in union with Christ and the Spirit as an ongoing present reality, without which all are slaves of this world and sit in darkness, whether emperors or patriarchs, prelates or priests, lay persons or monks (p. 298). All must be judged according to their fruits, including Symeon himself who claims to know of that which he is speaking (p. 298) and yet humbly submits his witness to the test of others and puts himself under anathema: "You, on your part, must see and test that which we say. If we have views different from those of the apostles and of the holy God-inspired fathers, if we speak contrary to what they said, if we fail to repeat what the Holy Gospels say about God, then let me be anathema from the Lord God Jesus Christ," p. 354.

Christ. However, faith at the tranformative level is not merely ζῶσα
formal faith, what some Church fathers call ψιλὴ πίστις (literally "thin faith"), that is, intellectual assent to biblical truths that
can be cleverly manipulated in one fashion or
another. Rather, it is what the fathers call "living faith" (ζῶσα
πίστις) in the profound biblical sense, an act of trust and commitment to the living God himself, which leads to repentance
and a life of righteousness. If faith at the interpretive level functions as assent to authoritative scriptural truth, faith at the
transformative level functions as personal appropriation of the
divine power of that truth. Living faith, energized by the Spirit,
involves an inner spiritual awakening that opens the believer in
varying degrees to direct and immediate experience of God in
his holy presence and forgiving love. Biblical faith is trust in and
obedience to the living God who calls for faith and obedience
precisely because of his giving evidence of himself and his moral
will. Biblical faith has to do with covenantal fidelity between
God and believer, which is tested in real life, even by way of
suffering and argument with God, yet one that can never be
coopted or manipulated by the human partner.

It is entirely regrettable that in ordinary human thinking, and
among many Christians themselves, faith is trivialized as a lower
form of knowledge, superficial or fanatical religiosity, naive or
vague optimism, or a risky leap into the unknown. Did not
Jeremiah and Ezekiel have evidence of God on the basis of their
own call and ministry in those turbulent times? Would not
Peter and Paul provide evidence for their faith in Christ, which
took them to martyrdom? Have not St. Symeon and countless
other men and women, instruments of God's work over the ages,
had evidence of God's presence and knowledge in their lives? It
is not a case of wisdom but of foolishness that "modern" or
"postmodern" men and women should set aside this bright cloud
of witnesses to the direct experience of God, especially the primary figures of Scripture and the great saints of history, and
replace it with some general and ambiguous "experience of
modern man" as an evaluative category. While these witnesses

may not provide "proofs" to satisfy the skeptic, the same skeptic should in turn know that, for the beholder of God in his light and love, the skeptic's search for controlling scientific or syllogistic "proofs" is childish in view of the immense mystery of life.

Hermeneutical reflection on the transformative level involves a deeper and more personal creative tension between faith and reason. It has to deal discursively and conceptually with the issue of the direct experience of God, which is beyond concepts and syllogisms – beyond but not against. Once again, we meet up with the need of a viable balance between experiential faith and syllogistic thought, as well as with the inseparability of the three hermeneutical levels. At the exegetical level, one can ascertain the fact that Scripture, as well as tradition, includes direct, eye-witness accounts of immediate experiences of God (Is 6:1-8; Gal 1:13-17) and more often secondary and tertiary reports of divine disclosures. At the interpretive level, one has to assess these accounts and reports from a systematic viewpoint and attempt to define criteria to determine the most authentic expressions of the faith experience of the living God according to Scripture and tradition. At the transformative level, one's own faith experience, positive or negative, yet not apart from reason, is inescapably engaged, which in turn gives the possibility of existential encounter with the living God and his blessings in varying degrees of spiritual discernment and transformative power. Such encounter or refusal of it, of course, colors one's whole life perspective, including one's most decisive view of Scripture and its value as sacred book; that is, whether Scripture testifies to true knowledge of God or to merely human religious constructs. To the degree that a reader or interpreter nurtures a faith life with God in the present, to the same degree he or she finds abundance of relevant meaning in the Scriptures.

Given these qualifications, transformative hermeneutics must further explore a number of questions, which can only be mentioned here. What are the dynamics of faith and unbelief in their practical, psychological, and spiritual dimensions? How are the Orthodox concept of θεωρία, the Roman Catholic notion of *sensus plenior*, and the Protestant view of inner illumination related; and, to what extent can they be comparatively discussed and defined for the sake of clarity in ecumenical hermeneutical discussion? What is the nature of mystical cognition pertaining to the immediate experience of God in his numinous presence and power, especially in biblical perspective?[39] How can the dynamic relationship between the experiential and cognitive dimensions in the saving experience of God be discussed according to recognizable terms or criteria? Can some bridge be constructed between two streams of hermeneutics inclined to go in opposite directions, namely, on the one hand toward the theological and experiential and on the other hand toward the philosophical and abstract? In what ways can our own paradigm of the three hermeneutical levels be clarified or revised toward a more satisfactory treatment of the "hermeneutical problem?" If hermeneutics at the deepest level is the translation or transference of meaning, and ultimate meaning is inseparable from a particular life stance, what guiding criteria can be offered either to justify or alter one's life stance?

From a patristic perspective, there are two major controlling references at the transformative level. One is the canonical biblical text itself as it stands and the other is the community of faith that bears the responsibility of assessing charismatic claims. These guiding references, too, require careful attention. With regard to the text, primary weight must be given to its grammatical and contextual meaning. Apart from this exegetical meaning, and apart from the interpretive norms or patterns chosen or assumed by the community, transformation may quickly become a matter of pure subjectivism. To repeat, the transformative, interpretive, and exegetical levels cannot be

---

[39] An extremely interesting effort to explicate Christology partly in terms of the category of "divine presence" is by Gerald O'Collins, *Christology: A Biblical, Historical, and Systematic Study of Jesus* (Oxford: Oxford University Press, 1995). See especially his Chapter 7 on "The Possibilities of Presence."

ultimately separated. Nor may the transcendent and cognitive aspects of the biblical religious claims be played off one another.

In this regard, those who hold to the authority of Scripture and seek a viable balance between faith and reason gravitate toward similar hermeneutical positions. According to the recent official statement of the Pontifical Biblical Commission, "the spiritual sense is not to be confused with subjective interpretations stemming from the imagination or intellectual speculation."[40] This is especially true with regard to the mystery of Christ and the life that issues from that mystery. "The spiritual sense can never be stripped of its connection with the literal sense ... [which] remains the indispensable foundation."[41] In a similar way, the Evangelical biblical scholar, Donald G. Bloesch, proposes a "historical-pneumatic hermeneutics" according to which the cognitive biblical•truth derived by historical critical exegesis, when received by faith, becomes a transformative personal revelation of God's word by the power of the Spirit. Bloesch develops a mediating hermeneutical position between Scripture as a storehouse of universal unchanging truths according to traditional Protestant orthodoxy and Scripture as a witness of human religious constructs according to various contemporary philosophico-literary hermeneutics.[42]

From the Orthodox side, John Panagopoulos is a strong advocate of holding together the exegetical and transformative dimensions of "the same biblical text" according to the model of the classic doctrine of Christ as "the one and same person" in two natures.[43] By means of a patristic hermeneutic, which he

---

[40] Pontifical Biblical Commission, "The Interpretation of the Bible in the Church," *Or* 23 (29, 1994), p. 512.

[41] *Ibid.*

[42] Donald G. Bloesch, *Holy Scripture: Revelation, Inspiration and Interpretation,* pp. 200-218.

[43] John Panagopoulos formulates a patristic hermeneutic on the basis of his magisterial three-volume work on the exegetical work of the Church fathers entitled Ἡ Ἑρμηνεία τῆς Ἁγίας Γραφῆς στὴν Ἐκκλησία τῶν Πατέρων of which the first volume has been published (Athens: Akritas, 1991). His hermeneutical position is presented in his Εἰσαγωγὴ στὴν Καινὴ Διαθήκη, pp. 430-459.

calls "christological, biblical, and ecclesial," Panagopoulos seeks to accommodate the pluralism of historical and literary methods and results under a unitive christological focus established exegetically from the New Testament and actualized in the life of the Church. For him, because Scripture is a historical document open to scholarly study through the accepted critical historico-philological standards, it cannot be absolutized as a self-sufficient holy book of eternal divine truths to be mined by theological reason. Rather, it is a record of revelation, that is, an interpretation of soteriological events and soteriological realities (τὰ πράγματα) to which Scripture bears written testimony and which are actualized in the community of believers, those who in faithful repentance receive the Spirit and constitute the body of Christ. Thus, primacy belongs not to the historical, biographical, ethical, or religious information derived from Scripture but instead to the soteriological mystery of Christ and his blessings, which can be known to the extent that the believer participates in that mystery "co-ascending" with Christ to the mount of the transfiguration. Neither is the Church master (κυρίαρχος) of Scripture, nor is Scripture the criterion judging the Church, according to false Western alternatives. Rather, Scripture and Church are identical in witness and function, manifesting the mystery of Christ. The Church is "the living Bible of Christ" (Χριστοῦ βίβλος ἔμψυχος)[44] because it is in its faith and practice – above all in its worship – that the fullness of Christ is actualized.

Panagopoulos formulates an ecclesial hermeneutic in idealistic terms. Would that the Orthodox Church in its visible life, that is, its institutional forms and the actual ways of its people, be the manifest fullness of the mystery of Christ! We Orthodox affirm that it is so and it should be so. But then, openly or subtly, we are challenged by the question: how are we to explain the reality of disputes in ecclesiastical politics and the obvious secular values among many Orthodox faithful, seemingly so distant from the spirit of Christ? Perhaps one answer is

---

[44] An Orthodox hymnological expression applied to the Virgin Mary which Panagopoulos knowingly applies to the Church.

perhaps

that the Church in practice has assumed, for many centuries, to be the master of Scripture and has not sufficiently allowed Scripture to be its primary guide, as the great Church fathers require for whom the authority of Scripture was direct and indisputable.

Did not Orthodox saints and fathers, from John Chrysostom to Symeon the New Theologian and Kosmas Aitolos, exercise a prophetic critique on the actual life of the Church on the basis of Scripture? Or, are we to assume that the visible Church and its countless written and oral traditions are not at all prone to error contrary to the implication of Florovsky's dictum that tradition has to do with truth rather than antiquity? Sorely missed in Panagopoulos' thought are hermeneutical elements on which to base a healthy critique of the Church in its actual life and practice. By virtually identifying Scripture and Church, and surrendering the dominance one-sidedly to the Church, the hermeneutic of Panagopoulos idealizes the Church and seems to silence the voice of Scripture. One wonders, then, on the one hand what happens to the patristic balance between Scripture and tradition, and, on the other hand, what is the purpose of biblical scholarship if not to keep the critical and prophetic voice of Scripture alive in the Church.

We agree with the fundamental thrust of Panagopoulos' hermeneutic but would insist that a greater balance between Scripture and tradition, as well as faith and reason, is a more accurate patristic hermeneutical position. The patristic concept of the "sufficiency" (αὐτάρκεια)[45] of the Scriptures according to their revelatory authority and canonical status must be given more weight. While the Church is the final authority in the interpretation of its Scriptures, it is also supremely accountable

---

sufficiency, not self-sufficient

[45] St. Athanasios, *Against the Greeks*, in the prologue. Cf. *The Life of Anthony*, 16. For the Church fathers, in practice and theory, Scripture was the sufficient source of saving truth and thus the primary guide of the Church's life. However, this principle does not mean that the Bible as Holy Scripture can stand by itself, or interpret itself, in isolation from the Church. The point is "sufficiency" and not "self-sufficiency."

to Scripture's inspired witness, a matter of utmost seriousness for the faith and practice of the Church. Among other things, this means holding to an integral connection between the cognitive meaning of the text at the exegetical level and its spiritual meaning and power at the transformative level in order to avoid subjectivism and arbitrariness.

In their many works, Athanasios, Basil, and Chrysostom for the most part derive their understanding of and teach the "soteriological realities" (τὰ πράγματα) from and through the biblical text, whether in matters of doctrine or daily living. They avoid the extremes of literalism and allegorism. They do not view Scripture as a deposit of platonic truths but they certainly derive clear and abiding teachings from it, which they fully expect God's people to obey. Moreover, these teachings pertain not only to doctrine but also to practical matters such as ownership and the use of property, leadership and the appropriate attitudes and conduct of shepherds as they tend to God's flock. It is somewhat paradoxical that, while recognizing that Athanasios marks a definitive departure from the platonic worldview as it influenced Alexandrian allegorism, Panagopoulos, in his overall hermeneutical thought, seems to incline toward an Origenist position by his excessive emphasis on the charismatic, mystical dimension of scriptural interpretation.[46]

In this connection, Orthodox biblical scholars need to pay closer attention and do greater justice to the nuanced positions of their Roman Catholic and Protestant colleagues. In particular, many Evangelical scholars such as Donald G. Bloesch, Gordon D. Fee, and James I. Packer, appear to have the closest

---

[46] Referring approvingly to a point made by T. F. Torrance, Panagopoulos, Ἡ Ἑρμηνεία τῆς Ἁγίας Γραφῆς στὴν Ἐκκλησία τῶν Πατέρων, p. 329, writes: "A first basic consequence and new element of biblical hermeneutics [in the Church fathers] is the definitive abandonment by Athanasios the Great of the platonic distinction between the visible and intelligible world, which is the basis of the Alexandrian allegorical method and consequently of the Origenist contrast between the letter and the Spirit." On the other hand, elsewhere, p. 280, Panagopoulos writes: "Origen was and remains the founder and pioneer of biblical hermeneutics, the inexhaustible fountain of sound ecclesial biblical interpretation."

affinities to Orthodox scholars, at least pertaining to Scripture. These and other Evangelicals form a kind of "golden mean" between fundamentalism and liberal Protestantism, working out their own kind of "neo-patristic synthesis" within the diverse world of Protestantism. To be sure, such Evangelicals need to rethink the "ecclesial principle" as expressed by the Orthodox tradition, and some are doing so. However, pertaining to the "scripture principle," leaving aside *sola Scriptura* and "inerrancy" as slogans, these Evangelical scholars, in their affirmation of the authority of Scripture and their demand for the visible actualization of its evangelical content and spirit in the concrete life of the Church, appear to be even more "patristic" than many Orthodox who think of the patristic heritage as their own inheritance.

Bull Crap!

For example, J. I. Packer centers an incisive critique of modern hermeneutical theories precisely on the integral connection between the cognitive and personal dimensions of the biblical word.[47] For Packer "to set propositional and personal revelation in opposition to each other is ... to enmesh oneself in a patently false antithesis."[48] The extreme in the former case depersonalizes biblical revelation into a kind of conveyance of "information one finds in official memoranda or company reports" and renders "evangelical rationality in interpretation to look like a viciously self-reliant rationalism."[49] The extreme in the latter case is to lapse into subjectivism. According to Packer, the critical error in modern hermeneutics since Schleiermacher and all who are dependent on his philosophical surrender of truth to the scientific method – and who, one might add, tend to think only of their own hermeneutical positions as being "modern" – is the abandonment of the classic Christian idea that Scripture provides true cognitive knowledge and instruction from God and about God. Once divine revelation is

---

[47] James I. Packer, "Infallible Scripture and the Role of Hermeneutics," in *Scripture and Truth*, ed. D. A. Carson and John D. Woodbridge, pp. 325-356.

[48] *Ibid.*, p. 334.

[49] *Ibid.*, pp. 335 and 347.

understood essentially in terms of feeling, religious consciousness, or imaginative understanding, the flood gates open to all kinds of subjective religiosity and empty theological speculation.[50] The end is predictable: the debunking of all hermeneutical systems on the premise that the possibility of accurate transcultural communication between the ancient and modern world is virtually non-existent.[51]

For Packer, revelation is wholistic and personal, and thus "embodied not only in propositions ... but also in the attitudes, wishes, invitations, appeals, and reactions that they [God's

---

[50] This is how Packer sums up modern hermeneutical systems which, after denying that the biblical text communicates true knowledge from and about God, end up grounding themselves on the "I guess" of subjectivity: "Examples of such systems are: the reconstructed gnosticism of Paul Tillich...; the modified deism of Maurice Wiles...; the dynamic unitarianism of Geoffrey Lampe...; the dualistic existentialism of Bultmann...; the process theology of John Cobb... an endless succession of diverging personal theologies... once the acknowledgment of Scripture teaching as revealed truth is given up," p. 338. His critique of the "new hermeneutic" of Ernst Fuchs and others is scathing: "The new hermeneutic is in truth the end of the Schleiermacherian road ... beyond which there is nowhere to go. Logically, the new hermeneutic is relativism; philosophically, it is irrationalism; psychologically, it is freedom to follow unfettered religious fancy; theologically, it is unitarianism; religiously, it is uncontrolled individualistic mysticism; structurally it is all these things not by accident but of necessity," p. 344.

[51] The position of Dennis Nineham in his *The Use and Abuse of the Bible* (London: Macmillan, 1976) which Packer critiques. Packer concedes that there are significant cultural and attitudinal differences between ancient and modern people, but disagrees that these are so radical as to make the biblical authors and their contemporaries unintelligible to us. Not only expert sociological opinion is lacking on this score but also the possibility of all historical knowledge, including Nineham's own confident exegetical work, is undercut by skepticism about transcultural communication which, according to Packer, is "nonsense." For Packer the cutting edge of Nineham's thesis is that modern people like himself are positivistic and antisupernatural and thus cannot make much sense of biblical theism. In reply Packer states that one of Scripture's jobs is precisely "to challenge and undercut 'modern' positivistic deism, panentheism, and atheism, just as it challenged and undercut the then 'modern' polytheistic paganism of the Greco-Roman world in the first Christian centuries. Presuppositional errors of cultures need to be nailed no less firmly than those of individuals," p. 331.

spokesmen] expressed by the way they put things."[52] Yet Packer, does not underestimate the cultural distance between modern and ancient people regarding such things as manners, attitudes, and assumptions. He takes note of H. J. Cadbury's warning of long ago about the peril of "modernizing" Jesus. However, according to Packer, skepticism about transcultural empathy and understanding is untenable unless one is prepared entirely to undercut the study of all religion, history, and literature. The deepest human experiences, such as love of a spouse, admiration for a hero, and knowledge of God are communicable across historical and cultural divides by empathetic understanding to those who are receptive. As much as Schleiermacher must be given his due, however, Gadamer's corrective is both appropriate and substantial. "Distancing" must precede "fusing" of cultural horizons in order both to understand Scripture on its own terms and to allow Scripture by its impact to extend or redraw our own horizons. Nevertheless, valuable as Gadamer's hermeneutical reflections are, so Packer states, they do nothing to bridge "the theological Grand Canyon that yawns between the evangelical and the Schleiermacherian views of Scripture"[53] pertaining to true cognitive knowledge of God gained by sound exegetical work.

We agree with Packer's critique about transcultural communication but would add the following qualification. Packer's critique applies chiefly at the level of historical understanding involving reason and empathetic imagination. This is a necessary and important part of human communication but secondary to the transformative appropriation of Scripture's saving message by the grace of the Holy Spirit, a truth with which we are sure Packer would agree. In the previous presentation of St. Symeon's views, it is extremely important to mark that Symeon was not talking merely about a cultural transference of the "religious understanding" or the "religious

---

[52] *Ibid.*, p. 334. What is said about Packer's thought in this paragraph derives from pp. 330-332 and 338-340.

[53] *Ibid.*

experience" of a particular biblical author in human terms, although he assumed that such understanding was generally possible in that the theologians of his time had indeed acquired sufficient informational knowledge of what the biblical authors experienced and taught. Rather, he was talking about the believer's own direct and personal experience of the risen Lord and his blessings in the present, actualized by initiative of the Holy Spirit, as the believer engaged the witness of Scripture and responded to the saving good news. Symeon's thesis was precisely that a theological expert could have correct conceptual knowledge by leaning on the "mere study of Scripture," but could woefully lack the experiential transformation granted by the Lord himself through the Spirit. He was astounded that churchmen and theologians could intellectually traffic in God's word but show no signs of the new life in Christ through living faith, genuine repentance, and prayerful obedience to the Lord.

Therefore, at the transformative level, the crucial hermeneutical point is not to relive the exact personal religious understanding or religious experience of Peter or Paul according to the hermeneutical ideal of Schleiermacher. Rather, the point is to open oneself to the Lord's active presence here and now as one encounters God's saving word and thus to be transformed by the Lord's living word in the context of one's own background, personal circumstances, and intimate understanding intellectually and emotionally. Packer himself affirms that the correct application of biblical knowledge is not a strictly rational process because the Holy Spirit, "the great hermeneut," leads and enlightens us in biblical study interpreting God's word in our minds and hearts.[54] The substantive continuity in the salvific experience between the biblical author and the contemporary believer is the Holy Spirit, whose nature and saving action cannot be essentially different in one age from another, but who acts contextually and intimately in the life of each believer. From the human side, the principle of transformational evaluation, one to which St. Symeon frequently appeals, is the Lord's: "You

---

[54] *Ibid.*, p. 347.

will know them by their fruits" (Mt 7:16). The Orthodox and Evangelicals would, of course, agree that an authentic contemporary experience of Christ, granted its peculiarly personal aspects, can neither be apart from the apostolic framework of scriptural truth nor yield different fruit than the fruit of the Spirit as attested by Scripture. Though distinguishable, the cognitive and transformative dimensions of God's word can never be disjoined.[55]

Next to the primacy of the biblical text, the second controlling reference at the transformative level is the community of faith, the Church, which is charged to "test the spirits" (1 Jn 4:1). We have already underscored the decisive hermeneutical function of the community of faith at the interpretive level where the ecclesial community inescapably selects, assesses, and develops norms of faith and life on the basis of its interpreted reading of Scripture. The Church is a critical "hermeneutical agent" at both the interpretive and transformative levels. During the last generation, the convergence of ecumenical discussion on the ecclesiological issue, that is, the nature of the Church not only in theory but also in practice, has been both welcome and promising. After all the biblical scholarship of the twentieth century, scholars and theologians can no longer in good faith minimize either the historical or theological importance of the community of faith in the formation of Scripture from the oral proclamation of God's word to the canonization of the Christian Bible through tradition, including church officials and councils.

The same is equally true about the actualization of God's

---

[55] Again I would stress that, if the "ecclesial principle" as well is brought into play, Orthodox and Evangelical scholars can support each other in substantive terms on the basis of their unanimity on classic Christian doctrine as a summary of abiding biblical truth. Their theological commitments and contemporary circumstances drive them together to work toward a common witness and common biblical hermeneutics beyond Schleiermacher and Gadamer, and beyond most modern hermeneutical theorists, including the so-called new literary critics, who still operate within the framework of "modern" hermeneutical assumptions.

living word in the Church's concrete communal faith and life.[56] Indeed, the biblical text itself in countless places underscores that faith and life according to the biblical tradition is communal rather than individualistic.[57] The reality of the community, "the Church of God" (ἡ ἐκκλησία τοῦ Θεοῦ, 1 Cor 1:1; 1 Tim 3:15), is a constitutive part of God's good news of salvation in incarnational concreteness.[58] With a touch of humor, Orthodox Christians, having learned from Protestant biblical scholars, now ask their Protestant brothers and sisters, especially those who hold to the authority of the Bible, to go back and underline those biblical passages about the Church and its life that they have apparently missed.[59] However, apart from humor and beyond sloganeering on all sides, the biblical

---

[56] The actualization of God's word in the Church's communal life is especially stressed by St. Basil according to Philip Rousseau, *Basil of Caesarea*, pp. 106-131. St. Basil, who distinguished between mere opinions and established positions on controversial issues, took his stand over against Eunomios on the all-sufficient truth of the gospel transmitted through the apostolic tradition and actualized particularly in the worship of the Church. For St. Basil, according to Rousseau (p. 122), tradition links epistemology and ecclesiology.

[57] A welcome hermeneutical conclusion drawn by Gordon D. Fee, *Gospel and Spirit*, p. 82, who among other things writes: "I think, for example, of such a simple thing as the recognition of our own personal histories in a thoroughly individualistic culture, and how differently – and more correctly – we will understand and apply [the biblical] texts when we recognize the essentially corporate – people as a whole people – presupposition that lies behind all the epistolary imperatives."

[58] Mt 16:18; 18:17; Acts 15:3ff.; 1 Cor 3:16-17; 10:16-17; 11:20-22; 12:12ff.; Eph 1:23-24; 3:10-11; Col. 1:24; 1 Tim 3:15.

[59] It is interesting to note that major Evangelical hermeneutical works such as *The Scripture Principle* by C. H. Pinnock and *Scripture and Truth* and *Hermeneutics, Authority, and Canon*, ed. D. A. Carson and J. D. Woodbridge do not contain a single chapter or section focused on the Church as hermeneutical context; but otherwise D. G. Bloesch, *Holy Scripture*, who includes a chapter on "Scripture and the Church" (note: not "The Church and Scripture" which is the correct historical and theological perspective). Equally interesting is that, when Evangelicals consider their own differences and differences with other Christians, they begin to raise the ecclesiological issue for themselves, as for example M. A. Noll, *Between Faith and Criticism*, second edition, 150ff.; 160ff.; 186ff.

witness itself requires that committed followers of Christ discuss together biblical teachings concerning the Church as well as the gospel, canonical order as well as inner illumination, sacramental life as well as justification by faith. All this applies simultaneously at the exegetical level of Scripture's witness, at the interpretive level of the normative forms of teaching worked out in various faith traditions, as well as at the transformative level of the immediate encounter with God and his gracious presence in the life of the faith community.

At the transformative level, we meet not abstract ecclesiology, important as this is, but the actual life of the Church, its worship and practice, its leaders and faithful, women and men, with all their particularities of circumstances, values, attitudes, and conduct. We have a right according to the witness of Scripture to behold, without being superficially idealistic, tangible expressions of the new humanity in Christ in the total *praxis* of the Church from worship and prayer to administration and finances, from theological scholarship to pastoral care. Whatever the problems of the Christians at Corinth, the Apostle admonished them that they were God's temple in which God's Spirit dwelt (1 Cor 3:16), the sacramental body of Christ (1 Cor 10:16-17; 11:27-29; 12:12). In Romans, he expounds justification by faith (3:21ff.) and renewal through baptism (Rom 6:3ff.), demonstrated by the transformed personal and corporate existence of believers "who have come alive as from the dead" – ὡσεὶ ἐκ νεκρῶν ζῶντας (Rom 6:13; cf. Rom 12:1ff.)!

What are the visible expressions of the "new creation" in the contemporary Church? Without signs of the renewed humanity, humbleness, holiness, justice, unity, love, and care for the downtrodden, the Church's witness to the accomplished work of Christ is seriously undermined and appears hollow to believers and unbelievers alike. The entire *praxis* of the Church – liturgy, preaching, teaching, order, pastoral care, moral conduct, service, witness, and mission – cries out for "hermeneutical reflection." Exegetical hermeneutics is reflection on how to glean the authentic message of Scripture in all its nuances.

Interpretive hermeneutics is reflection on how to arrive at the normative theological and moral aspects of the biblical witness. Transformative hermeneutics is reflection on how the saving message of Scripture and its normative aspects become living truth, God's living word, in the *praxis* of the Church. Although all three hermeneutics are necessary and integral to each other, the third is supremely important as the proof of the pudding. Whatever the exegetical methods, whatever the theological truths, and whatever the hermeneutical theories about communication and transference of knowledge, the actualization of God's saving work as attested by Scripture occurs at the level of actual life here and now as both clergy and lay pray, repent, think, and work, always looking for the Lord's personal presence and guidance in all things.

Transformative hermeneutics is critical in function as well as substance, seeking both spiritual discernment and existential access to new life. It calls the Church to be itself in, but not of, the world, a spiritual movement as well as a historical institution. It drives the Church to mission and service, which can be accomplished to the degree that the Church itself demonstrates unity in Christ and radiates the newness of the Spirit. The Church can try to hide from its own eyes but not from the eyes of the world, and certainly not from the eyes of God. The Church will inevitably have a hermeneutic of *praxis*; better to have a reflected and explicit hermeneutic, one that can be measured over against Scripture's witness. A dichotomy between *praxis* and *theoria* is inadmissible. Some gap between ideal and reality is part of the human condition in which we live eschatologically and see provisionally (1 Cor 13:12). But if the gap strains faith and truth, the community becomes a scandal to its own members and a spectacle to the world. The Lord speaks to his followers in each local church: "You are the salt of the earth; but if salt has lost its taste, how can its saltiness be restored" (Mt 5:13)? Similar words of the Lord may be found in the early chapters of the Book of Revelation, applicable corporately to local churches themselves.

Transformative hermeneutics becomes decisive also in

dealing with doctrinal differences and new questions under the inspiration of the Paraclete, whose function is to lead the Church to new insights and new actions amidst the struggles and divisiveness within its own life and that of the world. We have already mentioned that the most challenging aspect of the hermeneutical problem is that, while normative forms of faith and practice are grounded in the tradition of the past, the living community itself affirms its identity and tradition anew by means of reinterpretation in the face of new challenges. The total hermeneutical process, just as life itself, remains open-ended until the coming of the Lord. For each faith community, the crux of the hermeneutical challenge lies in the present, as circumstances change and new questions arise.

Discussion of issues, whether old or new, is never foreclosed among God's people. Debate and controversy may be signs of growth and vitality, not always confusion and disruption. Besides, God sometimes tears down in order to build up. Living tradition is creative and necessitates newly defined positions on old and new questions – faith and doctrine, word and sacrament, gender and liberation, racism and social justice – as long as these positions are consistent with the witness of Scripture and the core theological tradition of the Church which, under divine inspiration, has set canonical boundaries to the biblical tradition itself. However, what is consistent or inconsistent is not only a matter for experts to decide in formal deliberations. It is, above all, a matter of spiritual discernment involving the whole Church, lay and clergy in their respective ministries, being equally responsible before God and unceasingly invoking the present guidance of his Spirit, who is the very source of new life and correct discernment.[60] But the Spirit nei-

---

[60] Similarly, Thomas Hopko, "The Bible in the Orthodox Church," p. 9, appeals to the ultimacy and immediacy of the Holy Spirit and states: "Every 'external criterion of truth' has been denied over and over again, be it the Bible, council, magisterium, hierarchy.... There is no secure, automatic way to the knowledge of God or to certain, infallible truth; there is no way but the way of Christ in the Spirit in freedom and love and purity, the way shown in the Bible and the Church Tradition, the way to be realized and fulfilled in freedom by every generation

ther works mechanically, nor imposes itself on leaders and people. The Spirit radiates the wisdom and glory of Christ where it finds receptive and obedient hearts. In this manner, the Spirit is the chief interpreter, prompting critical assessment of the Church's entire heritage and inspiring discernment toward renewed witness by the Church in its ongoing communal, ecumenical, and cultural context.

Transformative hermeneutics exposes this significant fact: the hermeneutical problem is ultimately a spiritual issue for the Church itself, a matter of its own ongoing health and renewal in Christ.[61] Ecclesial renewal in the concrete sense has necessarily to do with living persons, each of us in particular, clergy and laity together, as we believe, repent, struggle against sin and the devil, grow in the new life in Christ, and seek to live in the kingdom of love. The tangible witness, criterion, and interpreter of transformative truth is the transformed Christian, not in splendid isolation, but in communion and mutual accountability with one's brothers and sisters, and in solidarity with the suffering world. The way to transcend our traditional differences and to converge in varying degrees of common witness in the third millenium is what Gordon D. Fee terms a "redemptive hermeneutic" based on "the gospel and the Spirit," a hermeneutic that calls us "to be simultaneously both affirming and critical of our tradition(s)," while holding to the common theological tradition of classic Christianity.[62] However, according to Fee, this goal cannot be achieved without a mutual willingness to be open, to reexamine, and to understand our traditions more deeply in the light of how we perceive each other,

---

working out its salvation in fear and trembling with God at work within it."

[61] The issue is most sharply evident in such cases as the public scandals involving religious leaders and the malevolent way Christians have treated certain kinds of sinners, for example, homosexuals and abortionists, whom they apparently wish destroyed in the name of the God of love. The worst aspect is not the moral failures of individuals within the churches, but that the churches themselves turn a blind eye to their own failures and resist dealing forthrightly with them in self-corrective truth and love.

[62] Gordon D. Fee, *Gospel and Spirit*, p. 80. Cf. pp. 47ff. and 64f..

and above all without the integrity and readiness to change as needed through the leading of the Holy Spirit.[63]

This brings us finally to the vision of Christian life and theology as celebration; the celebration of love and truth, expressed by the late patriarch of Constantinople, Athenagoras (1886-1972). Patriarch Athenagoras sought to promote ecumenical dialogue on the basis of transformative hermeneutics in which the living Christ himself is the Leader. Without ignoring our serious differences, the patriarch believed that ecumenical healing could occur only when the theological task is conceived of as a celebration of truth and not as a dialectical weapon. His words have a special ring and can serve appropriately as a conclusion to the present discussion of hermeneutics:

I do not deny these differences between the churches, but I say we must change our way of approaching them. And the question of method is, in the first place, a psychological, or rather, a spiritual problem. For centuries there have been conversations between theologians, and they have done nothing except to harden positions. I have a whole library about it. And why? Because they spoke in fear and distrust of one another with the desire to defend themselves and defeat the others. Theology was no longer a pure celebration of the mystery of God. It became a weapon. God himself became a weapon! I repeat: I do not ignore the difficulties. But I am trying to change the spiritual atmosphere. We Orthodox must express the truth which is dear to us - because it protects and celebrates the immensity of the life which is in Christ – we must express it, not so as to repulse the others, to force them to admit that they are beaten, but so as to share it with them, as a celebration of truth to which we invite all.[64]

---

[63] *Ibid.*, p. 82.
[64] Regrettably, I could not find in my files the bibliographical source from which Patriarch Athenagoras' statement is taken, nor have I been able to locate it otherwise.

Appendix 1
Concerning Scripture

by St. John of Damascus (eighth century)

The God proclaimed by the Old Testament and the New is one He who is celebrated and glorified in Trinity, for the Lord said: "I am not to come to destroy the law, but to fulfill" (Mt 5:17). For He worked our salvation, for the sake of which all Scripture and every mystery has been revealed. And again: "Search the scriptures: for these give testimony of me" (Jn 5:39). And the Apostle too, says: "God, who, at sundry times and in diverse manners, spoke in times past to the fathers by prophets, last of all, in these days, hath spoken to us by his Son" (Heb 1:1-2). Through the Holy Ghost, then, both the Law and the Prophets, the evangelists, apostles, pastors, and teachers spoke. Therefore, "all scripture, inspired of God, is quite profitable" (2 Tim 3:16), so that to search the sacred Scripture is very good and most profitable for the soul. For, "like a tree which is planted near the running waters" (Ps 1:3), so does the soul watered by sacred Scripture also grow fat and bear fruit in due season, which is the orthodox faith, and so is it adorned with its evergreen leaves, with actions pleasing to God, I mean. And thus we are disposed to virtuous action and untroubled contemplation by the sacred Scriptures. In them we find exhortation to every virtue and dissuasion from every vice. Therefore, if we are eager for

From Book Four, Chapter 17, of *The Orthodox Faith*, trans. Frederic H. Chase, Jr. in *The Fathers of the Church: Saint John of Damascus* (Washington: Catholic University Press, 1958), pp. 373-376, and used by permission.

knowledge, we shall also be rich in knowledge, for by diligence, toil, and the grace of God who grants it all things succeed. "For he that asketh receiveth: and he that seeketh findeth: and to him that knocketh it shall be opened" (Lk 11:10). So let us knock at the very beautiful paradise of the Scriptures, the fragrant, most sweet and lovely paradise which fills our ears with the varied songs of inspired spiritual birds, which touches our heart, comforting it when grieving, calming it when angry, and filling it with everlasting joy, and which lifts our mind onto the back of the sacred dove, gleaming with gold and most brilliant (cf. Ps 67:14), who bears us with his most bright wings to the only-begotten Son and heir of the Husbandman of the spiritual vineyard and through Him on to the Father of lights. Let us not knock casually, but with eagerness and persistence, and let us not lose heart while knocking, for so it will be opened to us. Should we read once and then a second time and still not understand what we are reading, let us not be discouraged. Rather, let us persist, let us mediate and inquire, for it is written: "Ask thy father, and he will declare to thee: thy elders and they will tell thee" (Dt 32:7). For not all have knowledge. From the fountain of paradise let us draw overflowing and most pure waters springing up into life everlasting (cf. Jn 4:14). Let us revel in them, let us revel greedily in them to satiety, for they contain the grace which cannot be exhausted. Should we, however, be able to get some profit from other sources, this is not forbidden. Let us be proved bankers and amass the genuine and pure gold, while we reject the spurious. Let us accept the best sayings, but let us throw to the dogs the ridiculous gods and unhealthy fables, for from the former we should be able to draw very great strength against the latter...

In the New Testament there are: four Gospels, those according to Matthew, Mark, Luke, and John; the Acts of the holy Apostles by Luke the Evangelist; seven Catholic Epistles – one of James, two of Peter, three of John, and one of Jude; fourteen Epistles of the Apostle Paul; the Apocalypse of John the Evangelist; and the Canons of the Holy Apostles by Clement.

Appendix 2
On Spiritual Knowledge

by St. Symeon the New Theologian (+1022)

How the treasure of the Spirit hidden in the letter of Holy
Writ is not plain to all, even if they are willing, but only to those
who possess Him who "opens the mind to understand the Scripture" (Lk 24:45).

[The Closed Chest of Holy Writ]

Brethren and fathers,
Spiritual knowledge is like a house built in the midst of secular and pagan knowledge, in which there is laid up, like a solid
and well-secured chest, the knowledge of the inspired Scriptures
and the inestimable riches they contain. Those who enter into
the house will never at all be able to see those treasures unless
this chest is opened for them. But it does not belong to human
wisdom ever to be able to open it, so that the riches of the Spirit
deposited in it remain unknown to all who are worldly.

A man might pick up the entire chest and carry it on his
shoulders without knowing what treasure is contained in it. So
a person may read the Scriptures and commit them all to memory
and carry them with him as if they were but one psalm, and yet
be ignorant of the gift of the Holy Spirit hidden within them. It

---

A discourse on the reading of Scripture and perceiving its spiritual treasures by
means of θεωρία or spiritual vision. Reprinted from *Symeon the New Theologian:
The Discourses* by C. J. deCantanzaro, 1980, copyright by The Missionary Society
of St. Paul the Apostle in the State of New York. Used by permission of Paulist
Press.

is not by the chest that its contents are exposed, nor is it by the Scripture that the contents of Scripture become clear. How is this so? Listen!

[The Treasure That Lies Within]

You see a small chest, firmly secured on every side. By means of its weight and its external beauty you conjecture, or perhaps believe from what you have heard, that it contains a treasure. You pick it up quickly and go off with it. But tell me, what will it profit you if you constantly carry it about closed and locked without opening it? As long as you live you will never see the treasure it contains; you will not see the sparkling of its precious stones, the luster of its pearls, the flashing gleam of its gold. What will you profit, if you are not found worthy to take even a small part of it to buy some food or clothing? But if, as we have said, you carry the chest about with you entirely sealed, even though it is filled with a great and costly treasure, will you not be worn out with hunger, thirst, and nakedness? You will not profit at all!

Pay heed to me, brother, and apply this to spiritual things. Think of the chest as the gospel of Christ and the other divine Scriptures. In them there is enclosed and sealed up eternal life together with the unutterable and eternal blessings which it contains, though unseen by physical eyes. As the Lord's word says, "search the Scriptures, for in them is eternal life" (Jn 5:39). As for the man who carries the chest about, think of him as one who learns all the Scriptures by heart and always quotes them with his mouth. He carries them about in the memory of his soul as in a chest containing God's commandments as precious stones wherein is eternal life. For Christ's words are light and life, as he himself says, "he who does not obey the Son shall not see life" (Jn 3:36). Together with the commandments [it contains] the virtues, like pearls.

[The Commandments, Gates of Knowledge]

From the commandments spring the virtues, and from them the revelation of the mysteries that are hidden and veiled in the letter.

From the fulfillment of the commandments comes the practice of the virtues; through the practice of the virtues the commandments are fulfilled. Thus by means of these the door of knowledge has been opened to us; or, rather, it has been opened, not by them, but by him who has said, "he who loves me will keep my commandments, and my Father will love him, reveal myself to him" (Jn 14:21, 23). When, therefore, God "lives in us and moves among us" (2 Cor 6:16) and perceptibly reveals himself to us, then we consciously contemplate the contents of the chest, the divine mysteries that are hidden in the divine Scripture. Let no one deceive himself – in no other way it is possible for the chest of knowledge to be opened to us, and for us to enjoy the good things that it contains and partake of them and contemplate them. But what are these good things of which I speak? They consist in perfect love (that is, toward God and our neighbor), contempt of all things that are visible, mortification of the flesh and "its members that are on the earth" (Col 3:5), including evil desire. Just as a dead man has no thought whatever and perceives nothing, so we ourselves shall have no thoughts of evil desire or of passionate sentiment at any time. We shall not feel the tyrannical oppression of the evil one, but be mindful only of the commandments of our Savior Christ. [We shall think of] immortality, of the incorruption of eternal glory, of the kingdom of heaven, of [our] adoption as sons through the regeneration of the Holy Spirit. Thereby we become sons by adoption and grace, we are called "heirs of God and fellow – heirs of Christ" (Rom 8:17), and together with these things we acquire "the mind of Christ" (1 Cor 2:16) and through him see God and Christ himself dwelling in us and moving among us in a way that we can know.

All these things are granted to those who hear God's commandments and do them; they enjoy them abundantly together with those unutterable and ineffable things that are above these things, through the opening of the chest of which we have spoken, that is, the uncovering of the eyes of our minds and the contemplation of the things that are hidden in Holy Writ. But others, who lack the knowledge and experience of any of the things of which we have spoken, have no taste of their sweetness, of the immortal life derived from them, since they lean on the mere study of the Scriptures. Nay, rather, this very study will judge and condemn them at their departure [from this life] even more than those who have not heard the Scriptures at all. Some of these men err through ignorance and pervert all the divine Scriptures as they interpret them in accordance with their passionate desires. They wish to commend themselves as though they were to be saved apart from the exact observance of Christ's commandments, and so they altogether deny the power of the Holy Scriptures.

[The Treasury of the Mysteries Opened by the Holy Spirit]

This is natural, for the things that are sealed up and closed, unseen and unknown by all men, are opened up by the Holy Spirit alone. When they have thus been unveiled they become visible and knowable to us. How then will those who claim that they have never known at all the Holy Spirit's presence, radiance, illumination, and his coming to dwell in them have the power to know or perceive or think of them in any way? How shall they apprehend such mysteries, who have never at all experienced in themselves the recasting, renewal, transformation, reshaping, regeneration, that he brings about? Those who have not yet been baptized in the Holy Spirit, how can they know the change that comes over those who have been baptized in him? Those who have not been "born from above" (Jn 3:3), how shall they see the glory of those who have been "born from above" (as the Lord said), those who have been born of God and have become the children of God (Jn 1:12-13)? Those who have refused to experience this, but by their negligence have missed this glory – for they have received the power to become such – tell me, what knowledge will enable them to understand or in any way imagine what the others have become?

God is Spirit, invisible, immortal, inaccessible, incomprehensible. Those who are born of him he makes to be such as himself, like the Father who has begotten them. They may be touched and seen in body only; in other respects they are known to God alone and know only Him; or, rather, they wish to be known to God alone and constantly strive to look to him and are anxious to be seen by him. To express it differently, just as the illiterate cannot read books like those who are literate, neither can those who have refused to go through the commandments of Christ by practicing them be granted the revelation of the Holy Spirit like those who have brooded over them and fulfilled them and shed their blood for them. The man who takes a sealed and closed book cannot see what is written in it nor can he understand its subject as long as the book remains sealed, even though he may have learned all the wisdom of the world. Likewise even he who, as we have said, has learned all the divine Scriptures by heart will never be able to know and perceive the mystical and divine glory and power hidden in them without going through all God's commandments and taking the Paraclete with him. [The Paraclete] will open to him the words like a book and mystically show him the glory they contain. Indeed, with the eternal life that causes them to spring forth, he will as well reveal the blessings of God hidden in them, blessings that are veiled and utterly invisible to the despisers and the negligent. This is to be expected, since they have nailed all their senses to the vanity of the world and are passionately attached to the pleasures of life and to physical beauty. But since the vision of their souls is dimmed, they are unable to see and contemplate the intellectual beauties of God's unutterable blessings.

[How the Eyes of Flesh Cannot See Spiritual Beauty]

One whose bodily eyes are weak cannot at all look on a brightly shining sunbeam; if he stares at it he at once loses such sight as he still has. So he whose spiritual eyes are weak and whose senses are subject to passions cannot contemplate the excellence or beauty of a body without passion or harm to himself. Whatever peace of thought he possessed before, whatever calm of evil desire, he loses them as he lingers to reflect on the passion. Consequently such a person is wholly unable to perceive even his own infirmity. For if he has thought that he was sick it was because he believed that there were others who were healthy, and perhaps he blamed himself for being the cause of his sickness and was concerned for getting rid of it. Now, however, such a person holds that all men are subject to passions and looks on himself as their equal, and claims that it is impossible for him to be better than all others. Why is this? So that this wretched man may with them succumb to passion, since he is unwilling to rid himself of such an evil. Had he been willing, he would have had the strength, for he would have received the ability from God. For as many of us as were baptized into his Name have received from him the power to divest ourselves of our past inborn corruption like an old garment, and to become sons of God and clothed with Christ (Gal 3:27).

[Final Admonition]

But far be it from us, brethren, to become like those who take this attitude and think such thoughts, men of earth, and utterly dried up. Rather, may we follow Christ, who has died for us and has risen and exalted us to heaven. Let us continually follow in his footsteps, being cleansed by penitence from defilement of sin and clothed in the bright garment of incorruption that belongs to the Spirit, in the same Christ our God, to whom is due all glory, honor, and adoration, forever and ever. Amen.

Bibliography

Agouridis, Savas, "Ἡ Ἐφαρμογὴ Νέων Μεθόδων στὴ Μελέτη τῶν Ἁγίων Γραφῶν, " *DeltBibMel* 4 (January-June, 1985) 5-23.

———, *"Ἆρά γε γιγνώσκεις ἃ ἀναγινώσκεις;"* Ἑρμηνευτικές καὶ Ἱστορικὲς Μελέτες (Athens: Artos Zoes, 1989).

———, "Biblical Studies in Orthodox Theology," *GOTR* 17, 1 (1972) 51-62.

———, "Ἡ Ἑρμηνεία τῶν Ἁγίων Γραφῶν καὶ ἡ Νεοελληνικὴ Θεολογικὴ Πραγματικότης," *Theologia* 56, 3 (1985) 504-518.

———, *The Bible in the Greek Orthodox Church* (Athens: University of Athens, 1976).

———, *Εἰσαγωγὴ εἰς τὴν Καινὴν Διαθήκην* (Athens: Gregoris Publications, 1991).

Aland, Kurt and others, *The Greek New Testament* (United Bible Societies, 1993).

Albright, William Foxwell, *From the Stone Age to Christianity: Monotheism and the Historical Process* (Garden City: Doubleday, 1957).

Anderson, B. W., editor, *The Old Testament and Christian Faith: A Theological Discussion* (New York: Harper and Row, 1963).

Andriopoulos, P., *Τὸ Πρόβλημα τοῦ "Ἱστορικοῦ Ἰησοῦ" ἐν τῇ συγχρόνῳ Ἑρμηνευτικῇ* (Athens, 1975).

Athanasios, "39th Festal Letter," in *Nicene and Post Nicene Fathers, Vol. 4, Athanasius: Selected Works and Letters*, ed. Philip Schaff (Grand Rapids: Eerdmans, 1975) 551-552.

Athanasios, *Against the Heathen* in *Nicene and Post Nicene-Fathers, Vol. 14 Athanasius: Selected Works and Letters*, ed. Philip Schaff (Grand Rapids: Eerdmans, 1975).

Baird, William, "New Testament Criticism," *ABD, Vol. 1*, ed. D. N. Freedman (New York: Doubleday, 1992) 730-736.

Barbour, Ian G., *Science and Religion: New Perspectives on the Dialogue* (London: SCM Press, 1968).

Barclay, William, *Educational Ideals in the Ancient World* (Grand Rapids: Baker, 1974).

Barr, D. and Piediscalzi, N., *The Bible in American Education* (Alfaretta: Scholars Press, 1982).

Barr, James, *The Bible in the Modern World* (New York: Harper and Row, 1973).

———, *Fundamentalism* (Philadelphia: Westminster Press, 1978).

———, *Beyond Fundamentalism* (Philadelphia: Westminster Press, 1984).

———, *Holy Scripture: Canon, Authority, Criticism* (Philadelphia: Westminster Press, 1984).

Barrois, G. A., *The Face of Christ in the Old Testament* (Crestwood: St. Vladimir's Seminary Press, 1974).

Basil of Caesarea, "Letter 90," in *Loeb Classical Library: St. Basil Letters,* trans. R. J. Deferrari (Cambridge University Press, 1962) 122-127.

Beker, Christiaan J., *The New Testament: A Thematic Introduction* (Minneapolis: Fortress, 1994).

Bloech, Donald G., *Holy Scripture: Revelation Inspiration and Interpretation* (Downers Grove: InterVarsity, 1994).

Bossey Seminar, *Science and the Theology of Creation* (Bossey: WCC Publications, 1988).

Braaten, Carl E., "Response to Manfred K. Bahmann," *LF* 28, 3 (1994) 11-12.

Bradshaw, Paul F., *The Search for the Origins of Christian Worship* (New York: Oxford University Press, 1992).

Bratsiotis, Panagiotis, "The Authority of the Bible: An Orthodox Contribution," *Biblical Authority for Today,* A. Richardson and W. Schweitzer, eds., (Philadelphia: Westminster, 1951) 17-29.

Breck, John, "Theoria and Orthodox Hermeneutics," *SVTQ* 20, 4 (1976) 195-219.

———, "Exegesis and Interpretation: Orthodox Reflections on the 'Hermeneutic Problem,'" *SVTQ* 27, 2 (1983) 75-92.

———, *The Power of the Word in the Worshiping Church* (Crestwood, N.Y.: St. Vladimir's Seminary Press, 1986).

———, "Orthodoxy and the Bible Today," in *The Legacy of St. Vladimir,* ed. John Breck and others (Crestwood, N.Y.: St. Vladimir's Seminary Press, 1990) 141-157.

———, *The Shape of Biblical Language: Chiasmus in the Scriptures and Beyond* (Crestwood, N.Y.: St. Vladimir's Seminary Press, 1994).

Bria, Ion, *The Sense of Ecumenical Tradition: The Ecumenical Witness and Vision of the Orthodox* (Geneva: WCC Publications, 1991).

Bright, John, *A History of Israel* (Philadelphia: Westminster Press, 1981).

Brock, S., *The Syriac Fathers on Prayer and the Spiritual Life* (Kalamazoo: Cistercian Publications, 1987).

Bromiley, Geoffrey W., "The Church Fathers and Holy Scripture," *Scripture and Truth,* ed. D. A. Carson and John Woodbridge (Grand Rapids: Zondervan, 1983) 199-220.

Brown, Raymond E., *Jesus: God and Man* (Milwaukee: Bryce Publishing Company, 1967).

———, *Biblical Exegesis and Church Doctrine* (New York: Paulist Press, 1985).

———, *The Birth of the Messiah: A Commentary on the Infancy Narratives in the Gospels of Matthew and Luke* (New York: Doubleday, 1993).

———, *The Critical Meaning of the Bible* (New York: Paulist Press, 1981).

———, "The Contribution of Historical Biblical Criticism to Ecumenical Church Discussion," *Biblical Interpretation in Crisis: The Ratzinger Conference on Bible and Church,* ed. R. J. Neuchaus (Grand Rapids: Eerdmans, 1989) 24-49.

———, "Church Pronouncements," *NJBC,* ed. by R. E. Brown and others (Englewood Cliffs: Prentice Hall, 1990) 1166-1174.

———, "Hermeneutics," *NJBC,* ed. R. E. Brown and others (Englewood Cliffs: Prentice Hall, 1990) 1146-1165.

———, *The Virginal Conception and Bodily Resurrection of Jesus* (New York: Paulist Press, 1973).

———, *New Testament Essays* (Garden City: Images Books, 1965).

——— and others, *Mary in the New Testament: A Collaborative Assessment by Protestant and Roman Catholic Scholars* (Philadelphia: Fortress, 1978).

——— and others, *Peter in the New Testament* (Minneapolis: Paulist, 1973).

Bruce, F. F. and Rupp, E. G., eds.,*Holy Book and Holy Tradition* (Grand Rapids: Eerdmans, 1968).

Brueggemann, Walter, "Biblical Authority in the Post-Critical Period," *ADB, Vol. 5,* ed. D. N. Freedman (New York: Doubleday, 1992) 1049-1056.

Bultmann, Rudolf, *Jesus Christ and Mythology* (New York: Scribner's, 1958).

——— and others, *Kerygma and Myth,* ed. H. W. Bartsch and trans. R. H. Fuller (New York: Harper and Row, 1961).

——— and Kundsin, Karl, *Form Criticism,* trans. F. C. Grant (New York: Harper and Row, 1962).

Burke, John, *Gospel Power* (New York: Alba House, 1978).

Burton-Christie, D., *The Word in the Desert: Scripture and the Quest for Holiness in Early Christianity* (New York: Oxford University Press, 1993).

Canévet, Mariette, *Grégoire de Nysse et l'herméneutique biblique: Étude des rapports entre le langage et la connaissance de Dieu* (Paris: Études Augustiniennes, 1983).

Carroll, E. R., "Mary in the Apostolic Church: Work in Progress," *One in Christ* 25, 4 (1989) 369-80.

Carson, D. A. *New Testament Commentary Survey* (Grand Rapids: Baker Book House, 1993).

—— and Woodbridge John D., eds., *Hermeneutics, Authority, and Canon* (Grand Rapids: Zondervan, 1986).

—— and Woodbridge John D., eds., *Scripture and Truth* (Grand Rapids: Zondervan, 1963).

Chadwick, Henry, "The Bible and the Greek Fathers," *The Church's Use of the Bible: Past and Present,* ed. E. E. Nineham (London: SPCK, 1963) 25-39.

——, *Early Christian Thought and the Classical Tradition: Studies in Justin, Clement, and Origen* (New York: Oxford University Press, 1966).

Charlesworth, H., *The Old Testament Pseudepigrapha, Vols. 1 and 2,* (Garden City: Doubleday, 1986).

Childs, Brevard S., *The New Testament as Canon: An Introduction* (Philadelphia: Fortress, 1985, 1984).

——, *Introduction to the Old Testament as Scripture* (Philadelphia: Fortress, 1979).

——, *Biblical Theology of the Old and New Testaments: Theological Reflection on the Christian Bible* (Minneapolis: Fortress, 1993).

Chilton, Bruce, *Beginning New Testament Study* (Grand Rapids: Eerdmans, 1986).

Chrysostom, John, *Homilies on the Gospel of John,* in *Nicene and Post Nicene-Fathers, Vol. 14,* ed. Philip Schaff (Grand Rapids, Mich.: Eerdmans, 1969).

Collins, J. J. and Crossan J. D., eds., *The Biblical Heritage in Modern Catholic Scholarship* (Wilmington: Glazier, 1986).

Congar, Yves, *The Revelation of God* (New York: Herder and Herder, 1968).

Coniaris, A., *Preaching the Word of God* (Brookline: Holy Cross Orthodox Press, 1983).

Conzelmann, Hans, *Interpreting the New Testament: An Introduction to the Principles and Methods of New Testament Exegesis,* trans. S. S. Schatzmann, (Peabody: Hendrickson, 1988).

Cullmann, Oscar, *Peter: Disciple, Apostle, Martyr: A Historical and Theological Study* (New York: Meridian Books, 1964).

Daniélou, Jean, *The Bible and the Liturgy* (Notre Dame: University of Notre Dame Press, 1956).

deCatanzaro, C. J., *Symeon the New Theologian: Discourses* (New York: Paulist, 1980)

de Margerie, Bertrand, *Introduction to the History of Exegesis* (Petersham: St. Bede's Publications, 1993).

Dennin-Bolle, Sara J., "Gregory of Nyssa: The Soul in Mystical Flight," *GOTR* 34, 2 (1989) 97-116.

Dibelius, Martin, *From Tradition to Gospel*, trans. B. L. Woolf (New York: Scribner's, 1965).

Doohan, Helen, *Leadership in Paul* (Wilmington: Glazier, 1984).

Dulles, Avery, "Tradition and Creativity in Theology," *FT* 28 (1992) 20-27.

Eichhorst, C. Jack, "There is a Deep Spiritual Sickness," *LF* 28, 3 (1994) 24-28.

Elliott, John Hall, *What is Social-Scientific Criticism?* (Minneapolis: Fortress, 1993).

Ellis, E. Earle, *Prophecy and Hermeneutic in Early Christianity* (Grand Rapids: Baker Books, 1993).

Epp, E. J. and MacRae, G. W., eds., *The New Testament and its Modern Interpreters* (Philadelphia: Fortress Press, 1989).

Evdokimov, Paul, *Struggle With God,* trans. Sister Gertrude (Glen Rock: Paulist Press, 1966).

Fackre, Gabriel, "Evangelical Hermeneutics and Diversity," *Int* 43 (1989) 117-29.

Fedotov, G. P., "Orthodoxy and Historical Criticism," *The Church of God,* ed. E. L. Mascall (London: SPCK, 1934) 91-104.

Fee, Gordon D., *New Testament Exegesis: A Handbook for Students and Pastors* (Philadelphia: Westminster, 1983).

————, *The Holy Spirit in the Letters of Paul* (Peabody: Hendrickson, 1994).

————, *Gospel and Spirit: Issues in New Testament Hermeneutics* (Peabody, Mass.: Hendrickson, 1991).

Flesseman-van Leer, Ellen, ed., *The Bible: Its Authority and Interpretation in the Ecumenical Movement, Faith and Order Paper No. 99* (Geneva: World Council of Churches, 1980).

Florovsky, Georges, "The Pattern of Historical Interpretation," *ATR* 50, 2 (1968) 144-55.

————, "The Ethos of the Orthodox Church," *Orthodoxy: A Faith and Order Dialogue* (Geneva: World Council of Churches, 1960) 36-51.

————, "The Function of Tradition in the Ancient Church," *GOTR* 9 (1963-64) 181-200.

————, "The Lost Scriptural Mind," *Bible, Church, Tradition: an Eastern Orthodox View. Collected Works of Georges Florovsky, Vol. 1*, (Belmont: Nordland, 1972) 9-16.

————, *Bible, Church, Tradition: An Eastern Orthodox View, Collected Works of Georges Florovsky, Vol. 1*, (Belmont: Nordland, 1972).

————, "The Predicament of the Church Historian," in *Religion and Culture*, ed. by W. Leibrecht (New York: Harper & Row, 1959) 140-66.

Fogarty, Gerald P., *American Catholic Biblical Scholarship: A History from the Early Republic to Vatican II* (San Francisco: Harper & Row, 1989).

Ford, M., "Seeing, But Not Perceiving: Crisis and Context in Biblical Studies," *SVTQ* 35, 2-3 (1991) 107-25.

Frei, Hans W., *The Eclipse of Biblical Narrative; A Study in Eighteenth and Nineteenth Century Hermeneutics* (New Haven: Yale University Press, 1974).

Freyne, Sean, *New Testament Message 2: The World of the New Testament* (Wilmington: Glazier, 1980).

Froehlich, K., *Biblical Interpretation in the Early Church: Sources of Early Christian Thought* (Philadelphia: Fortress, 1985).

Funk, R. W., *The Five Gospels: The Search for the Authentic Words of Jesus: New Translation and Commentary* (New York: Maxwell Macmillan International, 1993).

Gabel, John B., *The Bible as Literature: An Introduction* (New York: Oxford University Press, 1996).

Gamble, Harry Y., *The New Testament Canon: Its Making and Meaning, Guides to Biblical Scholarship* (Philadelphia: Fortress, 1985).

————, "Canon: New Testament," *ADB, Vol. 1*, ed. D. N. Freedman (New York: Doubleday, 1992) 852-61.

Goppelt, Leonhard, *Typos: The Typological Interpretation of the Old Testament in the New*, trans. D. H. Madvig (Grand Rapids: Eerdmans, 1982).

Grant, Frederick C., *Form Criticism* (Chicago: Willett, Clark & Company, 1934).

Grant, Robert M. with David Tracy, *A Short History of the Interpretation of the Bible* (Philadelphia: Fortress, 1984).

————, "The Appeal to the Early Fathers," *JTS* 11, 1 (1960) 13-24.

Greenspahn, Frederick E., ed., *Scripture in the Jewish and Christian Traditions: Authority, Interpretation, Relevance* (Nashville: Abingdon, 1982).

Greer, Rowan A., "Biblical Authority in the Early Church," *ADB, Vol. 5*, ed., D. N. Freedman (New York: Doubleday, 1992) 1026-28.

Gregory of Nyssa, *Answer to Eunomius, Second Book*, trans. M. Day, *Nicene and Post-Nicene Fathers, Vol. 5* (Grand Rapids: Eerdmans, n.d.) 276.

Hahn, Ferdinand, *Historical Investigation and New Testament Faith: Two Essays*, trans. R. Maddox (Philadelphia: Fortress, 1983).

Hanson, R. P. C., *Allegory and Event: A Study of the Sources and Significance of Origen's Interpretation of Scripture* (Richmond: John Knox, 1959).

Harrington, Daniel J., *Interpreting the New Testament: A Practical Guide* (Wilmington: Glazier, 1979).

———, *The New Testament: A Bibliography* (Wilmington: Glazier, 1985).

Harrisville, Roy A., "Introduction," in Peter Stuhlmacher, *Historical Criticism and Theological Interpretation of Scripture*, trans. Roy A. Harrisville (Philadelphia: Fortress, 1977) 7-15.

Harvey, Van Austin, *The Historian and the Believer: The Morality of Historical Knowledge and Christian Belief* (New York: Macmillan, 1966).

Hatch, N. D. and Noll, M. A., eds., *The Bible in America: Essays in Cultural History* (New York: Oxford University Press, 1982).

Hauerwas, Stanley, *Unleashing the Scripture: Freeing the Bible from Captivity to America* (Nashville: Abingdon, 1993).

Hausherr, Irénée, *Spiritual Direction in the Early Christian East* (Kalamazoo: Cistercian Publications, 1990).

Hayes, J. H., *Biblical Exegesis: A Beginner's Handbook* (Atlanta: John Knox, 1983).

Hays, R. B., "The Corrected Jesus," *FT 43* (1994) 43-48.

Henderson, Ian, *Rudolf Bultmann* (Richmond: John Knox, 1966).

Henderson, Ian, *Rudolf Bultmann, Makers of Contemporary Theology* (Richmond: John Knox, 1966).

Hengel, A., "Historical Methods and Theological Interpretation of the New Testament," *Acts and the History of Earliest Christianity*, trans. John Bowden (Philadelphia: Fortress, 1979) 127-36.

Hill, R. C., "St. John Chrysostom and the Incarnation of the Word in Scripture," *CTR* 4, 1 (1980) 34-38.

Hodges, Zane C. and Farstad, Arthur L., *The Greek New Testament According to the Majority Text* (Nashville: T. Nelson, 1982).

Hopko, Thomas, "The Bible in the Orthodox Church," *SVTQ* 14, 1-2 (1970) 66-99.

———, *Reading the Bible* (New York: Religious Education Department, Orthodox Church of America, 1970).

Hunter, D. G., ed., *Preaching in the Patristic Age: Studies in Honor of Walter J. Burghardt, S.J.* (New York: Paulist Press, 1989).

Issac the Syrian, *The Acsetical Homilies,* trans. by Holy Transfiguration Monastery (Boston: Holy Transfiguration Monastery, 1984).

Jaeger, Werner, *Early Christianity and Greek Paideia* (Cambridge: Harvard University Press, 1961).

Jellicoe, S., *The Septuagint and Modern Study* (Oxford: Clarendon, 1968).
———, *Studies in the Septuagint: Origins, Recessions, and Interpretations* (New York, 1974).
John of Damascus, "Concerning Scripture," An *Exact Exposition of the Orthodox Faith*, trans. Frederik H. Chase, *The Fathers of the Church, Vol. 37* (Washington: Catholic University of America Press, 1958) 373-376.
Johnson, Allan E., "The Methods and Presuppositions of the Patristic Exegesis in the Formation of Christian Personality," *Dial* 16, 3 (1977) 186-90.
Johnson, J. I., ed., *The Bible in American Law, Politics, and Political Rhetoric* (Alpharetta: Scholars Press, 1984).
Johnson, Luke T., *The Writings of the New Testament: An Appreciation* (Philadelphia: Fortress, 1986).
Jones, C., Wainwright, G., and Yarnold E., eds., *The Study of the Liturgy* (New York: Oxford University Press, 1978).
Justin Martyr, *Dialogue with Trypho*, trans. A. L. Williams (London: SPCK, 1930).
Kaiser, O. and W.G. Kümmel, *Exegetical Method: A Student's Handbook*, trans. E. V. M. Goetchius (New York: Seabuty, 1963).
Karavidopoulos, John, Εἰσαγωγὴ στὴν Καινὴ Διαθήκη (Thessalonike: Pournaras Publications, 1991).
———, Ἑλληνικὴ Βιβλικὴ Βιβλιογραφία 1961-1975 (Thessalonike, 1975).
———, "Οἱ Βιβλικὲς σπουδὲς στὴν Ἑλλάδα," *DeltBibMel* 4 (January-June, 1985) 73-87.
———, "Das Studium des Neuen Testaments in der griechisch-orthodoxen Kirche inVergangenheit und Gegenwart," *BTZ* 3, 1 (1986) 2-10.
Keegan, T. J., *Interpreting the Bible: A Popular Introduction to Hermeneutics* (New York: Paulist, 1985).
Keller, W., *Bible as History* (New York: Bantam, 1983).
Kelly, G. A., *The New Biblical Theorists: Raymond E. Brown and Beyond* (Ann Arbor: Servant Books, 1983).
Kelly, J. F., *Why is There a New Testament?* (Wilmington: Glazier, 1986).
Kelly, J. N. D., *Early Christian Doctrines* (New York: Harper and Brothers, 1960).
Kelsey, David, H., *The Uses of Scripture in Recent Theology* (Philadelphia: Fortress, 1975).
Kelsey, David, H., "Protestant Attitudes Regarding Methods of Biblical Interpretation," *Scripture in the Jewish and Christian Traditions: Authority, Interpretation, Relevance*, ed. by F. G. Greenspahn (Nashville: Abingdon, 1982) 133-161.

Kennedy, George, A. *New Testament Interpretation through Rhetorical Criticism* (Chapel Hill: University of North Carolina, 1984).

Kesich, Veselin, *The Gospel Image of Christ* (Crestwood: St. Vladimir's Seminary Press, 1991).

——, "Biblical Studies in Orthodox Theology: A Response," *GOTR* 17, 1 (1972) 63-68.

Koch, Klaus, *The Growth of the Biblical Tradition: The Form-Critical Method,* trans. S. M. Cupitt (New York: Scribner's, 1969).

Konstadinidis, Chrysostomos, "The Significance of the Eastern and Western Traditions within Christendom," *Orthodoxy: A Faith and Order Dialogue* (Geneva: WCC, 1960) 62-72.

Kugel, James L. and Greer, Rowan A., *Early Biblical Interpretation* (Philadelphia: Westminster, 1986).

Kümmel, W. G., *The New Testament: The History of the Investigation of its Problems,* trans. S. MacLean Gilmour and H. C. Kee (New York: Abingdon, 1970).

Lampe, G. W. H. and Woollcombe, K. J., *Essays on Typology* (Naperville: A. R. Allenson, 1957).

Lategan, B. C.,"Hermeneutics," *ABD, Vol. 3,* ed. D. N. Freedman (New York: Doubleday, 1992) 149-55.

Leiman, Shnayer Z., *The Canonization of Hebrew Scripture: The Talmudic and Midrashic Evidence* (Hamden: Published for the Academy by Archon Books, 1976).

Letty, M., ed., *Feminist Interpretation of the Bible* (Philadelphia: Westminster, 1985).

Lewis, Jack P., "Jamnia (Jabneh), Council of," *ABD, Vol. 3,* ed. D. N. Freefman (New York: Doubleday, 1992) 634-37.

Link, Hans-Georg, ed., *The Roots of Our Common Faith: Faith in the Scriptures and in the Early Church, Faith and Order Paper No. 119* (Geneva: World Council of Churches, 1984).

Linnemann, E., *Historical Criticism of the Bible: Methodology or Ideology?* trans. R. B. Yarbrough (Grand Rapids: Baker Book House, 1990).

Lohse, Eduard, *The Formation of the New Testament,* trans. M. Eugene Boring (Nashville: Abingdon, 1981).

Louth, Andrew, "The Hermeneutical Question Approach through the Fathers," *Sob* 7, 7 (1978) 541-49.

——, *Discerning the Mystery: An Essay on the Nature of Theology* (Oxford: Oxford University Press, 1993).

——, *The Origins of the Christian Mystical Tradition: From Plato to Denys* (Oxford: Clarendon Press, 1983).

Luibheid, Colm, trans., *Cassian, John: Conferences* (New York: Paulist Press, 1985.)

Maier, Gerhard, *The End of the Historical-Critical Method* , trans. E. W. Leverenz and R. F. Norden (St. Louis: Concordia Pub. House, 1974).

Manley, Johanna, ed., *The Bible and the Holy Fathers for Orthodox: Daily Scripture Readings and Commentary* (Menlo Park: Monastery Books, 1990).

———, *Grace for Grace: the Psalter and the Holy Fathers: Patristic Christian Commentary, Meditations, and Liturgical Extracts Relating to the Psalms and Odes* (Menlo Park: Monastery Books, 1992).

Marrou, Henri Irénée, *A History of Education in Antiquity*, trans. George Lamb (New York: Sheed and Ward, 1964).

Marrow, Stanley B., *The Words of Jesus in Our Gospels: A Catholic Response to Fundamentalism* (New York: Paulist Press, 1979).

Marshall, Howard I., ed., *New Testament Interpretation: Essays on Principles and Methods* (Grand Rapids: Eerdmans, 1977).

Martin, Ralph P., *Worship in the Early Church* (Grand Rapids: Eerdmans, 1974).

McGlasson, Paul, *Another Gospel: A Confrontation with Liberation Theology* (Grand Rapids: Baker Books, 1994).

McGrath, Alister, *Evangelicalism and the Future of Christianity* (Downers Grove: InterVarsity Press, 1995).

McGuckin, J. A., "'Perceiving Light form Light in Light' (*Oration* 31.3): The Trinitarian Theology of Saint Gregory the Theologian," *GOTR* 39, 1-2 (1994) 7-32.

McKenzie S. L. and Hayes, S. R., *To Each His Own Meaning: An Introduction to Biblical Criticisms and Their Application* (Louisville: Westminster/John Knox, 1993).

McKim, Donald K. "Biblical Authority in the Protestant Reformation, " *ABD, Vol. 5,* ed. D. N. Freedman (New York: Doubleday, 1992)

McKnight, Edgar V., *What is Form Criticism? Guides to Biblical Scholarship* (Philadelphia: Fortress, 1969).

———, *Post-Modern Use of the Bible: The Emergence of Reader-Oriented Criticim* (Nashville: Abingdon, 1988).

Metzger, Bruce M., *The Canon of the New Testament: Its Origin, Development, and Significance* (New York: Oxford University Press, 1987).

———, *The Text of the New Testament: Its Transmission, Corruption, and Restoration* (New York: Oxford University Press, 1992).

——— and Ronald E. Murphy, eds., *The New Oxford Annotated Bible with The Apocryphal/Deuterocanonical Books* (New York: Oxford University Press, 1991).

Middeleton, J. R. and Walsh, B., "How Pomo Can You Get," *Academic Alert* 4, 2 (1995) 1.

Mulholland, M. Robert, Jr., *Shaped by the Word: The Power of Scripture in Spiritual Formation* (Nashville: Upper Room, 1985).

Murray, Dick, *Teaching the Bible to Adults and Youth* (Nashville: Abingdon, 1993).

Neill, S. and Wright T., *The Interpretation of the New Testament 1861-1986* (Oxford: Oxford University Press, 1988).

Neuhaus, R. J., *The Bible, Politics, and Democracy: Essays* (Grand Rapids: Eerdmans, 1987).

Neuhaus, R. J., ed., *Biblical Interpretation in Crisis: The Ratzinger Conference on Bible and Church* (Grand Rapids: Eerdmans, 1989)

Neusner, Jacob, *Rabbinic Judaism: Structure and System* (Minneapolis: Fortress, 1995).

Nicole, R. R. and J. Ramsey Michaels, eds., *Inerrancy and Common Sense* (Grand Rapids: Baker Book House, 1980).

Nineham, D. E., *The Use and Abuse of the Bible: A Study of the Bible in An Age of Rapid Cultural Change* (New York: Harper and Row, 1977).

Nissiotis, Nikos, "The Unity of Scripture and Tradition: An Eastern Orthodox Contribution to the Prolegomena of Hermeneutics," *GOTR* 11, 2 (1965-66) 183-208.

Noll, Mark A., *Between Faith and Criticism: Evangelicals, Scholarship, and the Bible in America* (Grand Rapids: Eerdmans, 1991).

Norris, Frederick W., *Faith Gives Fullness to Reasoning: The Five Theological Orations of Gregory Nazianzen, Supplements to Vigiliae Christianae*, Vol. 13 (Leiden: E.J. Brill, 1991).

Noth, Martin, *The Old Testament World*, trans. V. I. Gruhn (Philadelphia: Fortress, 1966).

O'Collins, Gerald, *Christology: A Biblical, Historical, and Systematic Study of Jesus* (Oxford: Oxford University Press, 1995).

O'Neill, J. C., "History of Biblical Criticism," *ABD, Vol. 1*, ed. D. N. Freedman (New York: Doubleday, 1992) 726-730.

Osiek, Carolyn, *What are they saying about the Social Setting of the New Testament?* (New York: Paulist Press, 1984).

Packer, J. L., "Infallible Scripture and the Role of Hermenutics," in *Scripture and Truth*, D. A. Carson and John Woodbridge, eds. (Grand Rapids: Zondervan, 1983) 325-356.

Palmer, R. E., *Hermeneutics: Interpretation Theory in Scheiermacher, Dilthey, Heidegger, and Gadamer* (Evanston: Nortwestern University Press, 1969).

Panagopoulos, John, *Εἰσαγωγὴ στὴν Καινὴ Διαθήκη* (Athens: Akritas Publications, 1994)

——, *Ὁ Προφήτης ἀπὸ Ναζαρέτ* (Athens: Parizianos Publications, 1973).

——, *Ἡ Ἑρμηνεία τῆς Ἁγίας Γραφῆς στὴν Ἐκκλησία τῶν Πατέρων*, Vol. 1 (Athens: Akritas Publications, 1991).

Pannenberg, Wolfhart, *Basic Questions in Theology: Collected Essays* (Philadelphia: Fortress, 1970-71).

Patte, Daniel, *Structural Exegesis for New Testament Critics: Guides to Biblical Scholarship* (Minneapolis: Fortress, 1990).

Pelikan, Jaroslav, *The Christian Tradition, Vol. 2: The Spirit of Eastern Christendom (600-1700)* (Chicago: University of Chicago Press, 1974).

——, *Christianity and Classical Culture: The Metamorphosis of Natural Theology in the Christian Encounter with Hellenism* (New Haven: Yale University Press, 1993).

Percival, H. H., ed., *The Seven Ecumenical Councils, A Select Library of Nicene and Post-Nicene Fathers of the Christian Church, Vol. 14* (Grand Rapids: Eerdmans, 1991).

Peters, M. K. H., "Septuagint," *ABD, Vol. 5*, ed. by D. N. Freedman (New York: Doubleday, 1992) 1093-1104.

Pinnock, Clark H., *The Scripture Principle* (San Francisco: Harper & Row, 1984).

Pietarinen, Rauno, *A Bibliography of Major Orthodox Periodicals in English* (Joensuu, 1987).

Pontifical Biblical Commission, "The Interpretation of the Bible in the Church," *Or* 23 (29, 1994) 448-524.

Powell, Mark Allan, *What is Narrative Criticism? Guides to Biblical Scholarship* (Minneapolis: Fortress, 1990).

Price, James R., "Mystical Transformation of Consciousness in St. Symeon the New Theologian," *Diakonia* 19, 1-3 (1984-1985) 6-16.

Reese, J. M., *Preaching God's Burning Word* (Collegeville: Liturgical Press, 1975).

Reumann, J., *Righteousness in the New Testament: Justification in the United States, Lutheran-Roman Catholic Dialogue* (Philadelphia: Fortress, 1982).

Reventlow, H. G., "Biblical Authority in the Wake of the Enlightenment," *ABD, Vol. 5*, ed. D. N. Freedman (New York: Doubleday, 1992) 1035-1049.

——, *The Authority of the Bible and the Rise of the Modern World*, transl. J. Bowden, (Philadelphia: Fortress, 1985).

Richardson, Alan, *The Bible in the Age of Science* (Philadelphia: Westminster, 1961).

Robinson, Haddon W., *Biblical Preaching: The Development and Delivery of Expository Messages* (Grand Rapids: Baker, 1980).

Robinson, James M., *The Nag Hammadi Library in English* (San Francisco: Harper & Row, 1989).

Robinson, Maurice A. and Pierpont, William G., *The New Testament in the Original Greek According to the Byzantine/Majority Textform* (Atlanta: Original Word Publishers, 1991).

Robinson, Robert, *Bruce Roman Catholic Exegesis Since* Divino Afflante Spiritu: *Hermeneutical Implications* (Dissertation Series/Society of Biblical Literature; No. 111, Atlanta: Scholars Press, 1988).

Rollins, Wayne G., *Jung and the Bible* (Atlanta: John Knox, 1983).

Romanides, John, "Critical Examination of the Applications of Theology," *Procès-Verbaux du deuxième Congrès de Théologie Orthodoxe,* ed. Savas Agouridis (Athens, 1978) 413-441.

Rousseau, Philip, *Basil of Caesarea. The Transformation of the Classical Heritage* (Berkeley: University of California Press, 1994).

Ryken, L., *The New Testament in Literary Criticism. A Library of Literary Criticism* (New York: Continuum, 1985).

————— and Longmann T., eds., *A Complete Literary Guide to the Bible* (Grand Rapids: Zondervan, 1993).

Sadowski, F., ed., *The Church Fathers on the Bible: Selected Readings* (New York: Alba House, 1987).

Sanders, James A., *From Sacred Story to Sacred Text: Canon as Paradigm* (Philadelphia: Fortress, 1987).

—————, *Canon and Community: A Guide to Canonical Criticism* (Philadelphia: Fortress, 1984).

—————, *Torah and Canon* (Philadelphia: Fortress, 1972).

—————, "Canon: Hebrew Bible," *ABD, Vol. 1.* ed. by D. N. Freedman (New York: Doubleday, 1992) 837-852.

Santer, Mark, "Scripture and the Councils," *Sob* 7, 2 (1995) 99-111.

Schneemelcher, Wilhem, *New Testament Apocrypha,* Vols. 1 and 2 (Louisville: Westminster, 1990 and 1992).

Schoekel, Luis Alonso, *Understanding Biblical Research,* trans. Peter J. McCord (New York: Herder and Herder, 1968).

Schrenk, G., "Γραφή," *ThDNT, Vol. 1,* ed. G. Kittel, trans. G. W. Bromley (Grand Rapids: Eerdmans, 1964) 615-620.

—————, "Γραφή," *ThDNT, Vol. 1,* ed. G. Kittel, trans. G. W. Bromley (Grand Rapids: Eerdmans, 1964) 749-761.

Schuller, Robert Harold, *Self-Esteem, The New Reformation* (Waco: Word Books, 1982).

Schüssler Fiorenza, Elisabeth, "Toward a Feminist Biblical Hermeneutics: Biblical Interpretation and Liberation Theology," *A Guide to Contemporary Hermeneutics,* ed. McKim, D. K. (Grand Rapids: Eerdmans, 1986) 358-381.

——, *Searching the Scriptures,* Vol. 1, (New York: Crossroad, 1993).

——, *Searching the Scriptures* Vol. 2, (New York: Crossroad, 1994).

——, *Bread Not Stone: The Challenge of Feminist Biblical Interpretation* (Boston: Beacon Press, 1995).

Scouteris, Constantine, "Holy Scriptures and Councils," *Sob* 7, 2 (1975) 111-116.

Sheppard, Gerald T., "Canonical Criticism," *ABD, Vol. 1,* ed. D. N. Freedman (New York: Doubleday, 1992) 861-866.

Stambaugh, J. E. and Balch, D. L., *The New Testament in Its Social Environment* (Philadelphia: Westminster, 1986).

Stendahl, K., "Biblical Theology, Contemporary," *The Interpreters Dictionary of the Bible, Vol. 1,* ed. G. A. Buttrick (New York: Abingdon, 1962) 418-432.

——, "Method in the Study of Biblical Theology," *The Bible in Modern Scholarship,* ed. J. Philip Hyatt (Nashville: Abingdon, 1965) 196-209.

Stuhlmacher, Peter, *Historical Criticism and Theological Interpretation of Scripture,* trans. Roy A. Harrisville, (Philadelphia: Fortress, 1977).

Stylianopoulos, Theodore, "Scriptural Authority (Eastern Orthodoxy)," *ABD, Vol. 5,* ed. D. N. Freedman (New York: Doubleday, 1992) 1021-1023.

——, "The Biblical Background of the Article on the Holy Spirit in the Constantinopolitan Creed," *Études théologiques 2: Le IIe Concile oecuménique* (Chambésy: Centre Orthodoxe, 1982) 155-173, reprinted in T. Stylianopoulos, *The Good News of Christ: Essays on the Gospel, Sacraments and Spirit* (Brookline: Holy Cross Orthodox Press, 1991) 168-195.

——, *Bread for Life: Reading the Bible* (Brookline: Department of Religious Education, Greek Orthodox Archdiocese of North and South America, 1980).

——, "Tradition in the New Testament," *GOTR* 15, 1 (1970) 7-21.

——, "Biblical Studies in Orthodox Theology: A Response," *GOTR* 17, 1 (1972) 69-85.

——, "Historical Studies and Orthodox Theology or the Problem of History for Orthodoxy," *GOTR* 12, 3 (1967) 394-419.

——, "Faith and Culture in Saint Paul: Continuity and Discontinuity," in *Rightly Teaching the Word of Your Truth: Studies in Honor of Archbishop Iakovos*, ed. Nomikos Michael Vaporis (Brookline: Holy Cross Orthodox Press, 1995) 39–52.

——, "Faithfulness to the Roots and Commitment toward the Future: An Orthodox View," in *Orthodox Christians and Jews on Community and Renewal: The Third Academic Meeting between Orthodoxy and Judaism*, ed. Malcolm Lowe and published in *Immanuel* 26/27 (1994) 142-159).

——, *Justin Martyr and the Mosaic Law* (Missoula: Society of Biblical Literature, 1975).

Sweete, L. I., "The Revelation of Saint John and History," *CT* 11 (1973) 9-10.

Sundberg, A. C., *The Old Testament of the Early Church* (Cambridge: Harvard University Press, 1964).

Sugirtharajah, R. S., ed., *Voices from the Margins: Interpreting the Bible in the Third World* (Maryknoll: Orbis, 1991).

Tanakh, The Holy Scriptures: Torah (Philadelphia: Jewish Publication Society, 1985).

Thompson, J. A., *The Bible and Archaeology* (Grand Rapids: Eeerdmans, 1982).

Topkins, J. P., *Reader-Response Criticism: From Formalist to Post-Structuralism* (Baltimore: John Hopkins University Press, 1980).

Torrance, Thomas E., *The Relevance of Christology* (Striling: Drummond Press, n.d.).

Towers, T. J., "The Value of the Fathers," *COR* (July-September, 1965) 291-302.

Trakatellis, Demetrios, Οἱ Πατέρες Ἑρμηνεύουν, Ἀπόψεις Πατερικῆς Βιβλικῆς Ἑρμηνείας (Athens: Apostolike Diakonia, 1996).

Trigg, Joseph W., *Biblical Interpretation: Message of the Fathers of the Church* (Wilminghton: Glazier, 1988).

Tuckett, Christopher, *Reading the New Testament: Methods and Interpretation* (Philadelphia: Fortress, 1987).

Tzogas, Ch. S. and Papaevangelou, P. S., Ἑλληνικὴ Θεολογικὴ Βιβλιογραφία τῆς Τελευταίας Ἑκατονταετίας 1860-1960 (Thessalonike, 1963).

Ugolnik, A., "An Orthodox Hermeneutic in the West," *SVTQ* 27: 2 (1983) 93-118.

Valliere, P., "The Liberal Tradition in Russian Orthodox Tradition," in *The Legacy of St. Vladimir*, ed. John Breck and others, (Crestwood: St. Vladimir's Seminary Press, 1990) 93-106.

Vasileiadis, Petros, "Βιβλικὴ Κριτικὴ καὶ Ὀρθοδοξία," Ἐπιστημονικὴ Ἐπετηρίδα Θεολογικῆς Σχολῆς Θεσσαλονίκης (Thessalonike, 1980) 337-377.

Vawter, Bruce, *Biblical Inspiration* (Philadelphia: Westminster, 1972).

———, "The Bible in the Roman Catholic Church," in *Scripture in Jewish and Christian Traditions*, ed. Frederick E. Greenspahn (Nashville: Abingdon, 1982) 111-132.

Vellas, Vasileios, "Κριτικὴ τῆς Βίβλου καὶ Ἐκκλησιαστικὴ Αὐθεντία," Ἐπιστημονικὴ Ἐπετηρὶς Θεολογικῆς Σχολῆς Ἀθηνῶν (Athens, 1937) 150-160.

Von Campenhausen, Hans, *The Formation of the Christian Bible*, trans. J. A. Baker (Philadelphia: Fortress, 1972).

Wainwright, G., "Word and Sacrament in the Churches' Responses to the Lima Text," *One in Christ* 24: 4 (1988) 304-327.

Walsh, Brian J. and Middleton, Richard J., *Truth Is Stranger Than It Used to Be: Biblical Faith in a Postmodern Age* (Downers Grove: InterVarsity, 1995).

Ware, Kallistos, "How to Read the Bible," in *The Orthodox Study Bible*, ed. Peter E. Gillquist and others (Nashville: Thomas Nelson, 1993) 762-770.

———, "The Spiritual Father in Orthodox Christianity," *CC* (Summer/ Fall, 1974) 296-312.

———, "Ways of Prayer and Contemplation: Eastern," *Christian Spirituality: Origins to the Twelfth Century*, ed. B. McGinn and others (New York: Crossroad, 1987) 395-414.

———, "The Ecumenical Councils and the Conscience of the Church," *Kanon: Jahrbuch der Gesellschaft fur das Recht der Östkirchen* (Wien: Herder, 1974) 217-233.

Weidenfeld, G., ed., *St. Ambrose: Select Works and Letters* (New York, 1990).

Weinfeld, Moshe, "Deuteronomy, Book of," *ADB*, Vol. 2. ed. D. N. Freedman (New York: Doubleday, 1992) 168-183

Wiles, Maurice F., *The Spiritual Gospel: The Interpretation of the Fourth Gospel in the Early Church* (Cambridge: Cambridge University Press, 1968).

Williams, Michael E. *The Storyteller's Companion to the Bible*, 5 vols. (Nashville: Abingdon, 1991-1994).

Wink, Walter, *The Bible in Human Transformation* (Philadelphia: Fortress, 1973).

World Council of Churches, *Confessing the One Faith: An Ecumenical Explication of the Apostolic Faith as it is Confessed in the Nicene-Constantinopolitan Greed (381), Faith and Order Paper, No. 153* (Geneva: WCC Publications, 1991).

Wright, N. T., *Who was Jesus?* (Grand Rapids: Eerdmans, 1992).

——, *The New Testament and the People of God* (Minneapolis: Fortress, 1992).

Yannaras, Christos, *The Freedom of Morality,* trans. Elisabeth Briere (Crestwood: St. Vladimir's Seminary Press, 1984).

Zernov, Nicholas, *The Russian Religious Renaissance of the Twentieth Century* (London: Darton, Longman and Todd, 1963).

Zizioulas, John, *Being as Communion* (Crestwood: St. Vladimir's Seminary Press, 1985).

Index of Biblical References

Select Index